KEY THEMES IN YOUTH SPORT

Key Themes in Youth Sport is a comprehensive and easy-to-read guide to key concepts in the study of young people's relationship with sport, exercise and leisure. Drawing on a range of subdisciplines in the study of sport, including sociology, psychology, physical education and sports development, the book offers a basic grounding in the central ideas and debates in contemporary youth sport as well as a departure point for further study.

The book is arranged into 45 concise, introductory essays, each of which defines and explains a key concept and its significance for youth sport. The essays cover topics as diverse as:

- ability and talent
- drugs
- friends, peers, parents and family
- gender, ethnicity and disability
- health, well-being and physical activity
- motivation and participation
- youth cultures

Key Themes in Youth Sport is invaluable reading for all those involved in the field of youth sport, offering quick and easy access to the essential information as well as directions for investigating specific topics in greater depth.

Ken Green is Professor of Sociology of Sport and Head of the Department of Sport and Exercise Sciences at the University of Chester, United Kingdom. He is also editor of the European Physical Education Review and visiting professor at the Norwegian School of Sports Sciences.

KEY THEMES IN YOUTH SPORT

Ken Green

Routledge
Taylor & Francis Group

LONDON AND NEW YORK

First published 2010
by Routledge
2 Park Square, Milton Park, Abingdon, Oxon, OX14 4RN

Simultaneously published in the USA and Canada
by Routledge
270 Madison Avenue, New York, NY 10016

Routledge is an imprint of the Taylor & Francis Group, an informa business

Typeset in Bembo by Glyph International
Printed and bound in Great Britain by CPI Antony Rowe, Chippenham, Wiltshire

British Library Cataloguing in Publication Data
A catalogue record for this book is available from the British Library

Library of Congress Cataloging-in-Publication Data
Green, Ken, Ph. D.
Key themes in youth sport / Ken Green.
p. cm.
1. Sports for children—Cross-cultural studies.
2. Sports for children—Social aspects—Cross-cultural studies. I. Title.
GV709.2.G74 2010
796.083—dc22
2010008994

ISBN 13: 978-0-415-43539-0 hbk
ISBN 13: 978-0-415-43540-6 pbk
ISBN 13: 978-0-203-88540-6 ebook

In memory of Stan Green

CONTENTS

LIST OF KEY CONCEPTS

Ability and talent
Abuse
Activity and exercise
Age and life-stages
Body/bodies
Capital
Clubs and organized sport
Commercialization and
    consumption
Competition
Disability
Drugs
Ethnicity
Extra-curricular physical
    education
Facilities and venues
Friends and peers
Gender
Gender socialization
Globalization
Health, well-being and physical
    activity
Identity (self-)
Individualization

Informalization
Leisure
Lifelong participation
Lifestyle sports and activities
Moral panic
Motivation
Obesity
Parents and family
Participation
Physical education (PE)
Policy
Risk
Role models
Sedentariness
Social class
Socialization and habitus
Sporting repertoires
Technology/ies
Time
Transitions
Typologies
Work
Youth cultures and lifestyles
Youth's new condition

INTRODUCTION

Key Themes in Youth Sport consists of introductory essays exploring various dimensions of youth sport. It is written in a context of burgeoning interest in youth sport, ranging from concern with general levels of participation in sport through the identification and nurturing of young sporting talent to the potential for abuse in and through sport.

As the title implies, the book is primarily intended for those studying youth sport, in one form or another, at an introductory and probably, therefore, undergraduate level. Each essay is intended to provide a basic grounding in the relevant theme as a departure point for further study. In the process, the book endeavours to provide answers to questions such as 'What does this mean?', 'What are the central ideas and arguments?' and 'How is it relevant?' In each case, the central concept is defined and explained before its significance for youth sport is explored. The central concepts or definitions are not premised on any supposed essence to each term or theme. Rather, they are intended to serve as a proposal to use the relevant terms in particular ways – readers can then decide whether these definitions or concepts prove to be adequate. Links to related concepts are highlighted as and when they first occur or appear relevant in each theme. Among other things, the breadth of themes is intended to enable the reader to gain an impression of the ways in which things that are happening in one area of young people's lives (such as individualization) are likely to impact upon others (such as leisure and sport). The length of the introductory outline for each theme and, for that matter, each thematic essay in its entirety differs according to one or all of several criteria; in particular, the complexity of the theme, the breadth and multidisciplinary nature of the relevant material and the significance of the topic under investigation.

Self-evidently, *Key Themes in Youth Sport* is not a textbook. It does not and cannot replace a text that weaves individual themes into an integrated whole. Unpicking the various thematic strands from the wider tapestry of youth and youth sport inevitably results in the isolation of what are often interrelated aspects of broader social processes. It also results in the categorization and inclusion of some material under a particular heading which might justifiably be located elsewhere. In such cases, cross-referencing and occasional overlapping of content are offered as partial solutions to these issues.

It is inevitable with a book of this kind that decisions need to be made about what and, equally importantly, what not to include. This particular selection of key themes is, of course, entirely mine. There are some themes that readers might have reasonably expected to appear that do not show up. In some cases, these would-be themes turn up within other themes and I can only hope that the reason for treating them as sub-themes, as it were, becomes apparent. Some terms simply do not appear at all and this will no doubt be contentious. The book eschews, for example, use of the terms social inclusion and exclusion because, when unpacked, these terms appear more as fashionable and rhetorical devices than adequate analytical ideas. Nonetheless, given their currency in contemporary debate, I feel compelled to justify exclusion of these particular concepts in a little more detail.

When considering the significance of various social dynamics for youth sport, it has become increasingly commonplace to talk in terms of social inclusion and exclusion even though, for many, they simply amount to 'political shorthand for the consequences of poverty' (Payne, 2006: 15); in other words, a result of various social divisions. It is, therefore, a premise of this text that nothing is added conceptually or analytically by referring to those groups of young people whose representation in and experiences of sport is impacted upon by their class and gender, for example, as excluded. If, by excluded, we mean set apart, then they are apart because they are impoverished, disabled, elderly and so forth. These, then, are the key analytical concepts and themes insofar as they are the most adequate means of conceptualizing the causes of exclusion. In addition, while young males and females from differing social classes and ethnic groups may be disadvantaged in sporting terms they are seldom excluded from all active leisure and are most definitely not socially excluded per se. Even those young working-class, Muslim women, for example, who are not involved in sport cannot be said to be *socially* excluded in any meaningful sense – at the very least, they will have friendship and family support networks. Bundling such groups together under the label 'exclusion' blunts our understanding and obscures the real differences between groups.

Examples from England provide many of the illustrations for each of the themes. Nevertheless, it is possible to identify a great deal of commonality in the present-day characteristics of youth sport, internationally. Consequently, the cross-cultural and global relevance of the various themes will, even where self-evident, be highlighted by reference to examples of international research. Although it is written with an international audience in mind – and includes themes, issues, ideas and evidence to be found in European and non-European studies of youth sport – the book is inevitably biased towards the developed or Western world, even though 85 per cent of the world's young people live in the less developed countries (Roberts, 2008). The focus is on the West because while youth and youth sport is, in several respects globalized, in less developed countries youth research is sparse and youth cultures less pronounced; not least because young people in the developing world and even Eastern Europe have less to spend than their Western counterparts on leisure and sport and do not appear to be catching up (Roberts, 2008). Many, if not all of the features of Western youth are, nevertheless, present elsewhere in the world (and, in particular, among Eastern European youth) such as remaining in education longer, prolonged periods of underemployment, if not unemployment, and increasing individualization (Roberts, 2008).

Youth sport is inevitably a field with open borders and, precisely because it is impossible to capture from a single perspective, its study tends to be a multi-sometimes interdisciplinary undertaking. Many of the most salient issues in youth sport involve processes beyond the sports field and even beyond young people's lives as such. In order to begin to appreciate the forces shaping youth sport the book delves into territory some of which is adjacent to youth sport (such as physical education) and some of which appears further away (e.g. commercialization and technology). Consequently, *Key Themes in Youth Sport* incorporates research from across the sociological, psychological, physiological and epidemiological studies of youth, leisure and sport as the subject matter of each particular theme necessitates. It is, however, implicitly underpinned by a broadly sociological perspective. In other words, in making sense of youth sport, the book attempts to locate or set youth (and young people more generally) in their social contexts rather than treat them as isolated individuals. Starting with their contexts 'enables us eventually to best understand young people's minds and lives' (Roberts, 2008: 12). The intention is to show how youth sport is socially constructed by, for example, family and educational experiences as well as, to varying degrees, consumer industries, politicians and the media. At the same time, however, the book attempts to avoid accusation of sociologism – that is, the tendency to explain social phenomena simply in terms of deep-lying and relatively determining social forces or processes. It treats young people, in other words, as interdependent with a range of other people and organizations – in the words of the famous sociological dictum, as free to choose but seldom in conditions of their own choosing. Similarly, and as difficult as it can be at times, an attempt is made to avoid advocacy, let alone proselytizing. Much that is written about youth sport in policy documents, the media and even academic work on occasions is written in polemical terms and in the language of crisis. The message, whether implicit or explicit, often seems to be that 'something needs to be done'! Thus, the book endeavours to avoid value-judgements of the kind which pathologize young people – treating their (sporting) lives as in some way deficient and/or problematic.

Terminology

Although all the themes in the book are initially defined and interpreted, the two central terms – 'youth' and 'sport' – probably need some explanation at the outset. The age-band thought to constitute youth (or terms often treated as de facto synonym, such as adolescent and teenager) varies over time as well as within and between societies: 'The chronological ages when youth begins and ends have varied greatly by time and place, and both the beginnings and ends are "fuzzy" in all modern societies' (Roberts, 2009: 12). In *Key Themes in Youth Sport*, youth will be defined as a life-stage that in chronological terms can be very broadly mapped onto the middle-to-late teenage years, with some leeway at the upper end to include the post-teen years up to young adulthood. Thus, youth is regarded as a period of transition ranging from roughly 15–25 years. As Roberts (2008: 12) observes, 'The virtue of a transitional, life-stage conception of youth is that it reflects the reality of young people's lives – forever changing.'

Treating youth as 'a transitional period in the journey from childhood to adulthood' (Kehily, 2007a: 13) – rather than merely a developmental stage (denoted by preference for the term, adolescent), where physiological changes 'dictate' psychological states (usually the *sturm und drang* of intense emotions) – has the additional benefit of encompassing the abundant research on older youngsters. It also allows for coverage of those young people whose leisure lives are quite precocious and those young adults whose lives continue to resemble closely that of teenagers. It focuses attention on the roughly 1.2 billion young people between the ages of 15 and 25 in the world negotiating the crucial period when young people come to the end of compulsory schooling (and, therefore, compulsory school sport) or voluntary higher education and begin to experience key life transitions (e.g. from education to work and from family to single living arrangements). Maintaining fluid boundaries to the concept of youth enables the various thematic entries in the book to take young people's past (in other words, their childhood) into consideration as well as their (adult) futures and the significance of both of these for their relationships with sport. In the process, it implicitly encourages a relational view of youth sport: recognizing the many and varied ways in which young people are interdependent with a wide variety of people and networks (including, for example, their parents and family, schools, peers and friends, the countries they inhabit and, within these, the various governmental and regional policies towards sport as well as the dominant sporting and cultural practices).

With the flexibility of the age boundaries of youth in mind, the term 'young people' will also be used quite frequently in order to acknowledge where particular points or research relate to those 'below' youth, as it were, or who are not on the threshold of life-stage transitions. On occasions, the terms children and childhood will be added to incorporate the youngest age groups. The terms children, childhood, young people and the like are significant because it is in the earlier years that the predispositions that impact upon youth educational, working, leisure and sporting practices tend to be laid. Cutting across these intentions is the need on occasions to use the terms that the authors of cited research have, themselves, used in their studies: such as adolescents, teenagers and teens.

The second central term is 'sport' and this too requires some initial consideration. As Coalter (2009) observes, use of the word sport often 'disguises more than it reveals'. For Coalter, sports are best viewed as sets of social processes (doing different things like games and learning different skills). The various processes and practices typically labelled 'sport' tend, nonetheless, to display certain (empirically verifiable) common features: in particular, competition, physical vigour and institutionalization (the process whereby something – such as the game of football – takes on the characteristics of a structured, well-organized and established system) as well, some would argue, as physical skills. In this book, however, sport will (unless indicated) be used in a more general sense to incorporate not only competitive game-contests (that is to say, conventional sports such as football, hockey, basketball and badminton) but also less competitive, less organized, recreational versions of these sports as well as more recreationally oriented physical activities and exercises (swimming, aerobics, cycling, skateboarding, surfing, cheerleading, parkour and so forth) often referred to as 'lifestyle' or 'lifetime' sports and activities. On occasions, phrases such as sport and physical activities or active recreation will be used in order to highlight the significance of recreational or lifestyle activities to the point being made. Here again, these stipulated uses of the various terms will be cross-cut by the specific terms used in the research which provides the evidence-base for the particular themes.

When the two central terms – youth and sport – come together, the conceptual and thematic picture can become quite opaque. While the book endeavours to simplify things (somewhat artificially at times, it must be said) by dealing with a number of key themes in isolation, a thematic text inevitably begs questions about the interrelationships between the various component themes. One approach, among many, to identifying the relationships and reconciling the themes is presented in the next section by taking youth itself as a starting point and developing a thread intertwining the *Key Themes in Youth Sport*.

Key Themes in Youth Sport

Youth as a term is notoriously difficult to pin down. It tends to be linked with **age**. However, for various reasons, youth is better thought of as a **life-stage** during which significant **transitions** typically occur; transitions that, in the early part of the twenty-first century, have been made far more complex due to economic and social changes which have resulted in what has become known as **youth's new condition**. The changes in young people's labour market situations have had far-reaching consequences for their lives and lifestyles and, ultimately, their **participation** in leisure and sport. Two particular features of the new condition of youth – **informalization** and **individualization** – have exacerbated a tendency to view youth as a life-stage characterized by **risk** and associated with a series of **moral panics** – ranging from excessive use of **drugs** (including alcohol and tobacco) through to **abuse**. Prominent among these moral panics is a concern with the **health** of future generations and, in particular, the health consequences of the global pandemic of **obesity** brought on, or so it is claimed, by a surfeit of **sedentariness** and a deficit of **activity and exercise** among young people. As a consequence, 'heightened concerns with the emotional well-being, risk behaviour, sedentary habits and obesity of youth' (Zuzanek, 2005: 379) are a feature of youth research. Growing concern with so-called 'lifestyle diseases' and the alleged roles of activity, exercise and sport have led researchers to explore issues related to the **body** and the impact thereon of **technology** and the growing **commercialization** of life and **leisure** as well as the impact of **globalization** on global youth. It has also led to a greater focus on the place of sport in **youth cultures and lifestyles** vis-à-vis other uses of young people's spare **time**, prominent among which are the growing amounts of part-time **work** used by young people to fuel adult-like consumer-oriented lifestyles; hence, the heightened focus – in much **policy** towards youth sport – on the roles of **physical education** and sports **clubs and organized sport** as vehicles for **motivating** young people to engage with sport. Such policies have tended to emphasize sport (and especially sporting **competition**) and overlook the significance of **lifestyle sports and activities** in young people's **sporting repertoires** or, for that matter, for **lifelong participation** in sport and active recreation. Policy towards youth sport also tends to overlook, or at least downplay, the significance of a young person's (pre)dispositions (or **habitus**) – towards sport in general and particular sports as such – for participation. Young people's sporting habituses tend to stem from their **socialization** and the social and cultural as well as economic **capital** they accrue as a result. Among other things, **parents and family** can be particularly important **role models** in terms of socialization into (or away from) sport and, for that matter, sporting **ability and talent** – particularly as agents of **gender socialization** in relation to a young person's sporting (and self-)**identity**. While levels and forms of participation tend to stem from the social and cultural capital acquired, in the first instance, through parents and family, they are inevitably influenced, to a greater or lesser degree, by their subsequent relationships with **friends and peers**, physical education and **extra-curricular physical education**. In this regard, socialization during childhood and youth serves as a foundation for the rest of life: 'Childhood and youth are the life-stages when individuals build up leisure capital (tastes, skills and interests) on which they then base the rest of their lives' (Roberts *et al.*, 2009: 262). Indeed, the decisions young people have made by age 16 'are likely to affect the rest of their lives since many are unable to get a second chance' (Jones, 2009: 104). Thus, youth is the last major opportunity to encourage young people into sport. Once they are settled in adult roles, young people are far less likely to begin engaging with sport if they are not already doing so; if they have become, in other words, one of a number of 'non-sporty' **typologies**.

The significance of socialization and habitus notwithstanding, the availability, proximity and suitability of sporting **facilities and venues** can be a key variable in participation, albeit among marginal players more so than those 'locked in' to sport. Suitable facilities can be particularly important for girls (especially those from Muslim cultures) and youngsters with a **disability**. Even where appropriate facilities and venues are plentiful, however, sports participation continues to display the effects of structural dynamics such as **social class**, **gender** and **ethnicity** in isolation but especially in configuration. In simple terms, young, white, middle-class males are most likely and older, working-class, South Asian Muslim females least likely to be involved in sport. To the extent that young, white, working-class females are involved in sport, it is likely to be less than their middle-class counterparts, and it is more likely to be in particular forms such as soccer and dance than in horse-riding and skiing. Despite these caveats, in many areas of leisure and sport there has, nevertheless, been convergence such that there are fewer differences and more similarities between the sporting and leisure lives of males and females, middle- and working-class youngsters than hitherto. Convergence does not, however, amount to a leisure or sporting democracy among youth.

Acknowledgements

In concluding this introduction, I want to acknowledge the contributions of several people. First of all, I must thank Ken Roberts not only for casting an eye over the manuscript but also for being a constant source of inspiration over the best part of 20 years that I have known him and his work. Not for the first time, nor hopefully the last, I am deeply indebted to Miranda Thurston for her comments on various aspects of the manuscript. Last, but by no means least, I must thank Simon Whitmore at Routledge for his support and forbearance in seeing the project through to completion. *Key Themes in Youth Sport* is dedicated to my late father, Stan Green, who (along with my mother, Betty Green) was and remains the source of my enthusiasm for sport, among so many other things.

KEY THEMES IN YOUTH SPORT

ABILITY AND TALENT

Ability can be defined as possessing the means (in the form of a configuration of physical and/or mental behaviours and habits) to do something, such as performing sporting skills. As well as being a particular kind of (practised) ability, sporting skill is also a physical form of **capital**. Talent, on the other hand, is usually taken to refer to an individual's 'natural' or 'inborn' abilities of a particular kind, such as sporting talent. While physical capacities (such as genetic predispositions in relation to height and shape and even visual acuity) may be a 'gift', sporting skills are abilities inasmuch as they are behaviours that have been learned (and, almost invariably, practiced). Sociologists argue that many claims regarding 'ability' and 'talent' are inherently ideological in nature (see Evans *et al.*, 2007) insofar as they tend to individualize success and failure, encouraging those who do not succeed (at sport, for example) to internalize the belief that failure is entirely their own fault.

The significance of ability and talent for youth sport

Sport, by its very nature, highlights ability and talent and youth sport has always served as a conveyor belt for elite level sport, showcasing able and talented youth with potential to succeed. What marks contemporary (youth) sport out is the increasingly rationalized (calculated and systematic) nature of the process of talent recognition and development. Scientific approaches to sifting, identifying and systematically developing sporting 'talent' (as it tends to be generically referred to) from younger and younger **ages** have become a feature not only of elite sports organizations but also of **club** sport as well as **physical education** (PE) and various forms of sports development. Indeed, PE, club sport and sports development are frequently viewed as central to the identification and nurturing of sporting talent. Unsurprisingly, given their sporting backgrounds and **habituses**, PE teachers, club coaches and sports development personnel continually define, measure and interpret the nature of ability for their young charges, as well as the importance of talent, ability and hard work in achieving success and failure in the ostensibly meritocratic world of sport. PE teachers, for example, have long tended to group and stratify pupils within PE lessons in terms of 'gifted and talented' and 'low attainers' (Evans, 2004). Indeed, a tendency to focus upon ability and performativity (measuring something by its propensity to deliver results) when teaching and coaching sport is deeply entrenched in the practices of professionals. Such predispositions on the part of PE teachers tend to be reinforced by curricular demands for ongoing assessment of educational performance and attainment in which they are required to differentiate between different levels of sports performance and grade their pupils according to various multi-point scales (Evans *et al.*, 2007).

Practices that serve to identify and advance able and talented youngsters in sport are nothing less than politicians, the media and the general public would expect.

3

In the popular view, PE and sports development are expected to serve as vehicles for the flow of talented athletes into top-level, representative sport. This is particularly the case in the kinds of specialist sports schools and colleges to be found in regions and political regimes as far apart as Australia, the former Soviet-bloc countries and Scandinavia and introduced at secondary level in England and Wales in the 1990s. Here, governmental commitment to integrating school sport with talent identification and elite sporting development (Houlihan, 2002) lie at the heart of one of the flagship developments of the last decade or so, namely the *Physical Education, School Sport and Club Links* (PESSCL) strategy (DCMS/Strategy Unit, 2002) – latterly re-badged as the *Physical Education and Sport Strategy for Young People* (PESSYP). Within this strategy, schools in general and Specialist Sports Colleges in particular have been expected to identify and develop young sporting talent in partnership with sports clubs in their communities. The primary vehicle for this role is the 'talented' aspect of the so-called 'gifted and talented' (or G&T as it is known at school level) scheme, designed to profile and 'track' pupils with sporting ability. The G&T scheme is intended to encourage 'more talented young sports people to join junior sports clubs and develop and strengthen the relationship between schools and the National Governing Bodies of sport' (TNS UK, 2007: 39). Steve Grainger (Chief Executive of the Youth Sport Trust in England) (cited in Lightfoot, 2008: 25) described the identification and support of talented youngsters in schools as 'one of the pillars of a bridge' to sporting success, with local sports clubs as the next pillar. Ironically, in practice, talent not only tends to be recognized in terms of current achievement rather than the potential to achieve (Bailey *et al.*, 2009) but there is usually also a 'cap' on the numbers of youngsters who can be defined as talented. It is UK Department of Education (Department of Children, Schools and Families) **policy** that the proportion of pupils registered as talented – because of their ability in PE and/ or school sport – should be between 5 and 10 per cent. Indeed, the latest survey (Quick *et al.*, 2009) reveals 7 per cent of pupils between ages 9 and 16 years registered thus.

Systematic approaches to talent identification and nurturing are nothing new. Models for identifying then 'hot-housing' youngsters with sporting talent were synonymous with the communist regimes of the Soviet bloc (and the German Democratic Republic, in particular) in the second half of the twentieth century and have become increasingly commonplace more recently in Western capitalist democracies such as Australia and Canada. Indeed, the United States epitomizes the use of the education system as a vehicle for talent identification and development – attracting talented young sportsmen and women from around the world into its quasi-professional Collegiate sports system, which being a major spectator sport sector in its own right, ultimately acts as a nursery for elite professional sport. Nowadays, sports schools take a variety of forms. In Scandinavia, for example, schools can adopt a sporting orientation if they wish and sports-oriented secondary schools have been increasingly popular since the early 1970s (Annerstedt, 2008). Such schools choose a sports profile with a focus on either an elite approach – developing talents in different sports in conjunction with the sports confederations – or a sport-for-all orientation – where the focus of sporting activities is usually on health benefits. Schools with a sports profile (and especially those with an emphasis on elite sport) have grown substantially in recent years, especially in Sweden. In 2007, 51 per cent of Swedish state schools and 45 per cent of independent schools claimed a sports profile. Indeed, some independent schools have been created with the specific purpose of offering a specialism in sport (Annerstedt, 2008).

Despite the systematic character of talent identification and development in contemporary sport – and, for that matter, the various 'sport for all' policies (widely adopted in countries around the world) aimed at introducing all young people to sport and developing all sporting talent, irrespective of **social class, gender, ethnicity** and abilities – in many sports and in many countries elite (if not necessarily talented) youngsters in very many sports still tend to come from relatively affluent, middle-class households (and private or advantaged state schools) with disproportionately few from lower classes and deprived groups and areas (Collins and Buller, 2003). It seems that the many kinds of sporting **capital** which middle-class children are more likely to acquire at home, and which is usually reinforced in middle-class educational establishments, tend to lead to those with advantaged backgrounds being identified as able and talented; in other words, 'sporty'.

When it comes to more general involvement in **leisure**-sport, it seems that ability (or, at the very least, competence) may be crucial. Several studies have suggested that skill levels are a predictor of levels of **participation** in sport and increased (Iwasaki and Havitz, 2004) and sustained (Casper, 2007) engagement with particular sports. In the case of tennis in the United States, for example, Casper (2007) found that the higher the skill level, the more participants in tennis were likely to play throughout the year.

The differing self-**identities** (including sporting identities) young people develop tend to be influenced by their perceptions of competence in various arenas (such as sport and education) and based upon 'a combination of self-assessment and assessment by others (Jones, 2009: 83) including **friends and peers** and PE teachers. Because sport emphasizes physical performance and the acquisition and development of physical skills, a lack of these marks youngsters (whether disabled or not) out as inferior. In its effects, therefore, sport is a process within which teachers, coaches and their peers are prone to stigmatize young people (especially those with **disability**), not least because particular areas of sport (epitomized by contact games, such as rugby) remain enclaves of masculine, mesomorphic and able-bodied (in the sense of being both physically competent and unimpaired) young people. In other words, a normative paradigm prevails in sport that corresponds to what is often referred to as 'ableism' or discrimination on the basis of perceived ability or lack thereof.

5

All in all, while ability and talent are self-evidently central to sporting success, developing the means or ability to perform sporting skills (becoming competent, in other words) is also likely to be crucial for youth sports participation at a more general, recreational level, not least inasmuch as it tends to be a central feature of **motivation** and sporting capital.

ABUSE

In broad terms, child abuse refers to 'a range of harmful activities perpetrated by adults on children' (Lawson and Garrod, 2003: 30). These can include various forms of physical (including sexual) violence and mental abuse (such as emotional abuse in the form of tormenting, bullying and even simple neglect).

Child abuse is a modern idea. The gradual 'civilizing' of human behaviours in the modern world led to greater expectations that adults (and parents in particular) would regulate their behaviour towards children (Elias, 1994, 1997). The second half of the twentieth century (i.e. from the Second World War onwards), in particular, witnessed 'increasing concern in Western societies about the role of violence, sexuality and various forms of possibly abusive behaviour in adult–child relations' (Van Krieken, 1998: 157) including a 'heightening of the taboos against violence in relations between parents and children' (Elias, 1997: 207). As a result, in countries such as early twenty-first century England 'views about the status and rights of children are very different from those which prevailed in the seventeenth century ... when children were considered to be inherently bad and therefore in need of strict discipline' (Waddington, 2000: 48) – a view that justified what would now be considered extremely harsh, even cruel, forms of chastisement. Consequently, the modern conception of childhood entails 'an imputation of "specialness" to children (as cherished beings) and childhood (as a cherished state of being)' (Jackson and Scott, 2006: 220). Nowadays, there is a strong cultural expectation, in the Western world, in particular, that childhood will remain a protected state and children a protected group (Jackson and Scott, 2006). As a result, child exploitation and, in its extreme form, abuse (together with related issues of child protection and welfare) has become an increasingly salient topic in commentaries on youth sport over the past two decades.

Not only has **policy** and practice towards children developed apace in recent years, so too has the terminology employed to describe and categorize 'abuse', 'harassment' and 'exploitation'. Indeed, definitions – of exploitation and abuse, in particular – are steadily becoming more comprehensive and sophisticated (Van Krieken, 1998). Nevertheless, because definitions and interpretations of child abuse are associated with changing attitudes towards children they can, and often do, vary from one society to another as well as from one historical period to another (Waddington, 2000). In fact, not only do countries tend not to include children engaged in sports in the protection offered to children in ostensibly similar circumstances (such as child workers), 'existing international regulations are not sufficient to ensure effective protection of child athletes, either' (Weber, 2009: 67). The upshot is that in the same way that what could be considered exploitative child labour in Western Europe is often deemed a normal contribution to family economic activity in India and South Asia, in sporting terms what might be interpreted as child abuse in the West may be viewed as tough but necessary training in pursuit of sporting success in China. Consequently, it is likely that 'culturally-derived beliefs about what constitutes abuse' (Harthill, 2005: 295) will hinder and sometimes prevent recognition of abuse. Based on a study of female American and Israeli student–athletes by male coaches, for example, Fejgin and Hanegby (2001) concluded that perceptions of what is considered sexual harassment differ depending upon the national culture in which it is examined.

The significance of abuse for youth sport

Early studies of abuse in sport arose from work on harassment and discrimination (Brackenridge, 2008). In the sporting world, abuse typically takes either physical or mental forms (and sometimes both because young athletes may be subject to several forms of abuse at the same time [Waddington, 2000]). The most common forms of physical abuse involve physical punishment of one kind or another and forced exertion. Nonetheless, research has revealed instances of sexual abuse and exploitation particularly – but by no means exclusively (Harthill, 2005) – in relation to girls (and teenage girls especially). In this regard, Brackenridge (2008: 41) observes that evidence for child sex abuse in sport 'has been accumulated as much through the case files of governing bodies of sport as by primary research, with awareness of the issue having been raised through child protection policy, advocacy and training work since the early 1990s'.

Brackenridge (2001, 2006), in particular, has identified various forms of abuse during training. These are frequently expressed via intimidation and force, taking such forms as weight-loss programmes and rigid diets (in gymnastics, for example), burnout[1], violence, sexual abuse and the economic exploitation of able young athletes by their coaches, trainers and even parents. While some risks (such as bullying) are experienced by both boys and girls and shared across sport settings, there are both sport-specific and **gender** dimensions to the issue of abuse in sport (Waddington, 2000) and forms of abuse can vary from sport-to-sport. While dietary pressures are commonplace in gymnastics, for instance, gym and figure skating have been two sports particularly associated with the physical and sexual abuse of girls.

Although it is difficult to establish the prevalence and frequency of sexual abuse in sport, sexual harassment takes many forms – from sexual innuendo through intrusive physical contact and fondling to intercourse itself (Waddington, 2000) – and it is evidently more common than the sporting community has been prepared to admit. Indeed, sexual exploitation is increasingly cited as a, if not the, most prominent (if not the most prevalent) form of abuse perpetrated on young people in and through sport (Brackenridge, 2008). Girls appear particularly vulnerable to sexual abuse and especially susceptible to repeated bouts over protracted periods. Some researchers argue, however, that the dominance of the 'male perpetrator–female victim' paradigm (Harthill, 2005: 287; citing Mendel, 1995: 91) has meant that 'the experience of sexually abused males has largely been ignored' (p. 287). As a consequence, male-on-male and female-on-male physical and sexual abuse continues to be under-reported, frequently passing unnoticed (Harthill, 2005) – even though they have lower prevalence rates in official statistics and self-report studies, young males may well be as sexually victimized as females. This may be partially explained by the fact that, in general terms, boys are more likely to be abused outside and girls inside the home (Harthill, 2005; citing Mendel, 1995) and that physical force tends to be more normalized among males in sports setting than it is among females.

The tendency towards under-reporting of abuse is likely to be exacerbated by youngsters' differing **socialization** experiences and the concomitant ways in which young males and females experience abuse differentially: acknowledging passivity, helplessness and victimization (in other words, personal weakness) does not sit easily with boys' self-**identities**. Nor, for that matter, does the potential stigma of homosexuality (Harthill, 2005).

Although the term 'youth' sometimes encompasses those young people (i.e. those under 16 in the United Kingdom) who are classified as children under the law, the issue of sex abuse is complicated by the fact that the legal **age** of consent (in sexual matters) 'varies widely from country to country, from as young as 12 to as old as 21' (Brackenridge, 2008: 41). This situation has been compounded by developments in youth. Many researchers describe young people as increasingly at **risk** from pressures towards early maturity with the attendant likelihood of precocious sexuality (Jackson and Scott, 2006). The issue is made more complex by the fact that in sport, 'junior/senior distinctions also vary, meaning that there is no simple correspondence between chronological, developmental and sport age' (Brackenridge, 2008: 41). Indeed, the prevalence of exploitation and abuse may be exacerbated by the trend towards earlier and more intensive involvement of talented youngsters in sport and, in the process, in adult-like training schedules likely to involve significant risks of overtraining for young people whose bodies are growing rapidly and, as a result, are particularly susceptible to injury (Waddington, 2000). In this regard, Caine (2010) points up trends in the United States (in sports such as gymnastics) towards earlier sports specialization as well as increases in intensity of training and year-round training alongside increasing complexity in (and, thus, difficulty of) the skills to be practised and perfected.

In terms of the perpetrators, there is a tendency to assume that abuse is committed by coaches, trainers and those directly involved in sports; after all, sport is one way in which access to young people is both sought and gained

(Harthill, 2005). Nevertheless, it is worth bearing in mind that the vast majority of crimes of violence against children are perpetrated by parents and other relatives (Jackson and Scott, 2006). 'The darker side of father–child relationships' is especially evident 'in areas of competitive achievement' and the 'hypermasculine' domain of sport 'in which dominating and abusive behaviours can become normalised' (Kay, 2009a: 4). Parents who may have invested a great deal of **time**, energy and money in their children's sporting careers can be implicated in physical and emotional abuse in particular (Waddington, 2000). What Jackson and Scott (2006: 217) describe as 'the propensity of parents to live vicariously through their children, to treat them as carriers of their own hopes and dreams' is often writ large in the world of youth sport, especially in relation to talented athletes; infamous public examples of parental exploitation and abuse in sports such as tennis and swimming offer vivid illustrations of the issues. Such examples serve as a reminder, however, that in a context where talented young athletes stand to reap huge rewards from sporting success the issue of where appropriate (even necessary) support shades into exploitation and development becomes abuse is nothing if not complex. David (2005) rehearses some of the arguments surrounding what constitutes the best interests of the child in the context of children's early involvement in competitive sport, especially where they have pretensions towards elite level. The complex character of abuse is compounded by the difficulties inherent in determining where cajoling and motivating young athletes shades into bullying and abuse. What some might term psychological or physical abuse and political and economic exploitation (by those seeking to gain political kudos or financial reward) might be seen as going hand-in-hand with elite level sport and an unavoidable cost outweighed – in the minds of some of those involved as aspiring junior athletes as well as their parents and coaches – by the longer-term benefits. This is the inevitable paradox associated with the apparent necessity of earlier and earlier preparation for elite sport set against the physical and psychological dangers of involvement of youngsters in intensive training regimes at ages when their bodies are not fully developed and their life experiences are limited and narrow.

Among older youth, other forms of physical and sexual abuse have recently been explored such as 'hazing', 'whereby new players or "rookies" are induced into the sub-culture of a sport through sexually degrading or illegal initiation rituals, often alcohol-fuelled' (Brackenridge, 2008: 42). These are typically associated with team sports and higher education institutions in particular and constitute a particular and under-explored dimension of abuse – that of athlete-on-athlete.

Another dimension of abuse that has come under increasing scrutiny in recent years (see, for example, Rich, Holroyd and Evans, 2004) is that ostensibly perpetrated by young people (and young women in particular) on themselves but which may be encouraged in particular social (e.g. girls' friendship groups) and sporting (such as gymnastics and dance) networks in the form of what are commonly referred to as 'eating disorders'. The two most prominent eating disorders, anorexia nervosa ('the refusal to maintain **body** weight over a minimum normal weight for age and height' [Rich, 2008: 77]) and bulimia nervosa ('recurrent episodes of binge eating or recurrent, inappropriate compensatory behaviour to prevent weight gain' [p. 77] including fasting, vomiting, use of medications such as laxatives and excessive exercise) are particularly prevalent during adolescence and 'include psychological problems as well as concerns around dieting, weight and body image' (p. 77). Rich *et al.*'s (2004) research reveals the ways in which some sports – in emphasizing and exaggerating the desirability of lean physiques and celebrating the achievement of slenderness – heighten young people's concerns with their body. It is unsurprising, therefore, that those sports that place a particular premium on slenderness (for aesthetic and/or performance reasons) have 'a higher prevalence of participants exhibiting eating disorders' (Rich, 2008: 77).

Alongside eating disorders, an additional risk of sports **participation** – and another form of abuse seemingly perpetrated by young people on themselves – is compulsive over-exercising (anorexia athletica) (Rich, 2008). It is perhaps to be expected, therefore, that the majority of obsessive-compulsive disorders in relation to the complex of food and exercise are found among females where ideal (and often unattainable) bodily images appear crucial to both their sexuality and their sporting performances. The issue of dietary regimes and the prevalence of eating disorders among young women who play sport is a reminder that girls' relationship with sport and exercise tends to be related to their perceptions of their own bodies and their 'look'. School sport (see **physical education**) has a tendency to exacerbate any unease girls may feel with their bodies and the public display of their bodies can be crucial in their development of self-image (Hills, 2007): 'shared peer norms for thinness' (Dohnt and Tiggerman, 2005: 103) and possessing a desirable 'figure' are especially significant matters for many young women (Cox *et al.*, 2005). The potential for sport not only to highlight girls' self-consciousness (O'Donovan and Kay, 2005) but also to impact negatively on their self-esteem appears to be exacerbated during early adolescence. Indeed, embarrassment is viewed by teenage girls as a very real likelihood and a substantial cost of participating in sport in PE (Cockburn and Clarke, 2002). It is important to note, however, that concern with the shape and weight of their bodies is not simply the preserve of girls and women – although it is they who feel the constraints disproportionately because of dominant norms of femininity among girls (Gard and Wright, 2005). In this regard, messages about youth sport as a suitable vehicle for addressing not only the '**obesity** epidemic' but also youth concerns with body shape and image serve only to exacerbate the risk of eating disorders, in particular, among young people.

Some would say that the issue of exploitation in youth sport has developed into something of a **moral panic**, in the sense that the contemporary preoccupation with risk (Brackenridge, 2008) and children's 'rights' (as enshrined in the United Nations Children's Rights Charter and the Olympic Charter) has coloured judgements about the prevalence of abuse. Either way, countries such as Australia, Canada and the United Kingdom have developed policies[2] towards the maltreatment of children and young people in sport in order to constrain what are commonly viewed as exploitative power-relations, typically if not exclusively on the part of adults (and 'most frequently but not exclusively male coaches' [Brackenridge, 2008: 42]) – the ones usually in positions of authority. Ironically, however, it is the status and authority of coaches and parents (who are frequently one and the same), for example, that makes research difficult to conduct and concrete evidence hard to come by. This fact highlights just why young people are vulnerable to abuse. Waddington (2000) points to the relatively powerless position of young, aspiring athletes because of the adult–child character of the relationship (with all the connotations of authority and obedience) and the reluctance of youngsters to disobey authority figures (who may, at the same time, be held in high regard by their unknowing parents). He observes that power-differentials between adults and children tend to be exacerbated by the power-differentials associated with **gender** relations. These aspects of the power relationship between coach and young athlete can be further exacerbated by the significant position the coach occupies as a gatekeeper to sporting opportunities, **facilities**, knowledge and, ultimately, success. All of these features are compounded by (i) the likelihood of repeated and extended time spent together and (ii) the legitimacy and sometimes necessity for coaches to have physical contact with the young athlete for reasons of skill development and/or safety. This is why definitions of sexual harassment in sport are more problematic than that in other social settings – sport typically involves more physical contact and traditionally legitimizes male domination (Fejgin and Hanegby, 2001).

It seems ironic – when set against the seeming increased prevalence of abuse – that the quality of child welfare, internationally, is higher than ever before. Indeed, it may be that the growing concern for children's rights in a hitherto unexplored aspect of children's lives – sport – represents an expression of a civilizing process rather than a breakdown in moral standards and behaviours. Put another way, an increasing focus on child welfare in sport may reflect growing awareness of the prevalence of such issues and this, in turn, may be an expression of a general lowering of the threshold of repugnance towards the kinds of exploitative and abusive behaviours (on a continuum from, towards one end, sexual abuse of children in sport through to the administering of physical punishments as a means of 'training' physical skills at the other) sometimes found in youth sport. In short, this would amount to 'a socially-generated psychologically internalized, stricter taboo on acts of violence, which is characterized by the generation of feelings of guilt and anxiety on the breaking or infringement of such taboos' (Malcolm, 2008: 44). It may also be that the 'quest for excitement' (Elias and Dunning, 1986) – the controlled de-controlling of emotional controls – that is a feature of modern sports has hitherto enabled these now increasingly reviled practices to escape attention.

Notes

1 Burnout is a syndrome characterized by progressive disillusionment allied to diminishing **motivation** and, in extreme cases, loss of feelings of self-worth – 10,000 hours of training is often spoken of as a necessity to reach the elite level in many sports.

2 National governing bodies of sport in countries such as Australia, Canada, Norway, the United Kingdom and United States 'are at varying stages of developing and implementing child protection policies and procedures' (Harthill, 2005: 289), but these are the exception rather than the rule. Eighty-six per cent of **clubs** surveyed in Scotland (*SportScotland*, 2008) had designated child protection officers in place, and the United Kingdom has a dedicated unit for the protection of young people in sport. Nonetheless, even though many sports federations include child protection in their regulations, these regulations do not address day-to-day training, but only competitions, despite the fact that 'most of the harm suffered by child athletes originates from intensive training, not from participation in **competitions**' (Weber, 2009: 67).

ACTIVITY AND EXERCISE

The term physical activity tends to be interpreted in two quite different ways in relation to sport. For those (such as exercise physiologists) concerned with fitness and **health**, physical activity is taken to mean bodily movement produced by skeletal muscles resulting in the expenditure of energy (Marshall and Welk, 2008); in other words, being *physically* active. For those concerned simply with engagement in sport (such as sociologists), the term physical activity is often used in a context that implies **participation** and, in particular, participation in less competitive (or, at least, more recreational) activities. The two senses of the term physical activity are to be found more-or-less explicitly or implicitly in the vast body of research into the health and fitness of young people over the last 40 years or more. Concern with levels of physical activity in the sense of levels of energy expenditure is often juxtaposed with physical activity in terms of levels, rates and frequencies of participation in sport among young people.

Exercise physiologists distinguish between different forms of energy expenditure in relation to physical activity: the energy required to maintain basic physiological processes at rest, diet-induced energy expenditure, and physical activity itself – the latter comprising approximately 15–30 per cent of total energy expenditure for most people (Marshall and Welk, 2008). Physical activity in the form of bodily movement tends to be broken down into more or less energetic activities (ranging, in the case of young people, from sitting in classrooms or playing computer games, through standing or walking around with **friends**, to playing sport). In terms of young people's health, it is noteworthy that most spend much of their **time** in the less active, more **sedentary** forms typical of contemporary daily life. This is one of the reasons why those concerned with physical activity as energy expenditure in the service of fitness and health (such as the influential American College of Sports Medicine) prefer a more demanding threshold in terms of bodily movement involving a substantial increase in energy expenditure (Marshall and Welk, 2008).

The term exercise is taken to mean planned and structured physical activity (usually intended to have an effect on physical fitness and/or health). It is planned in the sense of being deliberate and structured in having a predetermined shape, form and limits. Both features are found in activities such as a 5-kilometre run, performing a particular number of 'sets' and repetitions of various gym activities or playing a game of squash. In cases such as these, exercise is a process whereby the **body** performs work of a relatively demanding nature in order to bring about physiological adaptations and improvements in performance. As well as for fun, exercise is often undertaken in order to strengthen the cardiovascular system (for fitness and/or health) or muscles (for strength) or to develop and improve sporting or physical skills. Exercise is seen as taking three broad forms depending upon whether it is predominantly aerobic, anaerobic or intermittent. Examples of aerobic exercise include brisk walking or running that requires the cardiovascular system (i.e. the heart and lungs) to work harder to meet the increased oxygen demands made on the body. Examples of anaerobic exercise include short bursts (<30 seconds) of high-intensity activity such as sprinting, throwing and jumping. In such cases, energy demands are met by the breakdown of high-energy phosphates and glycolysis as the demands exceed the rate at which energy can be produced aerobically. Intermittent exercise comprises periods of low intensity physical activity (e.g. walking and jogging) interspersed with periods of high-intensity, short-duration activity. Intermittent exercise is often associated with team sports (such as football and hockey) while also being commonplace among children during play (Twist, 2010).

Debates surrounding notions of 'sufficient' or 'appropriate' levels and forms of physical activity and exercise (or, more specifically, inactivity and **sedentariness**) tend to revolve around assumptions made in relation to **age** cohorts or age-related prescriptions. Judgements about whether young people are (sufficiently) active or not (including whether they are too sedentary) tend, in other words, to be either norm or criterion-referenced (Marshall and Welk, 2008); that is to say, made in relation either to a young person's peers or some predetermined threshold (such as minimum physical activity recommendations). Whereas norm-referenced approaches can result in young people being described (and, for that matter, describing themselves) as active in relation to their peers while still being insufficiently active to substantially benefit their health status, criterion-referenced systems can, and do, lead to youngsters being classified as inactive if they are not physically active for 30 (or even 60) minutes each day.

Attempts to measure levels of physical activity (and prescribe exercise accordingly) are made more complex by the fact that children's physical activity tends to be more spontaneous than that of adults and is usually accumulated

13

in small bursts throughout the day (Marshall and Welk, 2008). Indeed, it has become increasingly apparent that satisfactory measures of physical activity (and associated recommendations regarding health-related physical activity levels) are difficult to establish. Measurement of physical activity is problematic not simply because self-reported data can be unreliable but also because of uncertainty regarding the best kind(s) to measure as well as the problems associated with developing suitable technologies with which to measure it (Rowlands, 2009). While there is evidence of increased sedentariness (and especially TV viewing) and decreased walking (to school, for example) among young people, the reliance on notoriously inaccurate self-reported levels of physical activity means that a good deal of the available data – on which assumptions of decreased levels of physical activity are based – is questionable. More objective measurements using activity monitors (such as accelerometers) have only recently become available, and it is noteworthy that studies using accelerometers suggest pretty similar levels of total physical activity across the United Kingdom (Reilly et al., 2004) as well, for example, as between primary schools with different amounts of PE (Mallam et al., 2003).

Whatever the measurement, it is worthy of note that 'The number of children who experience physical activity of the duration, frequency and intensity recommended by expert committees decreases with age' (Armstrong and Welsman, 2006: 1067), especially during youth.

The significance of activity and exercise for youth sport

Research by Armstrong and Welsman (2006: 1067) reveals how 'European boys of all ages participate in more physical activity than European girls' and that 'the **gender** difference is more marked when vigorous activity is considered'. Nonetheless, the physical activity levels of both sexes tend to be higher during childhood declining as they move through their teenage years towards youth. Because physical activity patterns among young people also tend to be sporadic, 'sustained periods of moderate or vigorous physical activity are seldom achieved by many European children and adolescents' (p. 1067).

Despite the abundance of studies from around the world revealing the failure of youngsters to be sufficiently active in health terms, most young people indicate that they enjoy being physically active and many, indeed, are – at least in terms of **participation**. In their World Health Organization (WHO) study of seven European countries (Austria, Finland, Hungary, Norway, Scotland, Sweden and Wales), Samdal et al. (2006) found that over the course of the last 25 years of the twentieth century, levels of vigorous physical activity (four or more times a week) were stable across six of the countries (with a slight increase in the seventh, Finland). More specifically, the WHO study indicated 'stability or small increases in the levels of physical activity of boys and girls aged 11–15 years from the mid-1980s to the early 2000s' (Samdal et al., 2006: 242). In all countries, boys were more likely to report vigorous physical activity than girls as well as spending more time watching TV. In Britain, Philo, Mablethorpe, Conolly and Toomse's (2009) study of children's activities and **leisure** time in 2007 found that almost six in ten (58 per cent) youngsters aged 11–15 were reported as undertaking three or more hours per week of physical activity, with boys more likely than girls to exercise three or more hours per week (64 per cent compared with 52 per cent). Similarly, the Schools Health Education Unit's (SHEU, 2007) archive of 68,495 youngsters between the ages of 10 and 15 from 787 primary and secondary schools across the United Kingdom revealed that over 90 per cent of the sample reported exercising at least once 'last week'. Nevertheless, while up to 68 per cent of 10–11-year-old pupils considered themselves to be 'fit' or 'very fit', perceived fitness declined with age in males and females such that since 1991 there has been an upward trend (from 10–20 per cent) in 14–15-year-old females reporting being unfit, with 25 per cent of the 14–15-year-old females describing themselves as 'unfit' or 'very unfit'.

Negative self-perceptions of fitness among young people are consistent with the growing evidence of a decline in their cardiorespiratory fitness levels. It seems that youngsters who have low levels of physical activity alongside high levels of sedentary behaviour are also more likely to have lower cardiorespiratory fitness. Against the backdrop of an increase in reports highlighting a decline in aerobic fitness, Tomkinson and Olds' (2007) meta-analysis of secular changes in the aerobic fitness test performances of 161,419 Australasian (Australian and New Zealand), 6–17-year-olds (between 1961 and 2002) revealed a marked decline in recent decades and, in particular, a shift from improvements to declines in the early 1960s. Elsewhere, on the basis of a cross-sectional study of cardiorespiratory fitness levels in over 3,000 US youth aged 12–19 years of age between 1999 and 2002, Pate et al. (2006: 1005) concluded that 'Approximately one third of both males and females failed to meet recommended standards for cardiorespiratory fitness' and that 'those in the normal weight group had higher fitness levels than those at risk for overweight and overweight groups'.

Regardless of the trends that various studies appear to reveal, it is argued that many reflect a widespread misunderstanding involving the conflation of two independent variables: physical fitness and physical activity (Winsley and Armstrong, 2005). Fitness levels do not necessarily reflect and cannot be straightforwardly read-off, so it is claimed, from levels of physical activity. In addition, and notwithstanding the widespread belief that young people's fitness is in decline, there is in fact only limited evidence that young people's aerobic fitness – as defined by both endurance and maximal aerobic power (Harris and Cale, 2006) – is either 'low or deteriorating from generation to generation' (Winsley and Armstrong, 2005: 76). In short, it may be inaccurate and misleading to think that, as a consequence of their relative inactivity, children and young people are necessarily unfit; there is, it seems, only a weak relationship between their aerobic fitness and physical activity levels. Indeed, children and adolescents appear to be the fittest section of the population. This is because there is a significant genetic contribution to children's fitness which manifests itself during maturation. Indeed, 'when aerobic fitness is expressed relative to body size, children's aerobic fitness is at least as good as that of most adults' and 'has changed very little' since the 1930s (Winsley and Armstrong, 2005: 75). Most young people are, in other words, fairly fit by virtue of being young, the inevitable variations among them notwithstanding.

The particular significance of engaging in physical activity while young may, nonetheless, lie in its potential for health promotion over the life-course. High levels of physical fitness during adolescence and young adulthood appear positively related to a healthy **risk**-factor profile in later life and levels of physical activity while young are thought to be related to the major health issues for young people: overweight, type 2 diabetes, cardiovascular disease risk, skeletal health and mental health (Stensel et al., 2008). In particular, childhood and adolescence are crucial periods for bone development – in order to attain peak bone mass, young people 'need to be physically active prior to and through puberty' (Stensel et al., 2008: 43). Building the sport and physical activity habit early is also important because of the difficulty of enticing adults back into sport later on in life if they have been regular non-participants when young. In other words, if people do not find something they like doing and establish good exercise habits early on in their lives, it becomes progressively harder for them to build exercise into their lives and increasingly unlikely that they will do so, despite their best intentions (Roberts and Brodie, 1992; SHEU, 2007). All that said, and the various claims for the existence of a strong relationship between physical activity and fitness and health when young notwithstanding, in many quarters of the exercise sciences world there continues to be scepticism over whether physical activity habits carry over, or 'track', significantly from childhood and adolescence to adulthood (Marshall and Welk, 2008) – despite the fact that sedentariness clearly does.

When it comes to the 'recipe' for health promoting physical activity, contemporary recommendations and guidelines regarding physical activity tend to be more nuanced than a decade or so ago and more applicable to young people's lives than hitherto. They point out, for example, that requisite amounts of physical activity can be achieved in a number of short, 10-minute (minimum) bouts. Opportunities for moderate to vigorous physical activity include everything from competitive sport and formal exercise to active play and other physically demanding activities (such as dancing, swimming or skateboarding). They also include some of the activities that can form part and parcel of daily life (such as walking, cycling or using other modes of travel involving physical activity) (Stensel et al., 2008). In this vein, relatively recent government recommendations suggest that 'young people should engage in at least 60 min[utes] of moderate-intensity physical activity each day' (Marshall and Welk, 2008: 9) where moderate activity is defined as activity that makes young people breathe hard.

Often overlooked in discussion surrounding guidelines and recommendations is the nature rather than merely the amount of activity and exercise or even its form. The recommendations of the National Institute for Health and

Clinical Excellence in the United Kingdom (NIHCE, 2009) refer to opportunities for moderate to vigorous intensity physical activity. They suggest that children and young people should undertake a range of activities at this level for at least 60 minutes over the course of a day and at least twice a week; this should include weight-bearing activities that produce high-physical stresses to improve bone health, muscle strength and flexibility.

Despite the increasing detail of the various recommendations, many guidelines tend to result in swathes of youngsters being defined as inactive. McDermott (2007), for example, noted that because the cut-off point for being defined as 'active' is established by international guidelines, a large proportion of Canadian youngsters are deemed inactive. In their study of trends in vigorous physical activity among 14- and 15-year-old Icelandic adolescents from 1992–2006, Eiðsdóttir et al. (2008) identified a 6 per cent increase in the rate of vigorous physical activity. At the same time, however, they found that 'only' 53 per cent of boys and 37 per cent of girls achieved the recommended criterion for vigorous physical activity alongside 'an overall increase in the proportion of inactive adolescents, with girls consistently reporting higher levels of inactivity than boys even though the net increase in inactivity was higher for boys' (p. 289). While acknowledging an overall increase in vigorous physical activity and participation in sports **clubs** since 1992, Eiðsdóttir et al. (2008) observed that over half of all Icelandic adolescents were not achieving the recommended levels of physical activity (and that less than one-third of the adolescent population studied were achieving the recommended level of activity through organized sports clubs).

Although levels of physical activity tend to decline with age, the picture is not as straightforward as it is often portrayed. Ironically, while young people between the ages of 8 and 19 are most likely to play sport, they tend to be relatively inactive in the rest of their daily lives whereas those aged 65 years and over are more active overall (via gardening and walking, for example) (Fisher, 2002). Borodulin, Laatikainen, Juolevi and Jousilahti (2008) investigated time trends 1972–2002 in leisure, occupational and commuting physical activity across birth cohorts in 59,000 Finnish adults. They found that the prevalence of leisure-time physical activity increased between 1972 and 2002 from 66–77 per cent in men and from 49–76 per cent in women. In each study year, the younger people were more active than the older ones were. However, within the birth cohorts, physical activity tended to increase with age. The prevalence of physically demanding work decreased from 60–38 per cent in men and from 47–25 per cent in women and the prevalence of daily commuting activity decreased from 30–10 per cent in men and from 34–22 per cent in women, in the same period. In the 1970s and 1980s, the older people had more physically demanding work than the younger ones but, within the birth cohorts, occupational activity decreased with age. Borodulin et al. (2008) conclude that while, over the last 30 years, the prevalence of leisure-time physical activity among adults in Finland had increased, the prevalence of physical activity occurring while at work or commuting decreased.

Inevitably, there is a socio-demographic dimension to physical activity and exercise. Along with gender, there are **ethnic** and **social class** dimensions to activity and exercise. In their five-year longitudinal study of almost 6,000 11–12-year-olds from a variety of ethnic groups in London, Brodersen, Steptoe, Boniface and Wardle (2007) found that students from lower socio-economic neighbourhoods reported higher levels of sedentary behaviour while girls from lower socio-economic groups (but not boys) were less physically active than those from more affluent backgrounds. Similarly, in their review of young people's life-styles, sedentariness and sport in the European Union (EU) Brettschneider and Naul (2004) found consistent patterns in all EU countries: namely, boys were more active than girls with the former preferring intense activity and the latter favouring more moderate levels of intensity. From their study of 3,601 pupils in years 7–10 in six secondary schools in Leicester, England, Khunti *et al.* (2007) demonstrated that white European children in inner-city secondary schools were more likely to have walked to school than South Asians. At the same time, however, they identified high levels of inactive behaviours and low levels of active behaviours in both groups with over half (46 per cent) of respondents spending four or more hours each day watching TV or videos or playing computer games and a low overall level of active behaviour during school breaks particularly pronounced among girls. In the United States, Pate *et al.* (2006) identified black, Hispanic, and female students as substantially less likely than their white male counterparts to participate in vigorous physical activity at recommended levels. Exploring socio-economic differences in leisure-time physical activity through *The Malmö Diet and Cancer Study*, Lindström, Hanson and Östergren (2001) concluded that some of the socio-economic differences in leisure-time physical activity are likely to be due to differing social **capital** between socio-economic groups. Capital is, indeed, likely to be the key explanatory factor in relation to physical activity and exercise more generally.

AGE AND LIFE-STAGES

As a means of differentiation as well as a marker or indicator of social distinction, age has served as a basis for distinguishing between groups in all human societies (Payne, 2006). There are, nevertheless, a number of overlapping and potentially confusing terms commonly used to describe (and explain) the social significance of particular age-related groups and categories. The life-course is constructed through socially established calendars; in other words, 'people's ages are usually described in terms of calendar age – the number of years that have elapsed since birth' (Vincent, 2006: 196). The social significance of calendar age is, however, tied to the **transitions** between life-stages that tend or, rather, have tended to occur around particular ages; such as transitions from school to further or higher education or employment. Before exploring the significance of age – and the life-stage of youth in particular – for sport, it is worth saying a little more about age-related life-stages and the various terms (childhood and adolescence in particular) commonly employed alongside youth to make sense of early life (sporting) experiences.

Who and what a child is deemed to be have changed over **time**. Although in one form or another there has probably always been a concept of childhood, at least in terms of infancy, the current conception – as 'a human being in the early-stages of its life course, biologically, psychologically and socially' (James and James, 2009: 14) – is a modern invention. What is now regarded as childhood was, once upon a time, 'apparent only among the privileged classes' (Jackson and Scott, 2006: 220). The states of childhood and youth did not exist in the Middle Ages 'since children were absorbed into the adult world at an early age' (Jones, 2009: 2) and as recently as the nineteenth century, the term 'child' referred to a youngster's dependency on an adult rather than a particular age or stage (James and James, 2009). Not only was childhood not recognized as such but young people were afforded no special treatment. On the contrary, they were judged by adult standards instead – 'when no longer babies, children participated in society much as adults did' (James and James, 2009: 23). The idea and social practices now commonly associated with childhood (such as play) accompanied developments during the Industrial Revolution that, in effect, took youngsters out of the workplace, back into family homes and then into education. Thus, youth is the product not only of industrialization but also of nineteenth-century social and educational reforms such as child protection laws and the extension of education. Youth as a concept is, therefore, the unplanned outcome of adult policies in the creation of schools, the delineation of childhood, employment legislation and so forth; in other words, **policy** that defined life-stages by age (Jones, 2009).

The separation of the worlds of **work** and home led to working children becoming more visible 'and increasingly offensive to the bourgeois ideal of childhood' (Jackson and Scott, 2006: 220) and middle-class 'civilized' sensibilities (Elias, 1994). As work within the family and craft apprenticeships and training became obsolete, schools became the preferred means of controlling, occupying, socializing and educating children and young people. Consequently, the development of formal education systems across the developed world from the late nineteenth century onwards served to lengthen and, in the process, redefine the upper boundary of childhood in terms of the institutional arrangements (such as schooling and legal definitions) and social spaces (e.g. schools, playgrounds and youth **clubs**) that separate children from adults (James and James, 2009). Indeed, 'the scholarization of childhood (i.e. the expulsion of children and young people from "real work" in favour of education' (du Bois-Reymond, 2005: 382), and its concomitant prolongation, is currently advancing around the world via upward movements in the minimum school leaving age.

Overall, the division between childhood and adulthood is 'one of the key lines of social stratification along which [modern day] societies are organised' (Jackson and Scott, 2006: 231) and two overlapping terms – *adolescence* and

19

youth – are commonly used to describe the period of transition from one to the other. Indeed, the term adolescence is often used as a synonym for youth, and this confusion finds expression in debates between definitions of youth based on age or life-stage. Adolescence is, however, better reserved to denote the period between the onset of puberty and biological adulthood. Using adolescence as a synonym for youth is problematic in several respects. In the first instance, while adolescence appears relatively inflexibly rooted in the teenage years, trends towards earlier puberty are complicating this simple equation. This, and the fact that 'the chronological ages when youth begins and ends varies between and within societies' (Roberts, 2009: 324), further confounds any mapping of youth onto adolescence. In most countries, the term youth tends to be used to cover the period between around 15 years and the mid-twenties, 'though both these age "boundaries" are constantly rising' (Jones, 2009: 11). By contrast, a variety of studies (see, for example, Zuzanek, 2005) define adolescence in practice as the period between 15 and 19 years, although some have thresholds as low as 12. Finally, the term 'youth' is often used to refer to people who are no longer teenagers and who, in biological terms at least, have achieved adulthood. Youth and adolescence cannot, therefore, be usefully treated as interchangeable terms. Nowadays, social scientists tend to view adolescence as an aspect of one particular and very significant life-stage, youth; preferring the term youth to adolescence not merely because of the former's connotations of social construction rather than biological determination but also because while human beings age in chronological and biological terms, the significance of particular points and stages in the ageing process lies in their social significance. Their significance lies, in other words, in what these points and stages are taken to imply about, for example, transitions from home to school to work and, in the process, from childhood to youth to adulthood. The terms childhood, adolescent and youth are, therefore, socially constructed concepts that, nevertheless, have biological and chronological dimensions. Childhood and adolescence, for example, are biological and chronological in the sense that they refer to a period when young people have not yet reached full physical, psychological and social maturity. They are social in the sense that they refer to a period before adult status (with all that term implies) is attained. In this regard, childhood and youth are relational – they are only conceivable in relation to other life-stages such as adulthood (du Bois-Reymond, 2005).

Unsurprisingly, perhaps, the elastic and flux-like character of the period referred to as youth has led most sociologists to abandon trying to define youth in terms of chronological age[1]. Rather, youth tends nowadays to be conceptualized as the life-stage between childhood and adulthood – neither the first nor the last and, as such, inherently transitional (Roberts, 2003). Youth is associated with the period between leaving full-time education and becoming an adult in social and economic terms. In this regard, young people are acutely aware that moving into employment moves them 'out of the state of being a child and into the stage of a "serious person"' (du Bois-Reymond, 2005: 382) and that

'The process of becoming an independent adult is connected to the abstract idea of achieving the status of an individual' (Lahelma and Gordon, 2008: 210).

The typical sequence of life-stages and the roles or statuses (e.g. child, youth, adult) associated with them is commonly referred to as the 'life-cycle' (Vincent, 2006) insofar as at pretty much the same age most people are conventionally expected to move from one status to another and adopt the related roles of school pupil, worker, parent and so forth. It is more adequate, however, to talk of a life-*course* made up of life-*stages* rather than a life-*cycle*, not least because the life-cycle can change quite substantially between generations. In recent decades in many modern societies, for example, 'youth has been extended as a result of young people remaining longer in education, and marrying and becoming parents at later stages than formerly' (Roberts, 2009: 148). Put another way, boundaries between life-stages and ages are not fixed by objective criteria (such as chronological age) but, rather, are dependent upon the social, political and economic conditions at any one time (e.g. the collapse of youth labour markets and the concomitant growth in tertiary education). Youth is, therefore, best conceptualized as part of a life-course 'composed of successive identifiable life-stages – childhood, youth, adulthood and senior citizenship, for example' (Roberts, 2009: 148) which are characteristically associated with 'major status passages marked by "life events" such as leaving full-time education, marriage and retirement' (p. 148). In this sense, the concept of youth needs to be understood as a shifting social construction rather than any kind of absolute – 'Youth in late modernity is not the same as youth at the height of modernity, or youth in pre-industrial times' (Jones, 2009: 4).

Some transitions between life-stages are afforded special social significance. Transitions from one age or life-stage to another are usually associated with major life events such as leaving school and going to work. Thus, transitions can and do change as the preconditions change. A loosening of the social division of age has been apparent in shifts in the relationships between school, work and retirement that have been observable features of industrialized societies in recent decades and the age at which young people tend to leave school, start work and marry have changed for many young people. As a consequence, a characteristic of youth cohorts latterly has been riskier transitions from youth to adulthood (see **youth's new condition**): 'in most countries all over the world new life space has been created between young people completing full-time education on the one side, and entering full adulthood on the other' (Roberts, 2008: 15). This can be understood as an extension of youth rather than a new life-stage. As young people progress through the life-stage of youth 'they become increasingly divided from one another – into those who do and those who do not enter higher education, and into those who get good jobs, the under-employed, and the seriously unemployed, for example' (Roberts, 2008: 203). The upshot has been that youth, as a life-stage, has become more individualized (Hendry *et al.*, 2002).

Counter-intuitive as it may seem, processes of **individualization** among youth in recent decades point up the relevance of the concept of generations.

The fact that demographic cohorts or groups of people born at roughly the same time and of a similar age often tend to share particular characteristics (Vincent, 2006) enables researchers to talk of 'age classes', 'age strata' and generations – members of a society who were not only born in the same period but who, for example, also share similar and often distinct features in terms of such seemingly superficial things as dress, music and **leisure** tastes and habits and also more profound life-stage transitions. This is not to deny that the varying social and economic circumstances world-wide and over time render age-based definitions of youth problematic – not least because they imply a commonality of experience that often does not exist in practice. Rather, it is to observe that there can be a generational dimension to youth as cohorts experiencing the same historical processes (such as **globalization** and under-employment) (Jones, 2009), especially during their formative years, develop a more-or-less common sense of **identity** and interests and even share similar beliefs, predispositions and behaviours. Shared social and economic conditions can, in other words, result in a group or generational **habitus**.

The significance of age and life-stages for youth sport

Virtually everything of social significance is different for adults than it is for children (Roberts, 2003) and this is particularly true for games and sport. Age is strongly correlated with levels and forms of **participation** in many leisure activities and none more so than sport. The overall trend towards increased participation over the last quarter of the century notwithstanding, there is no escaping the fact that age has a deleterious effect on sports participation. In general, levels of sports participation decline with increasing age (especially among females) and this decline becomes more marked after the age of 45.

In addition, when compared with other uses of leisure, loyalty rates in sport are not good. Lessons from studies of adherence to sport through the life-course are pretty clear: it is much easier to keep people in sport – in other words, to stop them dropping out in the first place – than to bring them back (Roberts and Brodie, 1992). In their post-teens (i.e. age 20 onwards – older youth), people begin to relinquish more leisure activities than they take up: 'Lifestyles become more home-based, and this then becomes a lifelong trend' (Roberts et al., 2009: 274). Indeed, adults become more rather than less con-servative in their leisure tendencies and use the 'relative freedom' of leisure as they grow older to continue with their established routines. In other words, the ten-dency is for people to reduce what they did before rather than to increase it as they age (Roberts, 2006a). As a consequence, the supposed leisure renaissance often said to accompany the later life-stages simply does not occur in practice.

In all of these cases, the significance of age lies in the fact that it is a proxy for life-stages (being a child as opposed to an old-age pensioner, for example) and life-stage transitions (from school to work, for instance). Age can also be a proxy measure for subtle but profound (socially constructed) age-related changes within life-stages, such as from primary school to secondary school or across age-defined legal thresholds. This is why young people's leisure scenes are finely age-graded (Roberts *et al.*, 2009). Their inclination to take part in sport and physically active recreation in their leisure time is at its highest somewhere between the latter primary and early secondary school years, typically peaking between the ages of 9 and 13. Findley, Garner and Kohen (2009: 708) found that Canadian youngsters' participation in 'organized physical activity', while characterized by 'multiple patterns of participation', tended to peak in 'middle childhood' (between 9 and 12) and declined, thereafter, into adolescence. In England, in 2008–09, participation in out-of-hours school sport (see **extra-curricular PE**) gradually increased during the primary school years to reach a peak during the final year, around age 10 (59 per cent). A substantial drop-off as a consequence of the transition to secondary school was followed by incremental decreases between ages 11 (45 per cent) and 16 (35 per cent) and a final downturn during the last two school years, ages 17–18 (18 per cent) (Quick *et al.*, 2009). Although the largest drop in participation occurs at the end of compulsory schooling (around age 16 years in many countries), the decline in sports participation during early youth is steeper in some countries than others. While Canadian adolescents' participation in sports and outdoor activities declined sharply with age from 45 minutes among 12–14-year-olds to 24 minutes among 18–19-year-olds, in Finland 17–19-year-olds reported only 12 per cent less time for physical activities than the 12–14-year-olds (Zuzanek, 2005). Indeed, in Portugal, participation in sport has been relatively stable among 10–18-year-olds with participation in terms of time per month actually increasing with age (Seabra *et al.*, 2007). Notwithstanding the seeming inevitability of 'drop-out' from sport and physically active recreation among youth (in the post-school years) and adults (over the life-course), there is relatively little attrition across age groups in Norway. Among youth, the numbers of 16–19-year-olds participating three to four times per week (19–33 per cent) and almost daily (18–27 per cent) increased by roughly 50 per cent between 2001 and 2007. A similar pattern was evident among 20–24-year-olds where participation three to four times per week went up from 19 per cent in 2001 to 25 per cent in 2007 and almost daily participation increased by almost 50 per cent (13–18 per cent) (Vaage, 2009). Especially noteworthy were the ways particular activities fared among older youth (20–24-year-olds) in comparison with 16–19-year-olds in Norway. Within the trend towards a steady decline in participation levels in sport and active recreation generally from 16 years onwards, some activities fared noticeably less well than others at the juncture between upper-high school and university. There were big drops in participatory levels between 16–19 and 20–24-year-old groups in athletics, basketball, bandy, orienteering, handball and martial arts. At the same time there were relatively high degrees of continuity in some lifestyle activities – for example, jogging, cycling, weight training, cross-country and downhill skiing – and even some individual and team sports – such as golf, squash, tennis, football and volleyball.

23

Examples of sporting adherence during the early transitions to youth notwithstanding, changes in leisure behaviour between age 16 and 30 tends to separate youth into those likely to participate in little, if any, structured out-of-home leisure and those whose leisure will be characterized by relatively high and sustained participation in sport, high culture, going out to bars, cafes, cinemas, discos and so forth (Roberts *et al.*, 2009). Those with the lowest participation rates at age 16 will be the least likely to maintain or increase and the most likely to reduce their involvement in sport as they age. Thus, the inherently transitional life-stage of youth makes it a potentially critical period when dispositions towards participation or non-participation in sport tend to be reinforced or amended, with lifelong ramifications. Everywhere, participation rates tend to hit a ceiling around age 16. By no means all older youth, however, reduce their involvement in out-of-home leisure in general and sport in particular as they progress towards and through their twenties. Indeed, the likelihood of individuals maintaining or increasing their participation tends to vary considerably between socio-demographic groups (Roberts *et al.*, 2009). It seems that those with the lowest participation rates around age 16 will be the least likely to maintain or increase, and the most likely to reduce their involvement in sport as they age. This 'tendency for those who initially do least to do even less, thus widening the gap between the active and the inactive, is possibly international' (Roberts *et al.*, 2009: 274).

In attempting to explain the relatively sharp fall in levels of sports participation across youth and especially during the transition into adulthood in the United States, Zick, Smith, Brown, Fan and Kowaleski-Jones (2007: 125) speculated that 'role changes in late adolescence and early adulthood may be associated with declines in physical **activity**' (Zick *et al.*, 2007: 126). It is noteworthy, nevertheless, that some young people (and adults) are more likely than others are to persist in sport despite the various role changes they experience during the life-stage of youth. In this regard, there is evidence that **lifelong participation** (or, at least, a later exit from participation) is directly related to participation in childhood and youth and, in particular, to the number of sports played when young (Coalter, 1999; Roberts and Brodie, 1992). Such **sporting repertoires**, along with predispositions towards or away from sport more generally (and the concomitant likelihood that youth will successfully negotiate life-stage transitions still engaged in sport) are not only firmly embedded during childhood but appear highly dependent upon cultural inheritance from **parents and families** (Birchwood *et al.*, 2008). Although youth sporting experiences (and, in particular, school PE and sport programmes) may play an important, if not always crucial role in reinforcing predispositions towards (or, for that matter, away from) involvement in sport in later life (in a way that such experiences in early adolescence may not), the point is that the longer an individual is participating in sport 'the less likely s/he is to drop out from sports in later life' (Scheerder *et al.*, 2006: 426) – and family-inherited predispositions (Birchwood *et al.*, 2008) may be crucial in setting the parameters for this.

The extent to which levels of participation during youth are continued into adulthood and sustained will depend upon not only the quantity, quality and availability of sports **facilities** and sufficient leisure-time but also, and crucially, on the sporting **habituses** (or predispositions) that young people have or have not acquired by that age. Indeed, 'The extremely low rates of participation in physically active recreation within the present-day older age groups are not due solely to them having dropped out of sport during their adult lives but are also due to the poverty of their childhood sports **socialization** and the limited opportunities that were available for them to continue playing sport after leaving school' (Roberts, 1999: 139).

Note

1 It is important to remember, nevertheless, that as a classificatory marker that inevitably circumscribes young people's lives – legitimizing some things while sanctioning others – age remains very significant for young people.

BODY/BODIES

The modern Western liberal ideal of the autonomous (self-governing) indi-vidual revolves around the assumption that individuals can – along with the expectation that they will – control their bodily urges and subjugate them to rational will. Growing concern with the human body in the social sciences in recent decades has been a direct response to the tendency inherent in Western thought to overlook (or, at least, underestimate) the ways in which people are physical and emotional as well as mental and (potentially) rational creatures; in other words, *human* beings motivated by emotional impulses and a search for emotional gratification as well as capable of reasoning in order to achieve desired outcomes. Interest in 'the body' or 'bodies' has also been a response to the realization that the physical bodies of human beings are very much socially constructed in at least two senses. First, and in a more general sense, the ways in which people view their bodies and what they signify or 'mean' are expres-sions of collective, social beliefs about the body learned, in the first instance, via **socialization**. Second, and more specifically, the physical shape, condition and appearance of people's bodies not only have significance for their self-**identities** but can also be deliberately altered – in appearance (fake tans, tattoos and body-piercing, for example) and habitual behaviours (such as drug use and training regimes) – via various cultural practices.

It is necessary, therefore (so the argument goes), to conceive of our bodies as social products 'regulated', at least in part, 'into a desired shape and appearance by cultural norms' (Roberts, 2009: 19). Images of ideal bodies are normalized in contemporary Western societies and young people's reflection on their bodies takes place in the immediate context of their families, **friends and peers** but

25

also in the wider context of media and **commercial** interests – in effect, of market places in which they are encouraged to consume a variety of commodities. Many of these commodities are not only intended to connect young people 'to images of youthfulness, beauty and desired forms of masculinity and femininity' (O'Donnell, 2008: 137) but also presented as means by which they can become the kinds of people they want and/or consider themselves to really be. Concern with their bodies among young people is more exactly, however, a concern with their outer appearance rather than their 'inner' **health** and well-being. This is neatly illustrated by the increasing popularity of injected tanning potions.

The growing social science interest in bodies parallels post-modern claims that in highly developed consumer societies (in which traditional structural differences in the form of **age, social class** and **gender**, for example, are believed to have substantially diminished if not disappeared) people can treat their bodies as 'projects' to be sculpted, toned and fashioned in a manner that expresses a chosen **identity** – that, in other words, symbolizes who they think they are, their sense of self. The visible surface of people's bodies can be used to display 'signs' (regarding gender and sexuality, for example) or chosen identities (their individuality and taste) or express status and affiliation with particular groups (such as bodybuilders or 'Goths'). Young people are particularly inclined to use their bodies to communicate with gestures, bodily posture (the physical aspect of habituses, such as particular styles of walking associated with Afro-Caribbean youngsters, for example) and the ways in which they adorn their bodies (Roberts, 2009). The upshot is that young people's bodies are now a significant aspect of their lifestyles to be manipulated in the search for identity and meaning; to be displayed, pierced, trained, cosmetically and surgically enhanced or embellished. In the process young people endeavour to manipulate their identity in the eyes of others as well as in their own eyes.

Tattooing and body-piercing are said to be two recent examples of the trend towards young people treating their bodies as projects (Shilling, 2005). Other examples include the development of sharply honed, muscular physiques in health and fitness gyms or the use of cosmetic surgery and/or dieting in order to acquire more (sexually) attractive bodies. In ways such as these young people's bodies can be (but by no means always are) extensions – and, therefore, emblematic – of their more general **lifestyles**. Bodily appearance can be a particularly significant aspect of young people's **habitus** and the physical habits or behaviours (such as walking styles) of young, working-class males in particular. In this regard, the skills and knowledge that young people embody amount, in effect, to physical **capital**. Shilling (2005) argues that it is those people who have the requisite financial resources, spare **time** and cultural capital – in other words, middle-class youngsters – who are most likely to treat their bodies as projects to be moulded in line with their preferred images of themselves.

The significance of bodies for youth sport

Bodies are of particular significance in relation to sport. The popular Latin motto *mens sana in corpore sano* (a sound mind in a sound body) – so prevalent in nineteenth-century public school games traditions – neatly expresses the ideology that control over the body is an essential prerequisite for turning young people (and especially young males) into wholesome, 'rounded' and appealing adults. Nowadays, the shape and appearance of young people's bodies regularly feature in the **moral panic** surrounding the alleged **obesity** epidemic and debate about the consequences of **commercialized** leisure lifestyles (including, among other things, fast-food diets and alcohol consumption) for the health status of young people.

The contemporary preoccupation with exercise as a vehicle for bodily self-improvement is hardly surprising when one considers the ways in which young people are bombarded with messages about the necessity of gaining and maintaining lean, athletic-looking bodies. The cultural significance and, therefore, prominence of sport and the physiques of sporting stars means that young people in the developed world are especially likely to be dissatisfied with their appearance and desire to (whether or not they actually do – see **role models**) undertake 'body **work**' – physical exercise, enhancement and adornment – in an effort to improve the 'look' of their bodies. Young people frequently use their bodies (in terms, for example, of hairstyles and muscula-ture) to embellish other expressions (such as clothing) of membership of particular groups or subcultures (such as surfers, skateboarders, bodybuilders, and dancers).

For those youngsters committed to a particular sport or sports, **participa-tion** often involves disciplining their bodies to acquire some combination of strength, fitness, suppleness and shape. The control and shaping of their bodies by young people can be effected directly (e.g. through the kinds of **technol-ogy** and **activities and exercises** commonplace in health and fitness gyms, dance and various forms of aerobics) or indirectly (through the dietary regulation regimes commonly found in gymnastics and dance) (Malcolm, 2008). In some cases the necessary discipline will largely be a matter of personal choice (in preparation for recreational rock-climbing or football, for example). In other (usually competitive) contexts, however, there may be large elements of (more-or-less internalized) external constraint and/or discipline from coaches and **parents**. Sometimes such external constraint can amount to **abuse**. The increased rewards available to talented youth through sporting success brings with it concomitant pressures for them to discipline their bodies – developing and maximizing their physical and therefore sporting potential via, among other things, training as well as the products of performance-enhancing medical sci-ence (**drugs** or psychological training, for instance). These, in turn, can lead to the development of support networks likely to exacerbate the tendency for young people to treat their bodies as projects and aspects of themselves in need of constant surveillance and discipline. Perhaps unsurprisingly, there can be a number of unintended and undesirable consequences when young people discipline their bodies in pursuit of sporting achievement and success. O'Donnell (2008), for example, uses the term 'female athlete triad' to refer to the presence of the three related bodily conditions sometimes found among committed women athletes: disordered eating patterns, amenorrhea (loss of periods) and osteoporosis.

As well as enhancing their bodily appearance, sport also provides opportunities for young people (and males in particular) to display messages regarding their gender identities. Sports – like rugby union (Dunning, 1986; Dunning and Sheard, 2005; Light and Kirk, 2000), and boxing (Wacquant, 1995) among others – and physical activities – such as weight training, martial arts and climbing – are often used by young males to express and display toughness, courage, self-discipline, resolution, **risk**-taking and so forth. Similarly, albeit less frequently, sports (such as cheerleading, aerobics, dance and synchronized swimming) are used by some young women to express their femininity.

In conjunction with the personal traits thought to be necessary for (or developed by) participation in competitive games and contact sports, the consequences of some activities (such as rugby and weight-lifting) for bodily appearance – in the form of disfigurement through injury or highly developed musculature – while expressive of high status masculinity among young men can prove off-putting for some young women dissuading them from viewing such activities as suitable. The demands upon young women to model their bodies and appearance on stereotypical norms regarding femininity and attractiveness (Gard and Wright, 2005) means that where they do take part in characteristically male activities (such as football) they feel obliged to utilize 'apologetics' – emphasizing their femininity through the use of make-up and jewellery and generally feminizing their appearance. Inevitably, both 'sporty' and 'non-sporty' women 'monitor and survey their own bodies' (O'Donnell, 2008: 138) as they seek to avoid stigma and anxiety. Impression management tends to be of particular importance to young women (see gender) in relation not only to sport in general but also sport in schools (**physical education**) in particular. In a similar manner, their bodies are often central to the self-images and identities of young people with physical **disabilities**.

The relationship between sport and the body is especially keenly felt among youth. In focusing upon skilled sports performance and an ideal of slender, toned and fit bodies, sport (especially in schools) inevitably alienates some young people unlikely ever to be either or both of these (Evans et al., 2007). It needs to be borne in mind, nevertheless, that in addition to its significance for their identities, young people's bodies are vehicles in sporting terms for experiencing excitement. Indeed, young people are 'ingenuous in seeking ways to experience sensual pleasure, excitement, thrill' (Roberts, 2009: 20) and nowhere is this more evident than in their **leisure** and sport and physical recreations in particular (see risk).

CAPITAL

Most often used in an economic sense to refer to 'any assets that can be invested with a view to accumulation and profit' (Roberts, 2009: 25), the term capital can be defined more broadly as anything that has an exchange value and which can be used to acquire something else. In the social sciences, it finds employment in the terms of social and cultural capital and, increasingly, variants of these including physical, sporting, **identity** and symbolic capital.

Social capital consists of social relationships in which (in keeping with the economic analogy) people are said to 'invest'. The relationships that constitute social capital have value and provide advantages in the sense that they serve to facilitate such things as sports **participation**. Social capital is typically conceptualized as having two dimensions or forms: bonding (the ties and relationships between [similar] people and, in particular, 'valued, trusted relationships' [Roberts *et al.* (2009b: 74)]) and bridging (the links between individuals and different groups of people) (Putnam, 2000). Bonding capital is often witnessed among **friends** who enable and accompany each other when skateboarding, surfing and playing partner and team games and so forth. Bridging capital comes in handy when parents and relations, family friends and even friends' parents provide young people with access to their golf, squash and other sports **clubs**, for instance. The significance of social capital lies particularly in the manner in which it supplies opportunities – rather than pulls strings as it is commonly assumed to do in 'popular folk explanations' of access to, for example, employment and membership of particular clubs (Roberts *et al.*, 2009b: 75).

Cultural capital, on the other hand, consists of the skills, knowledge, beliefs, predispositions, tastes and values people acquire in their particular social milieu (Bourdieu, 1984; Roberts, 2001) and which serve as a kind of cultural coinage or currency (Field, 2003). Cultural capital is typically a product of early **socialization** experiences and conditioning within particular social networks and specific (often class-based) lifestyles (Kew, 1997). Cultural capital becomes literally and metaphorically embodied (and given tangible or visible form) in young people's dispositions, skills and abilities; in other words, their **habituses**. Shared cultural capital and experiences, leading to shared outlooks and knowledge, constitute group habitus (Elias, 1994). In this regard, references to the term subcultural capital are used to denote forms of cultural capital which develop within the subcultures and around particular activities such as rugby, martial arts, surfing, climbing and skateboarding. This subcultural capital might, for example, include the role of dietary supplements, recreation and performance **drugs**, dress codes, musical tastes and even language.

The significance of early socialization experiences notwithstanding, cultural capital is 'built up gradually' (Roberts, 2001: 218) and, in the same way that economic resources can be passed-down the generations, so too can social and

29

cultural resources – hence, the claims for the significance of **parents and families** in the intergenerational transmission of cultural capital (Gunn, 2005; Roberts, 2009) and the fact that the form it takes may change over time.

While both forms of capital can be significant, overall cultural capital is likely to be more significant in sporting terms than social capital; put another way, what a young person knows is likely to be more important than who s/he knows. If education is anything to go by, social and economic forms of capital are important but mainly insofar as they create access to crucial cultural capital (Roberts *et al.*, 2009a).

It is increasingly commonplace to identify specific forms of social and cultural capital. Coalter (2007: 57), for example, refers to 'sporting capital' to describe those social networks that provide 'access to sports-related technical skills and knowledge'. Similarly, the bodily or physical manifestations of young people's lifestyles are often referred to as 'physical capital' – in other words, physical abilities, skills and attributes. Identity capital (Cote, 2002) is used to refer to the abilities, appearance and interaction skills young people can draw on in constructing and refining their identities. All of these various and specific forms of capital may be viewed as aspects of social and cultural capital; that is to say, a dimension of *who* people know and/or *what* they know and can *do* – in terms of their physical and social skills and abilities.

While social and cultural capital is something that all young people possess – the generation of capital is an inevitable feature of all their social networks – the crucial differences lie not so much in the amounts of capital each possesses but rather in the types and how valuable these prove to be in particular social settings, such as sport and education (Roberts, 2001). Thus, capital has an **age and life-stage** dimension. Childhood and youth are periods of intense capital accumulation (Jones, 2009) and the more narrow and difficult childhood and youth experiences tend to be, the smaller will be the stocks of sporting capital which youth 'preserve or build up and then carry into later life-stages' (Roberts, 2005: 7). Interestingly, 'Life course effects on **leisure** during young people's **transitions** to adulthood appear impervious, almost completely unresponsive, to changes in the macro-economic and political contexts' (Roberts *et al.*, 2009a: 276) if and when leisure-related cultural capital is embedded early on in life.

The physical dimensions of cultural capital are particularly salient expressions of **social class** (Evans, 2004; Kirk, 2004; Shilling, 1998, 2005). Physical capital incorporates physical condition and **health** and because it has implications for health generally and health-related physical **activity and exercise**, in particular, socio-economic status is inevitably tied to health. Middle-class children, for example, have healthier diets, take part in more physical activity (Wanless, 2004) and become generally stronger and healthier than working-class youngsters; not least because 'Poorer households in poorer communities are less likely to have access to healthy, affordable food and suitable recreational **facilities**' (Royal College of Physicians *et al.*, 2004: 21). While all young people possess capital of one form or another, their 'horizon of possibilities' (Lane, 2000: 194; cited in Blackshaw and Long, 2005: 251) in sporting and leisure terms are constrained by their socio-economic backgrounds and expressed in their predispositions towards or away from particular activities. Indeed, the possibilities of those from lower socio-economic groups tend to be constrained by limited social networks which typically lead to 'a poverty of expectation' (Blackshaw and Long, 2005: 251). Put another way, 'At all subsequent life-stages, and in all spheres of life, the cultural capital that individuals bring to their situations affects their opportunities' (Roberts, 2001: 218). Hence, because the most privileged young people have the greatest opportunities to acquire social and cultural capital, they are far more likely to become sporting and, for that matter, leisure omnivores. The likely profound significance of social class notwithstanding, it is important to recognize that it is usually in the family where the groundwork of social and cultural (and, in particular, physical and sporting) capital is initially laid: cultural capital is especially significant in the intergenerational transmission of advantages and disadvantages (Roberts *et al.*, 2009a) and families act as mediators of (class-related) capital.

The significance of capital for sport

Some would argue that participation in sport is not only made more likely by the possession of social and cultural capital (knowing relevant people and possessing appropriate knowledge and skills) but it actually *requires* it. In other words, sports participation 'requires confidence, skills, knowledge, **ability** ... (and) a group of supportive friends and companions, including some who share the same desire to take part' (Collins, 2003: 69). In sporting terms, the bridging form of social capital can have a substantial influence on cultural capital insofar as it provides opportunities for young people to practice and develop competence as well as gain experience in situations they might never access otherwise. In other words, who they know can significantly impact upon the sporting opportunities available to young people and, subsequently, the sporting skills and experiences they acquire. Early opportunities for playing expensive sports such as golf and windsurfing are good examples of this. With the right kinds of social and cultural capital, young people are more likely to access and succeed in sport.

Golf provides an especially apposite illustration of the usefulness of the concept of capital for understanding youth sport. As well as requiring a relatively substantial amount of economic capital (in the form of disposable income) – not least because of the cost of equipment and club membership – access to a golf club also requires social capital: for both youngsters and adults joining a private members golf club requires an application for membership to be supported by current members. In this process, it helps immensely if the would-be members share similar forms of cultural capital, because groups tend to recruit members with similar dispositions to their own. In contexts such as golf,

31

hockey and sailing clubs, young people experience the virtuous circle of social and cultural capital. It is in such environments that young people add to the experiences, knowledge and skills (e.g. of appropriate dress codes, after-dinner speeches and even the role of alcohol in celebrations) that further develop their social and cultural capital as resources for future use (e.g. in university sports clubs).

There is no escaping the fact that structural factors (such as neighbourhood residence) remain influential in the generation and transmission of capital and, thus, in shaping the (sporting) identities and predispositions of some groups of young people (Shildrick, 2006). While all young people possess social and cultural capital in one form or another, the term capital is most often used to explain what amount to social class differences in sports participation. Particular social class locations make it more or less likely that involvement in differing kinds of sport (such as skiing or weight-lifting, rugby union or rugby league) will lead to young people acquiring particular forms of physical capital (e.g. in the form of skills and physical attributes) that have symbolic value and kudos and can prove to be valuable social, cultural and even economic resources (membership of a golf club or, for that matter, a sailing or polo club tends to confer a good deal of symbolic and identity value as well). In this regard, it is argued that young people's **bodies** have been, and continue to be, socially constructed in the sense that the programmes of sports and/or physical activities (from military drill in the nineteenth century through team games to 'body management' activities such as aerobics and HRE [health-related exercise] in the twenty-first century) they experience at their various class-differentiated schools (Gorard *et al.*, 2003) leads to young people developing particular skills and particular views of their bodies which serve to reinforce social class positions and orientations. The point is that social class does not just impact upon 'choice and preferences' (Evans, 2004: 102) in sport, it also has a substantial impact upon individuals' physical capabilities: in other words, their skills and abilities. Consequently, the distinctive sporting practices that characterize working- and middle-class people are far from arbitrary but arise out of their class-related physical capacities and dispositions (or **habitus**).

According to McDonald (2003), the body (and, by extension, physical capital) is pivotal in understanding the relationship between social class and sport and PE. In other words, 'How we manage our bodies in terms of diet and exercise, how we carry our bodies in terms of posture and deportment, how we present our bodies in terms of clothing, and how we use our bodies in social and physical activities, carry significant social and class meanings' (p. 170). In effect, young people's physical skills, experiences and even physical condition have a significant influence on their predispositions towards new or familiar activities and help shape their tastes in, among other things, sport. The ways in which young boys and girls from different social classes hold particular views of what sports and physical activities it is 'cool' – that is to say, socially appropriate or normative – to be involved in (e.g. boxing, football, skateboarding and surfing), as well as how they want their bodies to look (e.g. in relation to levels and forms of muscular development among boys and norms of thinness among girls) are, on this view, an expression of the cultural dimensions of social class and are reinforced not only by their peers but also, it is often claimed, by **role models** (from the worlds of sport and music, for instance).

All in all, notions of cultural and social capital help us to appreciate that while economic resources lie at the heart of social class, social and cultural relations and resources help create and reproduce differences and inequalities: money is not the sole reason for the less well-off having 'a narrower range of tastes and activities' (Roberts, 2001: 86), in sporting terms in particular. In this vein, Kew (1997) suggests that some sports – he probably had in mind such things as polo and sailing and, to a lesser extent, fencing, golf, skiing and sub-aqua – remain more or less socially exclusive whether or not they continue to be cost-exclusive. Similarly, Wilson (2002: 5) observes that findings from the *General Social Survey* in the United States suggest that 'those who are richest in cultural capital and those who are richest in economic capital are most likely to be involved in sports generally' and that 'these tendencies are independent of one another'. He adds that whereas economic capital has no bearing on involvement in what he refers to as 'prole' or working-class sports, 'those richest in cultural capital are least likely to be involved' in such sports in the United States (p. 5).

There are, of course, interrelationships between social and cultural capital in various dimensions of young people's lives. There is, for example, evidence that involvement with voluntary sporting, arts and other organizations (such as the church) when young, leads to integration into wider social institutions such as school and **work**. The medium for this may well be the social capital that young people (on upward life trajectories) acquire within these social networks (Roberts, 2008). In a similar vein, Pichler and Wallace's (2007) study of patterns of social capital in Europe, found that youngsters in Scandinavian countries and the Netherlands had the highest levels of all forms of social capital alongside some of the highest rates of youth sport participation. Engstrom's (2008) study of sport habitus and later exercise habits found an almost fivefold greater likelihood that an individual with 'very high' cultural capital at the age of 15 (as defined by their social background and grades in theoretical subjects at school) would still be an active exerciser 38 years later in comparison with an individual with 'very low' cultural capital. In short, it seems that 'Those who acquire the most leisure capital during childhood, will be the most likely to build on these foundations during the next life-stage' (Roberts *et al.*, 2009a: 274).

CLUBS AND ORGANIZED SPORT

A sports club can be defined as an association of more-or-less 'like-minded people ... coming together to produce and consume a common interest – a particular sport' (Coalter, 2007: 59). In the United Kingdom, sports clubs have tended to focus upon single sports. Occasionally, however, larger clubs – that often originated as single sport clubs – provide several sports. Such larger, multi-sports clubs lie at the heart of organized sport in mainland Europe where community sports provisions are overwhelmingly club-based and state support (for youth sport) is largely channelled through voluntary sports clubs.

Organized sport is usually taken to mean those types of sporting activities that have clear structures in the shape of governing bodies, national and regional networks of clubs, with **competitions** and fixtures, and regular scheduled training and practice sessions, team selection and so forth. Sports clubs are model examples of organized sport inasmuch as their activities tend to be characterized by being 'regular, methodological, programmed and guided' (Koska, 2005: 305), group-based and provide playing, teaching and coaching hierarchies. Historically, the term sport(s) club has been used to refer to the kinds of voluntary, not-for-profit associations commonly associated with 'traditional' organized sports such as football, rugby, cricket, netball, hockey, athletics and tennis. Nowadays, however, use of the term club in the sporting context has broadened to incorporate commercial variations such as squash and dance as well as **health** and fitness clubs.

The significance of sports clubs for youth sport

Since the emergence of modern sporting forms in the public schools of England in the second half of the nineteenth century, it has been conventional to view sports clubs as the bedrock of sports **participation** around the world. While in continental Europe it has been the norm for youngsters to attend (multi-sport) sports clubs, in Britain and other English-speaking countries many youngsters have been as likely to access sport by remaining at school beyond the school day for so-called **extra-curricular physical education**. Even in the United Kingdom, however, it has always been assumed that schools would provide opportunities for young people to access voluntary sports clubs in the vicinity as the most likely and/or suitable vehicles for ongoing involvement in sport – and organized and competitive sport in particular.

A study of the nature and extent of sports participation in the 25 EU member states over the previous 20 years (van Bottenburg et al., 2005) revealed that, in 2004, 70 million EU citizens (15 per cent of the EU population) were members of sports associations. Such figures are likely to represent a somewhat rosy picture not least because not all members of sports associations are active participants: golf and sailing clubs, for example, tend to have relatively large numbers of 'social' members.

Despite the existence of several anomalous studies – suggesting, for example, increases in active sports club participation among male and female 14- and 15-year-olds adolescents in Iceland between 1992 and 2006 (Eiðsdóttir et al., 2008) and an upward trend in Finnish adolescents' involvement in organized sport (Laakso et al., 2008) – overall levels of club membership among all **age** groups in Europe remain below the levels they were a quarter of a century ago. Since the 1980s, in countries such as Belgium, Finland, Germany and the Netherlands, there has been a decline in participation and membership among young and old alike. Kjønniksen, Wold and Fjørtoft's (2009) longitudinal study of Norwegian youngsters revealed that the proportion reporting being a member of a sports club declined with age from 13 years onwards among both boys and girls. Indeed, in Denmark, France, Germany, Great Britain, Italy and Spain, 'a large and rapidly growing proportion of the population is engaging somewhat informally in sport, in other words, independently from membership of a club' (Heinemann, 2005: 181–82). This overall longer-term decline in sports club membership has occurred alongside a decline in participation in organized sport among both young people and adults, as illustrated in countries such as Australia, Sweden and the United Kingdom (Dollman *et al.*, 2005). Using data from the *General Social Surveys*, Clark (2008) found that organized sports participation among children aged 5–14 also declined in Canada between 1992 and 2005. In 2005, 51 per cent of 5–14-year-olds (2.0 million children) in Canada regularly took part in sports during the previous 12 months with about 51 per cent of those taking part in more than one sport and involved in sports activities on average about 2.5 times per week per sport during their sport's season. As a consequence of trends such as these, sporting organizations worldwide can regularly be heard bemoaning the tendency of young people to turn their backs on sports clubs.

The decline in membership of sports clubs as well as involvement in organized sport among young people is, in part, due to changes in **youth cultures** and lifestyles. It is also a by-product of young people's longstanding tendency to desert (organized) sport and sports clubs as they grow older. As with levels of participation in sport more generally, participation in organized sport and sports clubs tends to rise steadily through the primary years to peak at or just before the early teens, declining markedly when young people reach the end of compulsory schooling (Breedveld, 2003; Quick, 2007; Roberts, 1996a, 1996b, 2004; Telama *et al.*, 2002). Despite the trend away from sports club membership among young people generally, in countries such as England, attempts continue to be made to develop and sustain links between schools and sports clubs in the expectation that these are likely to propagate participation among young people in both recreational and elite sport. In 2008–09, for example, schools in England had links to an average of eight sports clubs (Quick *et al.*, 2009). For the most part, these were football, cricket, dance, rugby union, swimming and athletics clubs; that is, predominantly conventional sports clubs.

It is important to recognize, however, that the decline in sports club membership among young people does not mean that they are abandoning physically active recreation or, for that matter, competitive sport altogether. The majority (59 per cent) of the 'active' Dutch teenagers in Elling and Knoppers (2005: 261) study 'participated in sport within an organized club context' and, at the

35

end of the 1990s, 'about 56 per cent' of Flemish high school pupils were actively involved in club-organized sporting activities (Scheerder *et al.*, 2005b: 325). Notwithstanding the fact that involvement in club sport declines with age, for a minority of youngsters competitive sports participation in club settings remains an important aspect of their **leisure**-sport lives. Indeed, while more young people are taking part in individualized activities as many as ever are playing team sports such as football. It is simply the case that today's young people are less 'clubbable' than their predecessors. Clubbability refers to 'young people's predisposition towards being involved in the more formal atmosphere of clubs and associations corresponding with organized forms of leisure provision' (Roberts, 2004: 91) and increasing numbers of young people seem to find the more informal, recreational, lifestyle activities – such as swimming, skateboarding and BMX (bicycle motocross) and mountain biking – more attractive than organized sports and their associated sports clubs. Rather than heralding the extinction of organized and competitive sport, therefore, current trends merely indicate 'a shift in the constantly moving boundary between club sport and self-organised recreation' (Roberts, 2004: 32) with youngsters increasingly likely to engage in recreational versions of traditional sports such as swimming and football – 'without joining clubs and teams, and participating in competitions' (p. 32) – as well as lifestyle activities such as surfing and free-running.

The shift is also partly attributable to processes of **individualization** and **informalization** among youth. Thus, the (adult-) determined and highly structured nature of much organized sport (in clubs, for example) – where activities almost invariably imitate the forms and structures of adult sport and tend to be organized by adults who act as gatekeepers for what is played, who plays, where, how often and with whom – has become increasingly unappealing and off-putting to youth in recent decades, especially in comparison with the newer **lifestyle sports**.

In addition, in all developed countries (including those with strong sports club traditions, such as Norway – where participation at sports clubs has declined since the 1980s) there has been a substantial shift towards commercial facilities – in keeping with the widespread trend towards lifestyle sports – since the late 1990s, with private provision having become larger than sports club provision. The increasing desire among young people (and adults) in many countries to engage in more **commercialized**, individualized and flexible sports and physical activities rather than regular, relatively structured forms of involvement – such as that required by a strong commitment to club-based sport – is consistent with the broader changes in the increasingly individualized lifestyles of participants (Coalter, 1999, 2004; Roberts, 2004). All told, young people's lack of involvement with sports clubs reflects a general tendency in youth leisure whereby 'in the late teens clubs tend to be replaced increasingly by commercially run venues such as cafes, pubs and discos as the setting for social life' (Feinstein *et al.*, 2007: 306) (see **facilities and venues**).

This is simply an expression of a more atomized involvement in many aspects of their leisure lives, including club membership, among young people.

The 'like-minded' people that continue to populate sports clubs are often from similar age ranges, educational backgrounds, sex, **social class**, **ethnic** and religious groupings (Coalter, 2007). Consequently, while sports clubs provide the context for the development of (or 'investment' in) bonding **capital** between the people from similar backgrounds who tend to populate such clubs, they tend to be less successful in the development of bridging capital: partly because clubs and their neighbourhoods or catchment areas tend to be 'socially and spatially isolated' (Coalter, 2007: 59) and partly because the more common sports for particular groups (e.g. of young working- and middle-class white males) can be quite different (soccer and martial arts compared with hockey and tennis). In such situations, some groups of young people (such as South Asian, Muslim, young women) are less likely than others to possess the kinds of social and cultural capital (whether in the form of connections with sports club members, particular sports skills, social skills or the kinds of 'business', voluntary or administrative skills) that would give them a bridge into new and relatively exclusive sports clubs. Because sports clubs recruit differentially according to class, **gender**, **ethnicity** and **(dis)ability**, the male-dominated world of organized and club sport has been a stumbling block for young women as well as ethnic and disabled groups for a long time. In Norway, for example, only approximately one in ten young women with an immigrant background from non-Western countries are members of sports clubs (Walseth, 2006a) while boys generally tend to report significantly higher participation in organized youth sport at ages 14 and 16 than girls (Kjønniksen *et al.*, 2009).

In addition to male domination of club-organized sporting practices (Scheerder *et al.*, 2005), it is likely that a perceived lack of competence in particular sports will impact upon young people's inclination (see **motivation**), if not desire, to participate. This is likely to be especially so in organized, competitive sports club settings and, in part, explains the relatively greater representation of young women in lifestyle sports.

COMMERCIALIZATION AND CONSUMPTION

Commercialization is the process by which something becomes increasingly monetarized. When turned into things to be bought and sold in the search for profit, areas of life such as sport are said to be commodified. In addition to the obvious examples in elite-level spectator sport, recreational **participation** in sport has also become an increasingly commercialized and commodified process, particularly in developed countries. Closely associated with commercialization and commodification is the process of consumption – the actual (purchase and) use of goods or services such as sport. A culture of consumption is said to be a distinctive and pre-eminent feature of contemporary society (Cook, 2006) and one that has 'assumed a stronger role in personal identity and maintenance' (Roberts, 2009: 44). Nowhere is this more prevalent than in the **leisure** lives of young people as they 'make purchases in order to align with and signal their membership of a particular sub-culture (of which there are many nowadays) or, more typically today … express their individuality' (Roberts, 2008: 77). Because leisure and consumer lifestyles are prone to quick disintegration (Jones, 2009), the significance of consumption for identity is, nevertheless, limited (Roberts, 2006). Consequently, although young people are unable to construct meaningful and enduring **identities** through what they consume, consumption can serve to publicize and reinforce the kind of person they see themselves as being at a particular point in time.

Commercial leisure becomes an increasingly prominent aspect of young people's leisure lives, as they get older and move through three broadly **age**-related stages: from organized leisure (up to approximately 13 or 14 years of age), through casual leisure (15–16 years) to commercial leisure (roughly 16 years and beyond) (Furlong and Cartmel, 2007; Roberts, 2006). At the same time, commercialization is becoming an increasingly prominent aspect of very many of the leisure (and sporting) activities young people engage with at all ages and stages. Despite the decline in full-time youth employment and the fact that commercial leisure is by its very nature rationed by the ability to pay (Roberts, 2008), 'young people collectively are spending more money than ever and have become a weightier consumer market segment' (Roberts, 2003: 21). Youth obtain their money from a combination of part-time jobs, paid house-work, pocket money, grants and loans (see **work**) in order to remain 'the most active age group in virtually every type of out-of-home leisure' (Roberts, 2003: 21). Increased levels of overall affluence and, in particular, the relative prosperity of young people from the middle classes have added fuel to the commercialization of leisure – as young people have acquired spending power a variety of fashion, music and leisure retailers and advertisers have identified commercial opportunities and targeted them. The 'young singles scene' is a large market for commercial leisure and a wide range of commercial enterprises have set about encouraging young people to see themselves as individuals in order that they might be further encouraged to utilize leisure consumption (whether cloth-ing, clubbing, musical tastes or sport) to highlight their distinctive, supposedly **individualized** leisure 'styles' (Furlong and Cartmel, 2007). One consequence of young people's increased access to consumer goods and the commercial ten-dency to package young people as 'kidults' or 'post-adolescents' (Jones, 2009) has been a weakening of the conventional boundaries between childhood, youth and adulthood (James and James, 2009) (see **age and life-stages**).

The significance of commercialization for youth sport

Developments in team games such as football, rugby and cricket neatly illustrate the effects of processes of commercialization, commodification and consumption increasingly apparent in virtually all forms of sport, especially since the latter decades of the twenty-first century. So too do recent developments in so-called **lifestyle activities,** such as fitness and **health** and even supposedly 'alternative' and adventurous activities such as surfing and rock-climbing. The rapid development of recreational (or leisure-) sport as a commodity has gone hand-in-hand with the diversification of leisure and sporting opportunities and the attendant emphasis upon encouraging young people to seek a distinct and individualized leisure style. Some areas of youth sport (e.g. blading, dancing, surfing and gyms) and their related subcultures are now popular and profitable markets for commercial enterprises. Similarly, the area of health and fitness has been transformed into a highly profitable commercial sector. The diversification of sporting activities (ranging from Ultimate Frisbee, through indoor 'bouldering' and climbing venues to Wii interactive game consoles) and the rapid growth of 'new' commercial activities (such as health and fitness gyms and paintballing) reflect the ingenuity of a breadth of commercial leisure enterprises in responding to and shaping the growing leisure and leisure-sport market. Animal, Billabong, Helly-Hansen, Quiksilver and The North Face are among many whose clothing and accessories make more money for their owners and shareholders than the sports equipment (for surfing, mountaineering and climbing) that they were originally associated with.

When it comes to the appeal of more commercialized forms of sporting activities to potential and current participants, in some areas of leisure-sport commercialization has gone hand-in-hand with both increased popularity and the preference among youth for commercial **facilities and venues.** Wheeler and Nauright (2006), for example, note that the tremendous growth of golf in the past three decades means that it is now the leading sport in the world in terms of total economic expenditure (there are well over 25,000 courses worldwide, collectively covering an area close to the size of Belgium) with 45 per cent of golfers in the United States aged between 18 and 39.

Elsewhere, it remains an open question whether or not the effects of commercialization on the development of shorter, quicker, more competitive, more action-packed even spectacular activities (such as small-sided and indoor variants of cricket and football) are likely to make them more attractive to youth in participatory terms to anything like the extent some of them (such as 20-20 cricket and indoor climbing competitions) appear to be becoming as spectator sports. In general, trends in participation over the last 40 years have been towards so-called lifestyle activities (such as skateboarding, blading, BMX and mountain biking, dancing and aerobics), many of which might be viewed as the antithesis of commercialized sport. Nonetheless, while some would argue that such new and different sporting sites enable expressions of subcultural 'resistance' to **globalization** and commercialization, such an argument is difficult to sustain in relation to the activities often cited as examples – such as surfing and climbing – which have themselves become increasingly commercialized (e.g. in clothing styles, equipment and venues) and globalized.

According to Coakley (2004), one consequence of youth sport programmes in the United States becoming subject to increased (commercialization and) privatization has been reduced availability of community-based 'sport for all' programmes. The implication that this will be damaging to youth sports participation is not straightforwardly corroborated by the available evidence, however. As young people grow older, they evidently prefer more casual and commercialized leisure and sporting forms over organized variants. That said, the ability of individual young people to access and engage with commercialized forms of participation – including not only private health and fitness **clubs** but also fee-paying voluntary golf, sailing and squash clubs, for example, will continue to be mediated by their ability to access economic as well as social and cultural **capital**. Material deprivation has a significant impact on young people's ability to access sport in the form, for instance, of equipment and families and the lowest income groups are more likely to go without certain leisure activities. In 2007 in England and Wales, for example, lone **parents** were seven times more likely to be unable to afford 'toys/sports gear for each child' than couples. Among lone parents, those working less than 16 hours per week were almost three times less able to afford such items than those working 16 hours or more (Philo *et al.*, 2009). Some young people are marginalized and, as a consequence, excluded from increasingly popular forms of commercial sport and leisure. Unemployed youngsters, for example, simply lack the financial resources to participate in (increasingly) commercial leisure and sport at an age (post–16) when these are becoming more central to the leisure and sporting lives of their peers.

For some observers, the spending power of youth nowadays and the appeal of adult-like lifestyles have made the pressure for young people to consume in their leisure a pressure towards precocious maturity (Jackson and Scott, 2006). Taking part in sport or attending a fitness gym – like slimming, having a haircut, acquiring a (fake) tan, purchasing particular items of clothing and footwear (including sportswear) – are means by which young people are encouraged and actively seek to construct lifestyles and embellish identities and, in particular, adult-like identities. One significant aspect of the pressure towards maturity is the commercially driven encouragement towards risky behaviours such as consuming alcohol and experimenting with adventure sports.

COMPETITION

In July, 2007, in the run up to the 2012 London Olympics, the UK Prime Minister announced a £100 million campaign to encourage sporting competition within and between schools at both primary and secondary levels. The campaign included a network of (225) 'competition managers', a new National School Sports Week, and greater use of sports coaches in schools, as well as charging governing bodies of sport with developing school sport competitions. But what do we mean when we talk of competition and why does such faith tend to be placed in competitive sport for young people?

Perhaps the most useful conception of competition defines it in terms of two people or groups of people, both seeking and striving for the same goal in the knowledge that one achieving it denies the 'prize' to the other. Sporting competitions are, by their very nature, zero-sum activities in which only one person or team can win and for one to win another must lose. The requirement that competition requires two mutually oriented participants (or groups thereof) necessarily precludes the possibility of climbers competing against the rock face, runners competing against the clock and sportsmen and women, more generally, competing against themselves. These latter cases clearly represent different phenomena to football matches, sailing regattas, cycling and athletic races and so forth. Indeed, they are better referred to as (game-) challenges (of the kinds associated with physical recreation) whereby participants seek to overcome a challenge according to a system of rules that make that challenge (such as free-running an urban space, performing a particular skateboard move and so on) possible and, as a consequence, enjoyment and/or satisfaction of one kind or another a likely as well as a desirable outcome.

The significance of competition for youth sport

Competition is significant for youth sport in two ways: first, the relative popularity (or otherwise) of competitive sport – not least in terms of the levels of young people participating; and, second, the assumptions commonplace among politicians, the media and the general public regarding the personal and social merits of competitive sport.

In relation to **participation** in competitive sport among young people, there are some noteworthy features. There is, for example, a marked **age** dimension. Like participation in sport more generally, competitive sport during the school years is distributed along a bell-shaped curve with the youngest (roughly 5–8 years) and oldest (14 and upwards) age groups the least likely to be involved and those in between forming the bulk of participants as well as the most enthusiastic age group. Thereafter, during the teenage years, participation in competitive sport (and, as a corollary, **clubs and organized sport**) declines markedly. According to Quick *et al.'s* (2009) *PE and School Sport Survey* of 21,464 primary and secondary schools in 2008–09, participation in any intra- and inter-school competitive sport in England increased gradually year-on-year reaching a peak between the ages of 9 and 13 years. In 2008–09, 69 per cent of young people in England aged between 5 and 16 participated in some form of *intra*-school competition during the academic year while 28 per cent of 5–19-year-olds participated regularly. Defined as three times or more during the school year 2008–09, 'regular' intra-school participation rose year-on-year

41

among upper primary school pupils (roughly 8–11 years) to reach a peak of 45 per cent by age 10–11. When the definition of regular rose to 12 times or more for 11–18-year-olds, participation in intra-school sporting competition dropped substantially to 28 per cent and continued to decline to a low of 6 per cent among 17–19-year-olds. In the case of *inter*-school sporting competition, 44 per cent of pupils across ages 5–16 years participated on at least one occasion in England during 2008–09 whereas 19 per cent of 5–19-year-olds participated regularly (three times or more for 8–11-year-olds and 9 times or more each year for 11–19-year-olds). Overall, although participation in intra- and, in particular, inter-school competition was high among youngsters between the ages of 7–9 and highest at ages 9–10, there tended to be a dramatic decline in competitive sports participation once children moved into secondary school.

Decline in the popularity of sporting competition among young people may be inevitable. By its very nature, the appeal of competitive sport is likely to be limited and, therefore, partial; not least because it inevitably involves failure for some (if not many) participants. On top of this, because young people's **identities** are inevitably intertwined with their perceptions of success and failure – in education and sport, for example – such experiences are not only likely to affect young people's (sporting) identities but also their self-esteem. As a corollary, perhaps, a significant feature of trends in sports participation among young people in recent decades has been a widespread shift away from competitive sport towards non-competitive, **lifestyle activities** (Coalter, 1996). In their study of the 'organised competitive' and 'recreational' sporting behaviours of 6,479 12- and 15-year-olds (3,270 males, 3,209 females) from six European countries (Belgium, Estonia, Finland, Germany, Hungary and the Czech Republic), Telama *et al.* (2002: 140) confirmed a shift towards such non- or, at least, less-competitive lifestyle activities among young people. Despite this general tendency, participation in competitive sport has not fallen in direct proportion to the increased engagement with less structured, more recreational lifestyle activities. Indeed, competitive sport remains an integral feature of the **leisure**-sport participation profiles of young people as a whole in many European countries (De Knop and De Martelaer, 2001; Scheerder *et al.*, 2005a; Telama *et al.*, 2005). Nor can the substantial shift towards lifestyle activities (or, for that matter, the fact that only a small minority continue to play competitive sport into their adult lives) be taken to indicate that competitive sport – and especially competitive games – is in terminal decline among young people. The trends in leisure-**time** sport among youth reflect a broadening and diversification of participation rather than a wholesale rejection of competitive sport per se. In the mid-1990s, Roberts (1996a) observed that most young people in England and Wales were competing at sport regularly both in and out-of-school. More recently (and as indicated above), Quick *et al.* (2009) found that, although their appeal waned considerably as they progressed into and through secondary school (i.e. towards youth), *intra*- and *inter*-school competitive sports remained popular among youngsters.

When it comes to the relationship between **gender** and competitive sport, there is extensive evidence that girls are less likely to be attracted to competitive sport than boys. While participation levels in inter-school competition for both girls and boys appeared to have 'steadily increased' [Institute of Youth Sport (IYS), 2008a: 13] in England in recent years, they have done little to impact on the long-established gap in participation levels between girls and boys in inter-school competition. In fact, the gaps in participation between school-aged young people 'has remained broadly the same with girls' participation equating to around three-quarters that of boys' (IYS, 2008a: 13). This is because girls tend to have individual, task-oriented and competence **motivations** for participation in sport (Biddle *et al.*, 2005) and are, therefore, more likely to choose to engage in non-competitive styles of sports. Interestingly, girls and young women who choose non-competitive styles of sports participation appear more likely to continue involvement in leisure-time sports than those focused on competitive sport (Scheerder *et al.*, 2006). That said, it is noteworthy that while Canadian boys between the ages of 5 and 14 years were less likely to regularly participate in sports in 2005 than they were in 1992, those who did compete were involved in fewer sports – an average of 1.8 sports versus 1.9 – whereas girls who participated played the same average number of sports in 2005, 1.7, as they did in 1992 (Clark, 2008).

In many countries, and across Europe in particular, it is conventional for voluntary sports clubs to be the main or even sole providers of sporting competition to young people. In North America, after-school sports clubs, organized and delivered by school coaches, provide the traditional setting for inter-school competitive sport (Curtner-Smith *et al.*, 2007) and Miller (2009) reports that, in 2007–08, 55 per cent of US high school students participated in organized high school sports. While not as overt a vehicle for competitive sport as in the United States, the bulk of extra-curricular school PE time in the United Kingdom continues to be devoted to competitive (usually coached) sport.

In relation to the second significant aspect of competition for youth sport – assumptions regarding the benefits of competitive sport for young people – the claims made are, to say the least, contentious. First, it is highly debatable whether competitive sport can be said to be meritocratic in the sense that those with most ability and/or who work hardest (those who, in other words, 'deserve' to win) are the ones most likely to succeed. Whether or not sport is meritocratic depends upon the answer to the question can merit (e.g. in the case of acquired skills) be divorced from other socially constructed advantages gained, for example, from being male and/or middle class? Put another way, 'Can merit be measured independently of socially transmitted advantages and disadvantages' (Roberts, 2009: 167)? If it cannot, or is not, then sporting success merely perpetuates a myth of individualism; it serves, in other words, to convince young people with **ability and talent** that success – which, by degrees, is likely to have been the consequence of socially constructed advantages accrued via, for example, their **parents and families** as well as their subsequent individual efforts – is simply a consequence of their talent allied to hard work. Second, there is the instrumental view of competitive sport as a vehicle for 'character development'. On this view, competitive sports (and particularly team games) provide young people with lessons in morality (e.g. in relation to fair play) as well as personal characteristics or virtues (such as self-discipline, perseverance and courage) and social characteristics (such as loyalty and civic virtues of subordination to the collective). Such taken-for-granted claims regarding the externalities of participation in competitive sport remain, nonetheless, 'vague and unexamined' (Coalter, 2005: 191) assertions for which there is little or no empirical evidence. Indeed, concerns regarding the potentially damaging effects of early introduction to sporting competition has led countries such as Norway to prohibit organized sporting competition before the age of 12 (Skirstad, 2009).

All in all, competition remains a pervasive and contentious aspect of youth sport.

DISABILITY

The increasingly successful application of science, in general, and medicine, in particular, in combating illness and disease over the past two centuries has resulted in the dominance of scientific models of **health** and illness. The corresponding privileging of what became known as the 'medical model' of **disability** (Barnes et al., 1999) meant that those medical and educational experts (such as doctors and educational psychologists) charged with the diagnosis of, and prescription for, disability tended to focus upon young people's particular mental or physical impairments in the medical terms associated with dis/functionality. Consequently, the term disability has come to be used to refer to biomedical conditions which limit a person's ability to perform specific tasks with the result that those with disabilities 'are often viewed in terms of their level of *functional* ability to carry out the routine tasks of everyday life' (Nixon, 2007: 419; emphasis in the original).

In response to the individualistic and decontextualized – and, correspondingly, partial and inhibiting (Meegan and MacPhail, 2006) – views of individuals with disability manifest in medical models, an alternative 'social model' emerged in the latter decades of the twentieth century to challenge the 'personal tragedy view of disability' (Fitzgerald, 2006: 756). From this perspective, disability (like other social dynamics such as 'race' and **gender**) was conceptualized as a social construct rather than a biological or medical category. Thus, it is now generally accepted that 'medicalized' diagnoses ignore wider social processes (e.g. of stigmatization) and the general socially constructed physical (e.g. sports **facilities** without disabled access[1]) and cultural (such as sports and games that, in unmodified form, are inaccessible to youngsters with disabilities) barriers to **participation** in wider, supposedly 'able-bodied', societies. In this manner, social models or explanations express a view of people with disabilities as constrained by situations that, in their effects, disable (and, as a consequence, oppress) them – not as an unavoidable consequence of their disability, as such, but rather because of the ways in which people and institutions respond or, more often, do not respond to them and their needs (Oliver, 1996). In practice, their engagement with various institutions (such as education and sport) is mediated by a wide variety of socially constructed restrictions – which often go hand-in-hand with impoverishment and multiple disadvantages – such as a lack of private transport and equipment and inaccessible school and sports buildings as well as discriminatory attitudes.

A consequence of the shift towards viewing disability as socially constructed has been a preference for the term special educational needs (SEN) over disability alongside calls for much greater incorporation of youngsters with SEN in sport. Consequently, two additional terms have come to dominate research into disability sport: integration and inclusion. Integration refers to the extent to which people participate while inclusion is said to denote the final stage of integration – in which young people with disability/ies are not simply involved but also accepted and respected and able to take part without being stigmatized (Nixon, 2007). What has occurred in practice, however, has not always met with the approval of those favouring inclusion, let alone those who question the logic underpinning claims that inclusion is inherently a good thing or that it is undesirable to differentiate or discriminate within sport.

The significance of disability/SEN for youth sport

The ways in which disabilities or SEN militate against participation in sport among young people are many and varied and more prevalent than commonly assumed. In the United States, for example, approximately 10 per cent of families have a child with a disability that can interfere with participation in sport and physical exercise (Sabo and Veliz, 2008). In England, the differences to be found between the general school **age** population and youngsters with a disability in participation in sport in school are mirrored in the differences out-of-school. Out-of-school, approximately half the number of young people with a disability (40 per cent) took part in sport in 1999 compared with the general population of young people (79 per cent) (Sport England, 2001a). Similarly, just over a third (37 per cent) of children and young people with a disability had taken part in sport during lunch-breaks on school days compared with two-thirds (67 per cent) of the overall population of young people, while half (47 per cent) had participated in sport at the weekend compared with three-quarters (74 per cent) of the general school population. The Sport England (2001a) study also revealed that approximately one in six

(15 per cent: 17 per cent of boys and 14 per cent of girls) 6–16-year-olds with a disability did no sport or physical **activity** at all out-of-school lessons in the previous year. More recently, Burgess' (2007) small-scale survey of 11–19-year-olds reported 27 per cent of wheelchair users did no sport at all, either in or out-of-school. By contrast, virtually all (98 per cent) primary- and secondary-aged youngsters in the Sport England (2003a) study participated at least once in out-of-school lessons in 1999.

The picture regarding the numbers of sports undertaken by youngsters with a disability and those without was similar out-of-school to within school. The average number of sports played frequently out-of-school, for example, was considerably less than half (1.7) the number played frequently by children and young people in general (4.5) (Sport England, 2001a). As with in-school participation, it was generally the case that the greater the number of disabilities (or the more complex the disability) young people had the lower the average number of sports they participated in, either at all or frequently, out-of-school (Sport England, 2001a). Similar to the general school population, the types of sports in which young males and females with disabilities took part frequently out-of-school lessons in England in 2000 consisted of an amalgam of team games and **lifestyle sports and activities**; albeit, with the balance tilted firmly in favour of the latter. The top five sports frequently undertaken by youngsters with a disability (or SEN) were:

- Swimming (35 per cent: made up of 40 and 36 per cent primary-aged boys and girls, respectively, and 34 and 32 per cent secondary-aged boys and girls).
- Football (18 per cent: 26 and 9 per cent primary-aged boys and girls, and 29 and 9 per cent secondary-aged boys and girls).
- Cycling (16 per cent: 20 and 17 per cent primary-aged boys and girls, respectively, and 17 and 12 per cent secondary-aged boys and girls).
- Other game skills (12 per cent: 19 and 18 per cent primary-aged boys and girls, and 7 and 9 per cent secondary-aged boys and girls).
- Walking (12 per cent: 11 and 13 per cent primary-aged boys and girls, and 11 and 13 per cent secondary-aged boys and girls).

(Sport England, 2001b)

The activities in which 11–16-year-olds with disabilities participated in frequently were similar for males and females: swimming (34 and 32 per cent, respectively), football (29 and 9 per cent), cycling (17 and 12 per cent), walking (11 and 13 per cent) and other games skills (7 and 9 per cent) (Sport England, 2001a). Approximately three-quarters (74 per cent of boys, 70 per cent of girls) did one or more of 21 different sports undertaken by the sample, of which basketball and swimming were the most popular.

Overall, the Sport England (2001a) survey revealed secondary-age youngsters to be involved in similar sports out-of-school as within school PE lessons.

As is the case with young people generally, the activity profiles of many youngsters with SEN were likely to include lifestyle activities alongside more conventional sport, including team games such as football and basketball. Indeed, the top five 'games' undertaken frequently out-of-school by youngsters with disabilities [football (18 per cent); skittles or tenpin bowling (5 per cent); rounders (4 per cent); cricket (4 per cent); basketball (4 per cent)] (Sport England, 2001a) all featured in the top 10 sports undertaken frequently by the general school population. It is not altogether surprising to find that more individualized activities tend to play a large part in the participatory profiles of those youngsters with disabilities engaged in sport both in and out-of-school lessons. Nevertheless, whereas in school this is often because youngsters with disabilities have little choice, out-of-school (that is to say, in their **leisure**) it is more an expression of their preferences. As with young people's sport, in general, however, and notwithstanding studies confirming swimming as disabled youngsters' favourite free-**time** activity (Fitzgerald and Jobling, 2004), it would be an oversimplification to assume that the popularity of individualized activities such as swimming means that youngsters with disabilities are avoiding sports and games. Basketball, for example, is very popular among wheelchair users (Burgess, 2007) as are disability-specific activities such as boccia.

For the vast majority of disabled youth, most sports provision has occurred through and in 'special schools' or a growing number of organizations such as the English Federation of Disability Sport (EFDS). It has been a feature of the last 20 years, however, that the mainstream sporting organizations that hitherto have typically catered only for non-disabled people have begun to offer opportunities to disabled people and youngsters in particular (Thomas, 2008). The popularity of sport among young disabled people and the involvement in provision of both special schools and the EFDS notwithstanding, Thomas and Smith (2008) point up the relatively weak provision of leisure-sport opportunities for young people with disabilities beyond formally organized sports **clubs** and national governing bodies of sport. Against this, and despite the limited opportunities available in school PE, as far as wheelchair users in Burgess's (2007: 38) study were concerned, 'the situation in the community was a good deal better' than in schools. Nevertheless, young people with SEN readily identify a number of 'barriers' to participation including:

- Lack of money/high costs.
- Lack of or problems with transport.
- Dependence on other people (especially family).
- The inaccessibility of sports facilities and equipment.
- Lack of adequate and knowledgeable coaching.
- Negative attitudes of those without disability.

(Blauwet, 2007; Sport England, 2001a)

Some of these (such as money, transport and facilities) are, of course, often identified as barriers to participation among the general population. Their effects tend, however, to be more pronounced and pervasive among disabled groups than among the population as a whole. The manner in which many of these barriers – cost (or lack of money), lack of transport and dependence on other people, for example – are not only strongly correlated but seemingly insurmountable becomes apparent when one considers that over half (53 per cent) of those youngsters surveyed in Sport England's (2001a) study were living in rented accommodation and approximately one-third (30 per cent) were from one-parent families. **Parents and families** are particularly significant in terms of access to sport and the general participation experiences of young people with disabilities (Nixon, 2007), particularly because they 'can easily become cut off from their friendship networks and wider communities' (Smith et al., 2007: 228).

The role of special schools in comparison with mainstream schools vis-à-vis disabled youth sport is worthy of particular attention. It seems that policies aimed at integrating/including disabled youngsters into mainstream schools (in order to challenge some of the stereotypical assumptions about youngsters with disabilities and breach the kinds of barriers that special schools, it was argued, simply perpetuated) have, in practise, amounted to 'segregated inclusion' whereby students with and without disabilities co-exist separately from one another within the same PE classes and school settings (Meegan and MacPhail, 2006). Not only do the needs of pupils with disabilities appear to have been sacrificed at the altar of 'inclusion', but also mainstreaming has merely served to perpetuate, even exacerbate, stigma attached to SEN. Indeed, it has been suggested that the much criticized and widely abandoned special school system may better serve the interests of young people with SEN: on average, more youngsters were involved in inter-school sports **competition** in special schools (46 per cent) than either primary (36 per cent) or secondary (34 per cent) schools (Quick, 2007) and the level of participation in 'at least three hours of PE and school sport' in England in 2008–09 was considerably higher in special schools (57 per cent) than secondary schools (42 per cent) (Quick et al., 2009). By contrast, mainstream schools with relatively high proportions of youngsters with SEN tended to have the lowest levels of participation in three hours or more PE and out-of-hours school sport. The commonplace criticism that sport (like PE) tends to be marginalized in special schools – in part because special school teachers tend to lack sporting expertise – can also be levelled at mainstream PE teachers who lack knowledge of disability sport and youngsters with SEN.

Although this section has focused on the significance of disability/SEN for youth sport, one interesting development in recent years has been what is referred to as 'reverse integration': the involvement of able-bodied people in disabled sports under 'disabled' conditions (e.g. wheelchairs).

Note

1 Access/accessibility refers to the ability to use facilities (such as playgrounds, parks or open spaces and sports centres) not only because they are physically accessible but because, for instance, they are free or affordable, do not require people to travel a long distance to use them and the environment and activities are suitable for those with disabilities.

DRUGS

Drugs (defined in general terms as any chemical substance that, when absorbed by the **body**, alters bodily functions, states and/or capacities) can, broadly speaking, be categorized as legal (e.g. alcohol and tobacco) and illegal or illicit (such substances as cannabis, amphetamines, cocaine, crack, ecstasy, LSD and heroin). In both legal and illicit forms, drugs are a large and widespread socio-economic phenomenon. Indeed, 'there has been considerable cultural accommodation among young people over the last 30 years' (Rojek, 2006: 471) to illicit drugs, so much so that youth view so-called recreational drugs (especially alcohol and cannabis) as a normal aspect of their **leisure** portfolios and one associated, in particular, with sociability.

As with many aspects of leisure, adult predispositions towards alcohol, illicit drugs and tobacco are typically established during youth. Across the 33 European countries in the *European School survey Project on Alcohol and other Drugs* (ESPAD) almost 90 per cent of the 15–16-year-olds had drunk alcohol at least once during their lifetime, with approximately two-thirds (61 per cent) having done so during the past 30 days (Hibell *et al.*, 2009). In England – one of the European countries in which youth consumption of alcohol is highest – drinking habits begin relatively young with up to 8, 19 and 37 per cent of 10–11-, 12–13- and 14–15-year-olds respectively having consumed at least one alcoholic drink during the previous week (SHEU, 2007). Around one in four young people between 14 and 16 years reported drinking at least once a month in Williams, Davies and Wright's (2010) UK study and this increased to over half of 17–19-year-olds. Although less pervasive than alcohol, similar patterns of early consumption are apparent in relation to smoking cigarettes and illicit drug use. Approximately one-third (29 per cent) of European 15–16-year-olds had used cigarettes and 2 per cent had smoked at least a packet of cigarettes per day during the past 30 days. Seven per cent reported smoking cigarettes on a daily basis at the age of 13 or younger (Hibell *et al.*, 2009). While 90 per cent of 10–11-year-olds in England say they have never smoked, this figure drops to 53 per cent of males and 44 per cent of females by the time they are 14–15 years old. Twenty per cent of the 14–15-year-old females and 13 per cent of the 14–15-year-old males in the SHEU (2007) survey smoked at least one cigarette during the previous week while 11 per cent of the older female smokers reported smoking up to 25 cigarettes a week. With regard to illicit drug usage, in 2007–08, 21 per cent of European 16–24-year-olds reported using illicit drugs in the previous 12 months and 7 per cent claimed to have done so in the previous month (The European Monitoring Centre for Drugs and Drug Addiction [EMCDDA], 2009). Similar figures were reported in the ESPAD. Roughly one-fifth of 15–16-year-olds across Europe (24 per cent males; 21 per cent females) reported using cannabis in 2007 and 11 per cent (13 per cent males; 10 per cent females) claimed to have used the drug in the last month (Hibell et al., 2009). Cannabis is also the most commonly used drug among 11–15-year-olds in England and the one most often 'tried' (Fuller, 2008). In England, approximately one in ten (12 per cent) 11–15-year-olds claimed to have ever used cannabis or used it in the past year (9 per cent: 10 per cent males; 9 per cent females), and 5 per cent (5 per cent males; 5 per cent females) reported having used cannabis in the past month (Fuller, 2008). In all cases, proportions of males and females were virtually identical.

All in all, the most prevalent drugs among young people are alcohol, 'soft' or 'recreational' illicit drugs (such as cannabis) and tobacco, in that order. 'Drinking', in particular, has become established as a significant leisure activity among youth (SHEU, 2007), and there has been a substantial growth in the numbers of young people consuming high levels of alcohol in recent decades. On average, half of the ESPAD 15–16-year-olds had been intoxicated at least once during their lifetime, to the point of staggering when walking, having slurred speech or 'throwing up'. For 39 per cent this had occurred during the past 12 months and for 18 per cent during the past 30 days (Hibell et al., 2009). In a large majority of the 33 countries in the ESPAD, beer was the dominant beverage among young 15–16-year-old males while spirits were the most important beverage among females in just over half of the countries. In the United Kingdom, as elsewhere, the most popular drink among 11–15-year-old girls tends to be 'alco-pops' (Williams et al., 2010).

Although increasing experience of alcohol and drugs with age is commonplace nowadays, most young people do not drink alcohol, use illicit drugs or smoke and those that do any or all of these things tend to do so in moderation. Indeed, most measures of general drug use among 15–16-year-olds in Europe reveal a stable or slightly downward trend on average between 1995 and 2007 (Hibell et al., 2009). According to the ESPAD (Hibell et al., 2009), the growth in cigarette smoking during the second half of the twentieth century and more recently, the use of illicit drugs – predominantly cannabis – among 15–16-year-olds across Europe had come to a halt by 2007. Smoking rates are said to have decreased dramatically in most Northern European countries over the last 50 years or so and, in England, the SHEU (2007) archive revealed a general decline since 1996 in the proportions of 14–15-year-olds smoking regularly. Despite the prevalence of drugs among youth, recent surveys of young people's use of illicit drugs also point to changes in usage over the last decade. In the United Kingdom, for example, lifetime prevalence use of at least one illicit drug fell among young people (10–25-year-olds) between 1998 and 2007. This is mainly due to the decline in the use of cannabis, which remains the drug with the highest lifetime prevalence use in this age group (Association of Public Health Observatories [APHO], 2009). Evidence from the ESPAD confirms this: the overall trend in cannabis use among 15–16-year-olds across most of the 33 European countries in the study was downward between 2003 and 2007 (Hibell *et al.*, 2009). Nevertheless, after the two most widely consumed drugs in the Western world – tobacco and alcohol – cannabis continues to be the drug of choice among young people. Indeed, evidence suggests that not only are people 'starting to use cannabis younger' there has been 'an increase in heavy cannabis use' as well as 'the availability of stronger varieties of cannabis' (RSA, 2007: 65–66). The one exception to the stable or downward trends in general drug use across Europe in the noughties has been 'heavy episodic drinking' (consuming five drinks or more per occasion) (Hibell *et al.*, 2009). On average, 43 per cent of the ESPAD 15–16-year-olds reported 'heavy episodic drinking' during the past 30 days. In effect, those young people who drink alcohol are drinking more. According to SHEU (2007), approximately a quarter of 14–15-year-olds in England were frequent drinkers (two or more drinks each week) and over a third were 'binge drinkers' (five or more drinks in any one 'session').

At the individual level, there is often a relationship between the usage of different drugs. In countries, for example, where many 15–16-year-olds reported recent (past 30 days) alcohol use and intoxication, more were likely to report experience of illicit drugs (Hibell *et al.*, 2009). Young people in Europe who smoked cigarettes (87 per cent) or had taken illegal drugs (94 per cent) were also more likely to drink. Thus, although alcohol is more prevalent than illicit drug use among youth (Smith, 2006) there appears to be a ratcheting effect: increasing numbers – up to 14 per cent of 14–15-year-olds according to SHEU (2007) – are mixing drugs and alcohol 'on the same occasion' and those youngsters who use drugs most frequently appear to be the ones who drink and/or smoke 'excessively' (Furlong and Cartmel, 2007). Higher cannabis initiation (or use) is also associated with greater smoking (Pampel and Aguilar, 2008) among young people and adults. This pattern is unsurprising among youth given that 'clubbers' are the group among whom drug use tends to be most prevalent. In such contexts, young people are more inclined than their predecessors were to experiment with drugs and to select different drugs (with their associated highs) 'according to mood, environment and occasion' (Furlong and Cartmel, 2007: 100) and, for that matter, mix drugs with alcohol and tobacco. Interestingly, however, given that it almost invariably takes place in their **free** time, young people do not consider smoking a leisure activity in the same way that they do alcohol and drugs (and especially not one associated with sociability).

Among young people, drug use is consistently associated with sociability. Indeed, there tend to be considerable pressures on young people in social situations to drink heavily on occasions in order to 'fit in' with **friends and peers**

(Furlong and Cartmel, 2007; Williams *et al.*, 2010). In England, young people who have friends and older siblings that use cannabis are also significantly more likely to report personal cannabis use and use of drugs other than cannabis (MacDonald and Marsh, 2002; Parker and Egginton, 2002; RSA, 2007). In their study of Mexican youth, Parsai, Voisine, Marsiglia, Kulis and Nieri (2009) concluded that the norms and intentions to use drugs among a group of Mexican heritage pre-adolescents in the south-west United States were more consistently related to peer variables than parent variables. In a similar vein, Svensson (2003) has observed how exposure to deviant peers is more important for the drug use of females in families where parental monitoring is poor.

One illustration of the process of normalization is the increasing evidence of a tacit acceptance of some aspects of general drug usage (such as drinking alcohol at home) among the **parents** of teenagers and youth: the majority of drinking reported by young people in the ESPAD was in private households, with young people who had drunk alcohol saying they had done so in their own homes (62 per cent) or other people's (41 per cent). Over half (53 per cent) of under-18s who drank said they were given alcohol by their parents, and this was the most common answer given by children of all ages. The tendency for young people to drink at home has become a feature of the normalization of alcohol. Drinking in the home is significant because, as Järvinen and Østergaard (2009) noted in relation to adolescents aged 14–16, the more lenient the parents' attitudes and rules are the more their children tend to binge drink.

As with other areas of young people's lives, there are structural dimensions to drug usage. Working-class youngsters, for example, are 'most likely to use a wider range of illicit drugs on a more regular basis' (Shildrick, 2002: 46), demonstrating higher illicit drug trying and usage rates up to mid-adolescence at which point greater proportions of youngsters from more middle-class backgrounds begin to experiment with drugs (Parker *et al.*, 2002). Higher rates of illicit drug use, particularly cannabis, are also found among young people living in single-parent as well as lower-income families. Smoking is also significantly structured by **social class**: manual working class groups are substantially more likely to smoke daily than are the professional and managerial classes (Layte and Whelan, 2009). Habitual smoking starts relatively early in life. Indeed, smoking is an example of primary **socialization**: at least 43 per cent of 12–15-year-olds who smoked lived in a 'smoky' home. Similarly, in Europe, young people who lived in households where other people smoked (57 per cent) or drank heavily (68 per cent) were more likely to drink alcohol (Hibell *et al.*, 2009).

In terms of **gender** and **age** differences, the available data suggest that young illicit drugs users are as likely to be female as male (Parker, Aldridge and Measham, 1998; Parker *et al.*, 2002) and, in the ESPAD study, the gender differences were negligible for smoking in the past 30 days. There has also been some convergence in drinking alcohol with increases in heavy drinking reported among girls in a number of countries (Hibell *et al.*, 2009). Young women from the middle classes, in particular, are drinking more. Heavy episodic drinking remains, however, more common among boys (47 per cent) than among girls (39 per cent) – with the notable exception of Norway.

In relation to **ethnicity,** youngsters from Asian backgrounds are less likely to try drugs compared with their White and Black counterparts, between whom there are no significant differences. In the United Kingdom, White youngsters are roughly five times more likely than Asians and three times more likely than Blacks to have ever had an alcoholic drink. Watt and Rogers' (2007) research in the United States confirmed that Black youth are less likely to use alcohol than White youth. Interestingly, these cultural differences in alcohol use were almost entirely explained by differences in the influence of peers and the family in particular.

Geographically, there is no clear pattern for high prevalence of cigarette smoking in Europe, but 15–16-year-olds in Central and Eastern European countries were often among those reporting higher rates of smoking and those in Scandinavian countries the least (Hibell *et al.*, 2009). Similarly, while high alcohol frequencies are mainly reported by 15–16-year-olds in Austria and Germany, the Nordic countries – Finland, Iceland, Norway and Sweden – belong to those with only very few of this age group drinking this often. The highest prevalence countries for cannabis use among young people tended to be in Western Europe while lower prevalence rates were often found among the Nordic countries and in Eastern Europe (Hibell *et al.*, 2009).

Unsurprisingly, much is made of the significance of drugs, in general, and alcohol, in particular, for youth **health**. Quite apart from the direct threat to life that alcohol (and, for that matter, drugs generally) pose – alcohol is the third largest **risk** factor for **disability** and death among adults in Europe (WHO, 2006) – in broader, more indirect, health terms most alcoholic drinks (including the increasingly popular alco-pops) are as calorific as high-sugar soft drinks. Up until the mid-1990s, alcohol sales had been falling among sections of the youth population, as they became more interested in the club scene and illicit drugs (Furlong and Cartmel, 2007). Subsequently, however, the popularity of alcohol has grown once more on the back of drinking fashions driven by the alcohol industries, as they attempted to capture the young adult market. Since the 1990s, age-related differentiation in the marketing of alcohol in the forms, for example, of alco-pops (e.g. 'Hooch'), spirit-mixers (such as 'Smirnoff Ice') and spirit 'shots' have exacerbated the trend towards higher and earlier alcohol consumption among young people.

Compared with other drugs, youth tend to view cannabis as a relatively safe drug and quite different from the rest. As they get older, however, young people increasingly view drugs as 'always unsafe', once again with the notable exception of cannabis, which is considered to be so by a considerably smaller percentage of the older age groups (SHEU, 2007). Increasingly aware of evidence which suggests that drugs such as ecstasy lead to memory loss and anxiety, young people view cannabis as potentially less harmful than either alcohol or tobacco. In this regard, it is interesting to note that, in keeping with the hypothesis that life as a whole has become increasingly medicalized (Waddington, 2000), general drug usage (rather than recreational use per se) has also become normalized among young people: around 28 per cent of 14–15-year-old males and 51 per cent of females, for instance, reported taking painkillers on at least one day during the previous week (SHEU, 2007).

All told, 'the introduction to alcohol forms an important part of normal **transitions** to adulthood and learning to use alcohol sensibly in social contexts is a necessary skill in most Western societies' (Furlong and Cartmel, 2007: 99). The same may be increasingly true for illicit drug usage but not smoking. Nevertheless, despite the normalization of alcohol and greater tolerance towards illicit drug usage among young people themselves, there is evidence of a growing **moral panic** as part of a public backlash against so-called binge-drinking and the 'anti-social behaviour' often attendant upon it. Driven by the media and the medical profession, moral panic related to drink and drugs draws on extremes in behaviour in order to infer general trends which inevitably tend to be inaccurate and exaggerated (Furlong and Cartmel, 2007).

The significance of drugs use for youth sport

The relationship between alcohol, illicit drugs and smoking and sports **participation** is two-way and the effects of one on the other are widely viewed as self-evident. It is commonly assumed, for example, that regular use of alcohol, illicit drugs and tobacco will be negatively correlated with sports participation and vice versa. However, the relationships tend to be nothing like as straightforward in practice. With youngsters involved in recreational sport rather than elite sport (where the consequences of drug usage appear self-evident) the effects of alcohol, drugs and tobacco usage are somewhat counterintuitive. The effects of alcohol and illicit drugs on participation, for example, can be marginal. In other words, many youngsters who drink alcohol and engage (albeit spasmodically) in illicit drugs such as cannabis still play sport (Smith, 2006). Once again, however, smoking is different. The *British Cohort Study* demonstrates how smoking at age 16 tends to be negatively associated with sports participation in adolescence (Feinstein *et al.*, 2005) – 'Adult smokers tended to be more likely to have spent their leisure time at 16 in youth **clubs**, and less often in sports and community centres' (p. 13).

When it comes to the assumed impact of sports participation on 'unhealthy' behaviours, the relationship is equally paradoxical. It is true that sport participants are more likely to engage in some other healthy lifestyle practices such as consuming healthy foods and abstaining from use of cigarettes and many ('hard') illicit drugs (Brustad *et al.*, 2008; Roberts and Brodie, 1992). The same is not true, however, with regard to alcohol and, albeit to a lesser extent, illicit drugs such as cannabis. Indeed, while engagement in sport tends to discourage youngsters from smoking, it has a habit of exacerbating alcohol consumption. Kokko (2005: 343) reports that the goal of many sports clubs in Finland to develop in young people a 'healthy and tempered lifestyle' has failed to achieve significant results. In fact, in some areas of their lives, such as heavy drinking, adolescent members of sports clubs manifested even more negative health behaviours than other adolescents (Kokko, 2005: 343). In the United States, Nelson and Wechsler (2001) studied a nationally representative sample of randomly selected college athletes. They found that student athletes reported more binge drinking, heavier alcohol use generally, and a greater number of drinking-related 'harms' than non-athlete students. Nelson and Wechsler (2001: 43) concluded that 'athletes are a high-risk group for binge drinking and alcohol-related harms' and that prevention programmes fail to significantly impact on the problem. Many youth sportsmen (and, increasingly, women) tend to consume alcohol in binges – often after **competition**. As a group of young people 'more likely to exhibit the strong social ties found to be associated with binge drinking' (Nelson and Wechsler, 2001: 43), those involved in team sports are also more likely to engage in excessive drinking as part of bonding rituals and ceremonies (such as 'hazing') (see **abuse**). All in all, 'Alcohol continues to be the most frequently consumed drug among athletes and habitual exercisers and alcohol-related problems appear to be more common in these individuals' (El-Sayed *et al.*, 2005: 257).

Being involved in sport tends not only to encourage consumption of alcohol among young people, it is often associated with other high-risk behaviours such as having unprotected sex while under the influence of alcohol. From their study of a 'bi-racial American middle-school population', Garry and Morrissey (2000) concluded that team sport participants were significantly more likely than non sports participants to demonstrate certain risk-taking behaviours including not only alcohol and cigarettes but also carrying a gun or a weapon as well as being in a physical fight. For their part, Metzl *et al.*'s (2001) study of creatine use among young athletes in the United States found that – despite recommendations against use in adolescents less than 18-years-old – creatine (often used as a nutritional supplement among aspirational adult sportsmen and women) was being used by middle and high school athletes (10–18 years of age) at all ages, and the prevalence in those around 16–18 years approached levels reported among collegiate (over 18 years) athletes. In terms of risk more broadly, a number of 15–16-year-olds in the ESPAD (Hibell *et al.*, 2009) reported problems during the past 12 months related to their alcohol consumption. On average, 15 per cent had experienced serious problems with parents and the figure was about the same (13 per cent) for 'performed poorly at school or **work**' or experienced 'serious problems with friends' and 'physical fights'. Risk-related alcohol or illicit drug-related problems were, perhaps unsurprisingly, more common among boys.

While sports participation is strongly associated with consumption of alcohol and 'soft' drugs such as cannabis, this is not so with tobacco and harder drugs. According to Charilaou *et al.* (2009: 969), 'Research suggests that physical activity protects against youth smoking. Their study examined the relationship between physical activity and smoking among 1,390 adolescents and young adults in Cyprus. They found a consistent and negative relationship between physical **activity** and smoking across both sex and age: 'The greater the intensity of youths' physical activity, the less likely they were to smoke' and 'Compared with inactive individuals, physically active individuals smoked fewer cigarettes and were more likely to be non-smokers or occasional smokers. Among physically active individuals, those engaging in more intense activity were less likely to be heavy or light smokers'. Using data from the 1997 Centers for Disease Control and Prevention *Youth Risk Behavior Survey*, Pate *et al.* (2000) examined the relationship between sports participation and health-related behaviours among a nationally representative sample of 14,221 American high-school students. They found that male sports participants were less likely than non-participants to report cigarette smoking, cocaine and other illegal drug use.

Nevertheless, over the last decade, it has become readily apparent that harder drugs are more commonplace in elite junior sport than is often assumed. In American high school and collegiate sport, so-called 'roid rage' among youths who feel constrained to engage with performance-enhancing as well as recreational legal and illicit drugs is well documented (Coakley, 2004). In more general terms, Greydanus and Patel (2002: 829) have observed how, in the United States, 'the drive toward success in sports and the need for a cosmetically acceptable appearance has driven many adolescents to take a wide variety of substances'. They point out that the consumption of a variety of chemicals in the hope of improved sports performance has been fuelled by an explosion of ergogenic dietary products commercially available to youth, including drugs such as anabolic steroids, beta blockers, human growth hormone, stimulants, and erythropoietin as well as dietary supplements such as creatine, androstenedione, protein and amino acids, minerals and antioxidants. The use of such drugs, Greydanus and Patel (2002: 829) conclude, 'has considerable potential to cause physical and psychological damage' to the young people using them.

Overall, the significance of alcohol, illicit drugs and tobacco for sport lies not only in their impact upon sports participation but also in what they tell us about the place of sport in **youth lifestyles**. It is one among a number of popular leisure activities some of which may appear somewhat contradictory but are, in fact, merely different dimensions to young people's leisure lives.

ETHNICITY

Despite the continued and widespread use of the term in the world of sport, the concept of 'race' has no scientific validity based, as it is, upon superficial, morphological differences in the form of observable physical features such as skin colour, facial features and hair texture. Populations cannot be meaningfully subdivided on this basis, not least because geographical boundaries have become less fixed over time as human societies have experienced widespread and massive movements of populations – leading, among other things, to the growth of 'mixed race' populations. In short, the lines of demarcation between supposed races are, at best, 'profoundly blurred' (Harrison and Belcher, 2006: 741) and, at worst, drawn arbitrarily and ideologically.

'Ethnicity', by contrast, is a far more useful concept with which to make sense of differences in relatively distinct cultures or, in other words, ways of life. Even though ethnic groups often share physical characteristics (such as skin colour), the term ethnicity draws attention to cultural traditions and heritage (Coakley, 2004). More specifically, it focuses upon membership of, and identification with, social groups or collectivities on the basis of country of origin, ancestry and history, family arrangements, language, religion and culture and the shared values, beliefs, customs and traditions and overall lifestyles these generate (Gabe *et al.*, 2004; Kay, 2005; Verma and Darby, 1994). Belonging to a particular ethnic group is, therefore, best viewed in terms of shared social experiences rather than shared genetic material and the concept of ethnicity helps make sense of the processes by which particular ethnic groups (even those sharing similar skin colour) learn to identify themselves as, for example, 'black' or Muslim.

Focusing upon ways of life in the form of customs and traditions as well as values and beliefs – rather than simply physical features – also helps in exploring an important dimension of ethnicity (especially in relation to **leisure** and sport); namely, acculturation – the process whereby people from one culture acquire or, at least, are constrained to engage with the way of life of another. In the twenty-first century, increased global flows of people as well as cultural artefacts is said to be the cause of a blurring between many ethnic **identities**. It may be, for instance, that the character of South Asian family life in the United Kingdom is changing as a consequence of being located in a dominant culture that not only differs in some important ways to its own but is itself also developing rapidly as global media mediate global cultural practices. Indeed, increasing numbers of young South Asian heritage women acquiring educational qualifications (Kay, 2005) – with all that entails in terms of movement away from traditional family values – are in the vanguard of changes in family life among some South Asian groups in Britain. Young women in Lowrey and Kay's (2005) study, for example, were fusing the Islamic traditions of their ethnic origins 'with elements of the majority culture' and this was reflected in a 'combination of small indications of movement towards more liberal lifestyles counterbalanced by … Islamic teachings' (Kay, 2005: 111). In Norway, Walseth (2006a: 449) points to the ways in which 'young Muslims settled in the West' commonly 'feel a sense of belonging to an "imagined community" of Muslims' and engage in renegotiating the content of their ethnic and religious identities

57

in their host environment. The complexities of acculturation notwithstanding, while **globalization** may well result in significant changes in the cultural practices of ethnic groups, these will inevitably occur alongside widespread and persistent continuities: 'The cultural menu in every country … is always a mixture of the international and the local' (Roberts, 2009: 138).

The significance of ethnicity for youth sport

Nearly everything that we do in our leisure is, as Roberts (2007a) observes, ethnic. It is, in other words, the product of one or another culture or cultures. Indeed, certain activities – cricket in England, baseball in the United States, Aussie rules in Australia and bandy in Norway, for example – often serve to express and consolidate the ethnic identity of particular (national) groups. Thus, ethnicity is not simply a minority issue even though it is usually treated as one – it is a facet of all sport. Consequently, regional, national and international sporting patterns have always to be considered in the context of ethnicity.

When it comes to sports participation among (minority) ethnic groups the limited extant research is restricted, for the most part, to adults. However, insofar as (i) it includes those aged approximately 16 years and over, and (ii) trends tend to be similar across **age** groups, data can be used to sketch a picture of the particular significance of ethnicity for youth sport.

In England, although a national survey reported 'relatively low levels of sports participation among ethnic minority groups' (Sport England, 2000: 37), the gap in **participation** rates between ethnic groups appears a good deal less considerable than commonly assumed. The frequent (10 times per year or more) participation rate among adult ethnic minority groups overall in 1999–2000 was 40 per cent compared with a national average of 46 per cent. Nonetheless, since the late 1990s, the 'gulf in participation' between white adults and ethnic minority groups appears to have grown in England (Sport England, 2005: 4). In 2002, '44 percent of white adults participated in at least one activity (excluding walking) compared to 35 percent of adults from an ethnic minority group' (Sport England, 2005: 4). Despite evidence (albeit limited and often indirect) of convergence between ethnic minorities and majority populations in relation to sports participation, one recent study of PE and school sport among 5–18-year-olds in England (Quick *et al.*, 2009) revealed that schools with the lowest levels of participation in three hours or more PE and out of hours school sport tended to have relatively high proportions of youngsters from ethnic minority (and especially South Asian Muslim) backgrounds.

The significance of ethnicity for youth sport lies, however, not so much in the overall levels of participation but in the specificities, and there can be considerable variation in the levels of participation not only between different ethnic groups and across different sports but also between men and women (Sport England, 2000). Consequently, despite evident differences, the picture of participation among ethnic groups is a good deal more complex than common sense, stereotypical generalizations suggest. For example, even though they 'tend to congregate in their own districts, teams, **clubs** and ... groups', many ethnic minorities are by no means under-represented in 'most "normal" forms of British leisure' (Roberts, 1999: 217). This is particularly true for Chinese and African-Caribbean males (Verma and Darby, 1994). It is less true for young Asian (and especially female) Muslims. In broad terms, Sport England's (2000) findings confirmed Verma and Darby's smaller-scale research in the mid-1990s in which Chinese and White British adults were the most active sports participants and Pakistani and Bangladeshi the least. Among minority ethnic groups, the Sport England (2000) survey found that, when walking was excluded, Black African (60 per cent) and Black 'Other' (80 per cent) males had higher frequent or regular participation rates than the national average, with Black Caribbean (45 per cent), Bangladeshi (46 per cent) and Pakistani (42 per cent) males less likely to participate in sport than men generally. The picture is similar in the United States, where Trost (2006) points to studies indicating that White children reported higher levels of both sports participation and physical **activity** than African-American or Hispanic youngsters.

The complexity of the constantly developing youth sport landscape (not to mention the attendant danger of turning empirical trends into stereotypes) is highlighted in a number of studies of sports participation among young people. Not only, for example, do pool and snooker tend to have a reasonable following among several ethnic minority female groups (Verma and Darby, 1994; Sport England, 2000), but some activities have also tended to be relatively more popular with females in particular minority ethnic groups than the population overall. Basketball, for example, has tended to be more popular with Black Caribbean and Black African females, cricket with Pakistani women, and weight training with black females in general. Keep-fit/aerobics/yoga was by far the most popular activity after walking among all women except Bangladeshis. In their study of Dutch youngsters, Elling and Knoppers (2005) found that although minority ethnic girls' participation levels generally were low, their participation in traditional masculine sports (such as soccer, basketball, and martial arts) – that also attracted many ethnic minority boys – was relatively high and Ratna (2007) has pointed to the growing numbers of young South Asian girls and women playing football, in particular, in England.

Despite the prevalence of very many different ethnic groups across a wide range of sports, there can, nevertheless, be substantial differences in the kinds of sports minority ethnic groups undertake. In England, for example, African-Caribbeans are hugely over-represented and Asians under-represented in athletics and soccer. While by no means the preserve of one particular ethnic group, cricket, badminton and basketball tend to be particularly popular among Asian, Chinese and African-Caribbean and 'black' males, respectively (Sport England, 2000). Similarly, in the United States, athletics and basketball are populated by proportionately more African-American and African-Caribbean males and activities such as golf and hockey by more European–Americans.

The complexity and diversity of patterns of participation notwithstanding, sex/**gender** and ethnicity combine to affect participation in sport markedly. The overall participation rates among ethnic groups camouflage substantial discrepancies between males and females, and especially among females from Pakistani and Bangladeshi backgrounds compared with females from white, black or mixed ethnic groups (Department for Children, Schools and Families [DCSF], 2008; Sport England, 2000; Trost, 2006; Verma and Darby, 1994). Using national data, Hanson (2005) examined Asian–American women's participation in sport during the high school years and, while they were virtually invisible in the sport literature, the findings suggested considerable diversity across groups of Asian–American women. The data revealed, for example, that while they were no less involved in sport than women from other ethnic groups, Asian–American women, as a whole, tended to display a different pattern of sport participation from other women. They remained, however, less involved in sport than young Asian–American men did.

Altogether, to be female and a Muslim, Hindu or Sikh from any of the South Asian groups – Bangladeshi, Pakistani and Indian – is likely to result in a lower participation rate in sport. Nevertheless, even here, change may well be occurring as increases in participation among female Muslims is being driven by increased involvement in so-called lifestyle activities. Dagkas and Benn (2006: 33), for example, observed that Greek Muslim young women in their study were more likely to participate at weekends and 'preferred a more relaxed way of exercising, for example visiting local fitness clubs or playing informal games with their **friends**'. In this regard, Walseth's (2006a) study of young Muslim women in Norway noted that sport can sometimes be experienced as a 'place of refuge' from difficulties experienced elsewhere in their lives for minority youth. Overall, it seems that young women from ethnic minority groups tend to be constrained more by their gender than their ethnicity (Jones, 2009) – or, rather, the interaction between the two – when it comes to engaging with leisure and sport. Muslim girls, in particular, face significant gender-specific barriers in the form of household and family responsibilities. In addition, being a young Muslim woman and participating in sport challenges the boundaries of their ethnic identities (Benn, 2005), not least because it draws attention to women behaving in an unfeminine manner when sport is not viewed as an expression of respectable femininity (Walseth, 2006b). In this regard, sport is typically seen as antithetical to adhering to the norms for South Asian, especially Muslim, young women (Walseth, 2006b).

The significance of ethnicity in general and the interrelationship between gender and religiosity (the degree to which people regard themselves as religious and the centrality of religion to their lives) in particular for young people's engagement with physical activity was apparent in a recent five-year longitudinal study of almost 6,000 11–12-year-olds from a variety of ethnic groups in London. In broad terms, the study revealed how vigorous physical activity decreased while hours spent in **sedentary** behaviour increased between the ages of 11–12 and 15–16 years, with a larger decline in physical activity in girls than that in boys. More specifically, it showed that Asian youngsters were substantially less physically active than their white counterparts with Asian girls, in particular, exhibiting faster increases in sedentary behaviour between ages 12–13 and 15–16 years than white girls. Sedentary behaviours were higher among black students generally while black girls engaged in less physical activity than white girls (Brodersen *et al.*, 2007). Similarly, in the United States, Latino and Asian youth reported lower levels of physical activity than that of any other ethnic group (Martinez *et al.*, 2008). It seems that when added together, ethnicity and gender can be an especially potent mix in relation to participation in sport and physical activity.

But gender is by no means the only social dynamic which, when configured with ethnicity, has significant ramifications for youth sports participation. The situation is made more complex by the fact that the patterns of sports participation within each ethnic group need to be subdivided by **age** and **social class** as well as gender (Roberts, 2007a). The interactive effects are evident in the form of young black males' prominence in sports such as football, boxing and athletics. Such complexity notwithstanding, the sporting implications of these social dynamics are pretty consistent across ethnic groups: young, middle-class males are more likely to participate in sport and one particular group – female Muslims – frequently appears under-represented in youth sport.

Patterns of participation among ethnic groups highlight, above all, the significance of one particular aspect of ethnicity – religion and religiosity – for sports participation. The more emphasis is placed upon religion among particular ethnic groups, the lower the levels and rates of participation in sport tend to be (Verma and Darby, 1994). In contrast to the other former Soviet states in their study of the South Caucasus region, Birchwood *et al.* (2008) point to the steep decline in sports participation after age 16 in Azerbeijan Baku. This, they suggest, is best explained in terms of a dearth of genuine interest in Western sports in Muslim countries, where cultural, non-material barriers to sport participation can prove highly resilient irrespective of the existence of suitable preconditions for sports participation in the form of economic growth and political intervention. Nevertheless, diversity in religious practices and beliefs to be found among Christians is also to be found among Muslims, as are the corresponding consequences for youth sports participation. Elling and Knoppers' (2005) study of Dutch youngsters revealed wide variation across ethnic groups and even between Muslim groups – Turkish girls (19 per cent), for example, participated half as frequently as Moroccan (40 per cent) girls.

The centrality of religiosity to ethnicity should not, however, overshadow the potential effects of the family among minority ethnic groups in particular. The recent findings of Sabo and Veliz (2008) in the United States and Birchwood *et al.* (2008) in the South Caucasus suggest that although **socialization** into (or, for

61

that matter, away from) sport are shaped by structural factors such as ethnicity and social class, they tend to be mediated by **parents and families** – opportunities in particular activities and encouragement in sports and physical activity more generally are often promoted in the family albeit within ethnic parameters.

Generation effects on sports participation among ethnic minorities not-withstanding, recent immigrants to any given society are the ones least likely to engage with the dominant (sporting) culture (Clark, 2008; Walseth, 2006a, 2006b). Clark (2008) shows how data from the 2006 census revealed that one of the problems confronting recent immigrants to Canada was achieving eco-nomic stability and, because participation in sports often requires economic as well as cultural **capitals**, children of recent immigrants tended to face substan-tial barriers to sports participation. Clark (2008) observed how children of recent immigrants (residing in Canada for less than 10 years) were a good deal less likely to participate in sports (32 per cent) than children of Canadian-born parents (55 per cent). While internationally popular sports such as soccer may provide the children of recent immigrants with a familiar place to integrate into Canadian society, even in soccer participation was lower (10 per cent) than among those whose parents were Canadian-born (23 per cent).

All in all, the sporting choices of all, and not just minority, ethnic groups are made in relation to other lifestyle preferences. It is just that some aspects of ethnicity – and most notably religion and the centrality of family – are par-ticularly significant. Many young Asians are fusing the cultural practices of their families and ethnic groups with the host cultures and **globalization** is not straightforwardly resulting in greater similarities in general or sporting cultures. All of this points up the dangers inherent in ethnocentric (judging another culture against the norms of one's own ethnic group) **policy**-making towards sport wherein, local and national sporting practices (such as 'traditional' team games) are viewed as inherently more suitable and appropriate for young people – via school **PE**, for example.

EXTRA-CURRICULAR PHYSICAL EDUCATION

Extra-curricular PE is best defined as the organization and provision by teach-ers of activities beyond the formal PE curriculum, typically after school and at lunch times but also, in some schools, before the school day begins or at week-ends (Penney and Harris, 1997). In this form, extra-curricular PE or sport is more common in English-speaking countries such as the United Kingdom, Australia and New Zealand. In North America, extra-curricular provision tends to take the form of after-school sports **clubs** oriented towards inter-scholastic sporting **competition**, organized and delivered by school coaches rather than PE teachers (although these can sometimes be one and the same). Thus, in the United States, extra-curricular sport is not so much an extension of the PE curriculum as a quite distinct setting for inter-school competitive sport

(Curtner-Smith *et al.*, 2007). Elsewhere, and in mainland Europe in particular, it is conventional for voluntary sports clubs to be the sole or main providers of sporting opportunities to young people after school. Nevertheless, even in Europe, there are instances of a merging of the various types of after-school or extra-curricular provision. In Flanders, for example, 'sports academies' provide multi-sport programmes after school without the requirement that young people be members of sports clubs as such (De Martelaer and Theebom, 2006). Indeed, in Scandinavian countries such as Norway, extra-curricular sporting opportunities for older children occur not only in sports clubs but also in recreational multi-activity clubs (usually for those aged 10 or younger) typically located in school sports **facilities** and administered by adults other than teachers. Despite differences in format, extra-curricular PE in Britain is not as different, qualitatively, from its counterparts in the United States and Europe as it might seem at first glance. Traditionally, extra-curricular PE in secondary schools has been almost exclusively oriented towards sport and competitive team games in particular (Daley, 2002).

The significance of extra-curricular sport for youth sport

The significance of extra-curricular PE for youth sport is said to lie in its role as the 'fundamental link' (Penney and Harris, 1997; De Martelaer and Theebom, 2006) between curricular PE and young people's participation in sport in their **leisure**. Put another way, extra-curricular PE is meant to bridge the gap between what young people are obliged to do in school PE and what they choose to do out of school in a manner that will enhance and reinforce their ongoing involvement in sport. This is one of the reasons that in England and Wales extra-curricular PE tends nowadays to be referred to (in **policy** documents at least) as 'school sport'.

In marked contrast to media and political portrayals of extra-curricular PE in the United Kingdom, the picture provided by the now abundant research is of a strong and developing aspect of school sport. According to Sport England (2003a), between 1994 and 2002, opportunities for extra-curricular PE in England and Wales improved significantly, and there was a steady climb in the percentage of secondary schools in England reporting an increase in the number of sports offered to pupils – a trend corroborated indirectly by the 2008–09 *PE and School Sport Survey* in England (Quick *et al.*, 2009). In terms of **time** allocation, several studies have suggested that an average of over 20 hours of extra-curricular PE is provided each week in primary schools and between 30 and 35 hours in secondary schools (Qualifications and Curriculum Authority [QCA], 2001; Sports Council for Wales [SCW], 2002, 2006).

Notwithstanding the seemingly widespread provision of extra-curricular PE in secondary schools, estimates of actual rates of participation among pupils tend to vary. If, as the available evidence indicates, somewhere between one-third (at secondary level) and one-half (at primary level) of school-**age** youngsters in the United Kingdom take part in extra-curricular PE on a weekly basis, then between half and two-thirds of youngsters are doing very little on a regular basis and about one-quarter are doing nothing at all. Daley (2002) notes that the numbers of pupils taking part in extra-curricular PE have always been relatively low and continue to be so despite an upward trend through the 1990s: 'Most pupils are given the opportunity to participate in physical activities outside of formal PE lessons, but ... many choose not to do so' (p. 38) – or, at least, choose not to do so on a regular basis. This is particularly so at either end of the school-age continuum; that is to say, in the early years of primary and the latter years of secondary schooling. As with sports participation and, for that matter, involvement with sports clubs, frequent (weekly or more often) participation in extra-curricular PE declines as pupils move from lower- through to upper-school: from about age 10–16. Participation once a week or more in Wales (SCW, 2006), for example, declined steadily across the secondary age range from 51 per cent for Year 7 pupils (11–12-year-olds) through to 38 per cent for Year 11 pupils (15–16-year-olds). The 2008–09 *PE and School Sport Survey* in England (Quick *et al.*, 2009) revealed 35, 20 and 18 per cent of 16-, 17- and 18-year-olds, respectively, taking part in 'out of hours' school sport, compared with an overall average of 45 per cent of youngsters aged 5–18. According to Sport England (2003a: 64) this pattern of participation across the year groupings has 'remained fairly consistent year-on-year' since 1994.

Sex differences in participation in extra-curricular PE are negligible during the primary years (Sport England, 2003a; SCW, 2006) with approximately two-thirds of children in England and Wales, for example, taking part on a regular (at least weekly) basis. Participation declines sharply, however, during the early years of the secondary phase among girls, in particular, and more steadily thereafter. Although the sex gap is wider at secondary level, average levels of at least weekly participation in extra-curricular PE have narrowed over time, even though the general age-related decline in participation continues to be more marked among girls than boys and widens substantially around ages 14–16. In terms of frequency of participation among boys and girls of secondary age, Daley's (2002: 42) study found that 'boys [in England] were involved in extra-curricular activities on more occasions and for longer periods each week than girls'. The 2002 Sport England (2003b) survey suggested, nevertheless, that the 'frequency' gap between the sexes is a good deal closer than that one might expect, with the figures for participation only drawing apart substantially at five days or more per week (7 per cent for boys compared with 2 per cent for girls). Despite these trends, there remains a gap between curricular and extra-curricular PE programmes and young women's active leisure lifestyles out of school (Flintoff and Scraton, 2001). Nevertheless, most of the Australian young women in Wright's (1996; cited in Flintoff and Scraton, 2001) study were physically active out-of-school and, in general, 'more women than ever before are taking part in physical **activity** in out-of-school contexts' (p. 5).

Despite increases in girls' participation in traditionally male games, such as football, the types of extra-curricular PE participated in by boys and girls overall remains fairly consistent as does the tendency for sex differences in extra-curricular participation in specific activities to be more pronounced at secondary level.

Whatever the true figure for levels of participation in extra-curricular PE in the United Kingdom are, there tend to be large differences in the amount and nature of provision as well as the range of sports on offer across schools and regions (Littlefield *et al.*, 2003; SCW, 2001). The same appears to be true in North America, where Braddock *et al.* (2005) observed wide variations in access to and involvement in interscholastic sports and teams between boys and girls in many states in the United States.

A salient feature of extra-curricular PE is the strong sporting (and team game) orientation or 'bias' (Penney and Harris, 1997) amid burgeoning provision – what Penney and Evans (1998) term the 'privileged' position of school sport within PE. As a consequence much concern has been expressed regarding the *kinds* of activities on offer and for *whom* these are intended rather than merely *how much* extra-curricular PE is available per se. Penney and Harris (1997) were particularly concerned with the manner in which extra-curricular PE was, in their eyes, 'dominated by traditional team games', typically had 'a competitive focus' and remained highly 'gendered' (p. 43). Accordingly, they argued that this 'particular focus' resulted in extra-curricular PE 'offering limited opportunities to only a minority of pupils' (p. 43). In the first decade of the twenty-first century, the bulk of extra-curricular PE time in the United Kingdom continued to be devoted to coached and competitive sport (Littlefield *et al.*, 2003; SCW, 2003, 2006; Sport England, 2003a, 2003b). Despite the broadening of programmes to incorporate more recreational sporting forms and lifestyle activities in many schools – not only in the United Kingdom but also elsewhere in Europe, such as Flanders (De Martelaer and Theebom, 2006) – extra-curricular PE continues to have a competitive sport orientation. In the United States, the focus upon competitive sport is taken to what some would view as a logical conclusion in the form of extra-curricular sport delivered by coaches and/or teachers hired primarily as coaches. As a result, 'the goals of American school sport … are generally more concerned with providing entertainment for the local community, sending their players on to a "higher level", and (using their teams) as a means of increasing school funds and as a vehicle for promoting school and community cohesiveness, spirit, and pride' (Curtner-Smith *et al.*, 2007: 133). In countries where extra-curricular PE revolves almost exclusively around competitive sports, such as Greece, this orientation is believed to be a major reason for what are viewed as relatively low levels of pupil engagement (Dagkas and Benn, 2006).

It is important to note, however, that while the readily apparent 'sporting bias' in extra-curricular PE may be a major reason why more youngsters do not take part, it is far from being the sole reason. In addition to the family and religious constraints facing some minority ethnic youngsters and the transport problems experienced by those with a **disability**, many young people have commitments that make attendance at extra-curricular PE difficult. Many of the boys in Bramham's (2003) study of 22 15-year-old boys in four inner-city schools, for example, held 'substantial evening and week-end part-time jobs' and were, as a consequence, reluctant to become involved with extra-curricular PE and enter into commitments towards school sport. Similarly, many reported having to reduce involvement in school sports as well as out-of-school active lifestyles because of the growing demands of public examinations.

It is particularly interesting to note the consistent patterns (over Sport England's three data collection points of 1994, 1999 and 2002) in participation in particular types of extra-curricular PE activity as young people move from primary to secondary schooling. Perhaps unsurprisingly, the activities that show a marked increase in participation rates are, for the most part, those traditionally associated with the expanded provision for, and greater focus upon, sport at secondary level (e.g. games such as rugby, hockey, rounders and basketball). A notable omission from that list, however, was football which repeatedly experiences a drop-off in participation as youngsters move from primary to secondary school (Sport England, 2003a) and for which club provision expands markedly around this age. Other activities that experience a decline in participation as youngsters move to secondary school include netball, gym, dance, cross-country and, interestingly, given the dearth of pools in primary schools, swimming.

All in all, extra-curricular PE continues to be characterized by a large amount of continuity. In England, the most popular extra-curricular PE activities in secondary schools continue to be sports and games such as football, athletics, netball, rounders, hockey, rugby, cricket and basketball (Sport England, 2003a). The only 'lifestyle' or recreational activities offered consistently and pervasively tend to be swimming and dance at primary level and swimming at secondary level (SCW, 2006). Despite the fact that the range of activities provided by schools in extra-curricular PE is changing as such diverse activities as archery, cycling, martial arts and orienteering are introduced (IYS, 2008a, 2008b), the contribution of extra-curricular PE (as with PE itself) to young people's leisure sport is highly likely to be limited for the most part to those youngsters already committed to sport. Even here, it may simply be reinforcing already well-established sporting capital.

FACILITIES AND VENUES

When people speak of sports facilities they tend to be referring to specific, specially constructed types of venues (or places in general) used for sport. Broadly speaking, these can be categorized in terms of indoor (e.g. sports halls, squash courts and climbing walls,) and outdoor facilities (such as football pitches, mountain bike trails and water-sport venues). Underpinning the different types of facilities are three main forms of provision: voluntary, public and commercial. In the voluntary sector sports facilities are provided for their members by sports **clubs** made up of subscribing volunteers of the kind historically associated with sports such as football, hockey, tennis and golf. From the middle of the nineteenth century, public facilities in the form of swimming pools and bathhouses, outdoor pitches for team games and even municipal golf courses became increasingly plentiful in the United Kingdom and, to varying degrees, in other Western countries. In the last quarter of the twentieth century, another wave of sport and physical recreational facilities were added to public provision in the United Kingdom and elsewhere in the form of large numbers of indoor sport and **leisure** centres. In the early years of the twenty-first century, public provision has broadened further to incorporate those facilities provided for some of the newer **lifestyle activities** such as skateboarding (parks), cycling (cycle ways) and mountain biking (trails). Over the last 25 years or so, however, it has been in the commercial (or private) leisure sector where facilities have grown most substantially. Commercial facilities tend to be prevalent in the **health** and fitness industries as well as those sports and activities that lend themselves to making a profit such as squash, tenpin-bowling and dance. In this regard, many countries around the world have experienced the emergence of **body**-image oriented, consumption-based, commercial clubs in tune with the highly **individualized** fashions for jogging, aerobics and the use of mechanized health and fitness equipment (Dunning and Waddington, 2003).

In the United Kingdom, public facilities that were new in the 1970s and 1980s are now inevitably beginning to appear dated and 'run down' and in need of investment; an impression exacerbated by the rapid growth of attractive commercial sports and fitness centres over the last two decades. The kind of investment subsidy required to achieve substantial improvements in these public facilities – and to maintain similar standards of provision to those found in the private sector – is very probably unaffordable by local or central governments. Collins (2008: 87) notes that Sport England estimates '£110 million a year would be needed just to keep existing facilities legal and functioning'. Nor, for that matter, is such spending politically viable, particularly when the welfare states of Western industrialized countries are confronted with funding crises (Heinemann, 2005). Governments, as well as the sporting and health lobbies, keen to endorse active lifestyles need, therefore, to consider the viability of the required levels of recurrent expenditure as well as capital investment not to mention whether they would be able to provide enough facilities necessary to accommodate everyone if all youngsters and adults were keen to play sport regularly (Birchwood et al., 2008).

Many of the wealthier membership-based voluntary sports clubs in major games (such as rugby union, tennis, squash and golf) own their own pitches, courts, courses and clubhouses. The less well-off clubs rent or hire their facilities. Many football, cricket and badminton clubs, for example, hire public facilities for their practice sessions and matches while outdoor sports clubs – such as sailing and climbing clubs – may own their own club houses but rely upon public facilities (reservoirs and national parks) as venues. Other clubs – in the martial arts, for example – are reliant on public or community sports centres, village halls and the like. Many of the newer **lifestyle sports** depend on a mix of public and commercial facilities and venues ranging from local government funded or commercial sports centres (in the case of aerobics and health and fitness gyms) through to town and city centre landscape venues, in the case of parkour/free-running and various forms of skating and blading.

The prevalence of voluntary, public and commercial facilities in the Western world notwithstanding, it is worth noting that the range and type of sporting or physical **activity** venues can differ according to political contexts. In China, for example, popular venues include not only sports clubs and commercial facilities but also the **work** place, home, public places, parks and the local neighbourhood (Xiong, 2007). In many former (such as Armenia, Azerbaijan and Georgia) and current (e.g. North Korea and Cuba) communist countries, facilities are provided by the state, and because there are no voluntary or commercial sectors to speak of, there are no voluntary or commercial sports facilities. This is, of course, changing – particularly in relation to commercial provision – in the wealthier ex-Soviet bloc countries (and Russia in particular) and changing quite rapidly in those communist countries that are, by degrees, embracing capitalism, such as China. Such facilities are inevitably the preserve of the middle and upper classes. The exception to this pattern tends to be in the education system and universities in particular and students worldwide still have more opportunities (in terms of facilities) to play sport than non-students.

Leisure and sporting venues are affected not only by political and cultural conventions in terms of sporting practices but also by geography. Indeed, the two tend to go hand-in-hand. Semi-arctic, heavily forested environments in Scandinavian countries and year-round warmth in the Far East and Australia make particular outdoor sports more feasible and, consequently, more popular. Thus, outdoor venues for activities like cross-country skiing, walking, mountaineering, surfing, beach volleyball and swimming tend to be more plentiful in these regions. One of the more interesting recent developments in the commercial sector has been the provision of 'urban nature' venues in the form, for example, of indoor winter sport facilities and indoor and outdoor climbing venues. The significance of urban areas for the supply of indoor and outdoor facilities and venues in close proximity to potential participants is illustrated by China, where 55 per cent (77 million) of regular sports participants were from urban areas compared with 45 per cent (63 million) from rural areas (Xiong, 2007).

Although it remains the case that rural communities face the biggest barriers to uptake of sport among young people and adults alike – due, in part, to a dearth of some facilities – the *PE and School Sport Survey* of 2008–09 in England revealed that **participation** in at least three hours of PE and out of hours school sport among 5–18-year-olds was higher in rural (56 per cent) than urban (48 per cent) areas (Quick *et al.*, 2009). This suggests that school provision for sport may, to some extent, be compensating for a relative lack of facilities and provision elsewhere.

The significance of facilities and venues for youth sport

The provision of both indoor and outdoor facilities is significant for two aspects of young people's sporting lives: sport in schools and sport in leisure time. Although 'Provisions per capita outside education never match those available in education' (Birchwood *et al.*, 2008: 297), the distinction between facilities for school sport and those for leisure sport is sometimes blurred. 'Many continental schools', for example, 'use clubs' playing fields whereas in Britain clubs are more likely to use schools' sports halls and other facilities' (Roberts, 2004: 91).

As far as school sport is concerned, the provision of suitable and well-maintained sports facilities in schools is not only an issue in Britain (CCPR, 2001) and Europe (Hardman and Marshall, 2005) but also worldwide (Hardman and Marshall, 2000). Many PE teachers in England, for example, subscribe to a view commonplace worldwide, namely that sporting and PE facilities have declined over time in both quantity and quality. Nonetheless, in practice, the vast majority of secondary schools in England own or have access to outdoor pitches and sports fields, approximately two-thirds have access to a multi-purpose sports hall and almost half own or have access to an indoor swimming pool (Sport England, 2003a). Put another way, while the quantity and quality of sporting facilities in schools in England (and, for that matter, the developed world) may not be optimal (and may well, in some places, be deteriorating) they are evidently a good deal better than they were half a century or more ago let alone prior to that.

In terms of their impact on participation, the provision of sporting and physical recreation facilities undoubtedly has the potential to increase involvement in sport and active recreation. They tend, however, to be far more likely to impact upon latent demand rather than create demand. Put another way, they provide more convenient opportunities, more appealing venues and more specialist facilities for those already predisposed towards participation and, as a consequence, are most likely to impact upon the participatory patterns of those already established in sport. The findings from Roberts and Brodie's (1992) study of inner-city sport in the United Kingdom suggest that (in addition to expanding the opportunities and repertoires of 'sporty' youngsters) where facilities might also make a difference to the sporting participation of young people is with marginal players; in other words, those who are interested but are not inclined to go to a great deal of trouble in order to take part in sport. Either way, as evidenced by the substantial growth in private sector provision, facilities tend not to be a source of **motivation** in their own right (Roberts and Brodie, 1992):

69

membership of private health and fitness clubs, for example, has skyrocketed in recent years, but overall rates of participation in the activities provided by these gyms has not risen commensurately.

The evident increases in sports participation in the United Kingdom in the 1980s is best explained in terms of young people who were to some extent predisposed towards sport having been given more opportunities to play a wider range of sports and this, in turn, would have been a partial consequence of developments around the same time in terms of improvements in facility provision for sport in schools as well as in the community generally (Roberts and Brodie, 1992). In a similar vein, from their study of the South Caucasus, Birchwood *et al.* (2008) concluded that the relatively high loyalty rates among young people around 16 years of **age** in the capitals of Armenia and Georgia were probably due to the superior community facilities available to those predisposed towards participation when compared with what was on offer in the non-capital regions. In short, it seems that facilities need to be local and modern if they are to attract marginal youngsters.

In order to impact upon youth sport participation, in addition to being accessible and up-to-date, facilities need to be in tune with young people's preferred activities and participatory styles. The kinds of indoor public facilities provided in recent decades and available for general public use, on a 'pay-as-you-go' basis, 'appear more congruent with present-day young people's and adults' lifestyle preferences than the stronger commitment involved in club membership' (Roberts, 2004: 91) (see lifestyle sports). Where facilities are out-of-kilter with the leisure-sport culture of young people (e.g. school rugby pitches and 'Olympic' gymnasiums), they are unlikely to encourage participation in the way that indoor climbing walls, multi-gyms, indoor swimming pools, dance studios or even skating and BMX 'parks' might. In other words, facilities also need to correspond to popular sporting forms and participatory styles if they are to sustain anything remotely approaching school-age levels of participation in sport during youth leisure.

Historically, children's ability to play has been limited to clearly defined social spaces usually regulated by adults. Activities, facilities and venues organized and patrolled by adults, while prominent and relatively popular among children and early teenagers (often as an extension of schooling) tend to be replaced – as the setting for social life in general and sporting involvement in particular – by commercially run and informal venues during the late teens (Feinstein *et al.*, 2005). Thus, in order to be effective **policy** towards facility provision also needs to recognize young people's preference for creating their own places on their own terms (James and James, 2009) while recognizing the limited public space actually available to young people (Jones, 2009). The difficulties associated with the provision of facilities in tune with **youth cultures** is perhaps best illustrated by local government provision of facilities for the new lifestyle activities such as skateboarding and free-running. In an attempt to corral these activities (partly in response to the **moral panic** engendered by local media) into particular areas of towns and cities, some local authorities have built skateboard and 'free running' parks. Nonetheless, the appeal of ledges, handrails, walls, benches, ramps, steps and other such physical features of the urban landscape for these activities – because of the challenges they provide and the public nature of the venues – means that such facilities are only ever likely to supplement rather than replace cityscapes. Youngsters' latter-day tendency to populate sites hitherto seen as out of bounds, such as urban landscapes, for some of their lifestyle sports reflects the growing level of **informalization** in modern societies and the concomitant preparedness of young people to **risk** social disapproval in order to access suitable public spaces. 'Traceurs' who practice parkour or free-running – a form of athletic performance focusing on uninterrupted, flowing and spectacular gymnastics over, under, around and through obstacles in urban settings – provide a relatively recent example of this phenomenon.

A particularly noteworthy feature of the increased participation evident among young people since the 1970s has been a clear trend within the evidently high retention rate among post-compulsory schooling (the 16-plus) age groups; that is to say, while participation (particularly casual participation) in outdoor, competitive and performance-oriented sport begins to tail off among 16–21-year-olds, participation in facility-based, more recreationally oriented indoor sport does not follow the same pattern. Indeed, as Roberts (1996a: 52) observed in the mid-1990s in relation to England, 'As many 18–21 as 11–15-year-olds were going to sport and leisure centres'. It is playing sport elsewhere (such as outdoor games pitches) that appears to decline with age. As with adults generally, there has been a marked movement indoors in sporting terms among young people (Sport England/UK Sport, 2001); the age group, it is worth noting, that tends matter-of-factly to be associated with heavy involvement in outdoor, team-based sport.

Even though there is less structural differentiation in terms of participation nowadays, differences are visible in the places people play. Different kinds of leisure and sporting venues tend to attract different groups in terms of **social class**, **gender** and **ethnicity** and, for that matter, **age**. Voluntary sports clubs are largely populated by the middle classes. The working classes, on the other hand, are to be found in disproportionate numbers in local public sports centre or on playing fields. While affluent youngsters populate commercial health and fitness centres, less well-off youngsters (and males in particular), by contrast, tend to be found either in public fitness facilities or 'hard core' bodybuilding gyms. Clark (2008) reports that sports participation in Canada is lowest among children in high-density areas where low-income families are more likely to be found and highest in low-density suburban areas of large and mid-sized metropolitan areas. The facilities young people utilize to play sport not only reflect the cultural as well as economic **capital** they possess but also reinforces it. This is because the physical context in which sporting activity takes place inevitably influences the social groups young people mix with and, in circumscribing the groups young people interact with when participating in sport,

71

clubs and facilities influence the nature and form of social and cultural capital young people acquire.

The nature and location of facilities are particularly constraining for women, ethnic minorities and disabled youngsters. While public spaces are important to boys, in particular (primarily in order to play soccer), young women and some ethnic minorities view particular facilities and venues as risky and this, in effect results in a process of self-surveillance (Seabrook and Green, 2004). In Holland, for example, ethnic minority girls 'tended to participate more often in commercial settings such as fitness centres' (Elling and Knoppers, 2005: 262). Thus, as well as being in tune with youth cultures more generally, facilities need to correspond to the surrounding ethnic cultures if they are to have a positive impact upon sports participation. In the South Caucasus region, Birchwood et al. (2008) observe how Azerbaijan is currently constructing a range of Olympic-grade sport facilities to support a bid for the 2016 summer Olympics. Such sporting provisions are, however, unlikely to lift levels of participation among local young people, simply because few Olympic sports coincide with the sporting predispositions and interests of youth in the region. The trend towards lifestyle activities among young people and adults across Western Europe is particularly significant, because these kinds of involvement are typically provided by public or commercial venues rather than by the (multi-) sports clubs associated with Central European countries and even the most successful sporting countries in the Western world: Australia and the United States.

There is reason to believe that a good deal of drop-out from sport occurs, because participation is less convenient during adult lives (Roberts and Brodie, 1992). The best way to change this would be to make sport more compatible with people's lifestyles; that is to say, more convenient. On the face of it, this would involve more and better facilities. Nevertheless, while sports facilities can make a difference to levels and rates of participation in sport, for the most part, this tends to be by enabling those predisposed to do so to take part. Explaining differences in sport participation rates among young adults in the South Caucasus, Birchwood et al. (2008) observed that the superior sports facilities in the capital cities offered the most plausible explanation for the higher rates of age 16 sport participation (except in Armenia: see ethnicity), and more so for the relatively steep drop-out after age 16 in all the non-capital regions. They concluded that participation in regions of Armenia fell steeply after age 16 because, while sport was strongly encouraged while young people remained in education, afterwards 'there were neither the facilities nor **motivation** among the population to sustain participation at close to the age 16 level'. While supply-side changes are unlikely to make a strong or quick impression on either overall levels or the forms of participation nor the types of people involved, over the longer term persistent incremental improvements in the range and quality of sports facilities and venues may well make an impact on the overall level of participation and the types of people involved

(Roberts and Brodie, 1992). The potential significance of appropriate facilities notwithstanding, participation in sport depends far more upon predisposition (see motivation) to take part than facilities per se and the source of sporting predispositions or **habituses** for most young is their **family**. Put another way, while what young people can do in the name of sport is inevitably limited by what is available, demand tends to be more influential in sporting provision than mere supply and sporting demand is largely a product of youngsters' **socialization** and their interests often vary according to structural factors (Roberts, 2010).

FRIENDS AND PEERS

The term friend refers to those whose company young people choose and seek out (rather than being bound to as in the case of family members) and with whom they develop mutual emotional and reciprocal bonds. Peers, by contrast, are young people's 'social equals' (Roberts, 2009: 198) defined in terms of shared social status or characteristics such as educational background, sports **club** membership or **age** (James and James, 2009). The age, **social class, gender, ethnic** and geographical make-up of young people's peer networks forms the particular contexts in which their friendships are formed. The 'communities of choice' – often based on similarities of interest as well as proximity (James and James, 2009) – that make up friendship groups tend to have stable patterns of interaction and young people derive important aspects of their self-**identity** from these and other similar peer groups (Arai and Pedlar, 2003; Robb, 2007a).

As young people move into the teenage years, there tends to be a loosening of parent–child relationships as the balance of significance in their lives shifts away from **parents and family** (and, for that matter, adults more generally) towards friends and peers. This process strengthens as they approach the youth life-stage when other young people, and youth culture more generally, become major points of reference (James and James, 2009). Around this time, young people increasingly exchange 'the emotional and social supports previously provided by the family for those provided both by friendships with individuals and friendship groups comprising the young person's peers' (James and James, 2009: 96). Indeed, the teenage years not only 'signal the growing role of the peer group as an influence on young people's choices' they frequently involve 'clashes between the continuing role of parents as a major source of advice and that of friends' (Feinstein et al., 2005: 1). While peers generally play a more and more prominent role in young people's lives, it is friends in particular who become the single-most influential element in their daily lives (Carter et al., 2003). This is because young people 'place a lot of importance on belonging, on being included, on being "normal", and on being part of a group' (O'Donovan, 2002: 1). Thus, a prime concern for young people is making and keeping friends and the meaning of what they do lies in no small measure in

73

what it means to their friends. Young people invest a great deal of energy in group social life in order to make and keep friends and tend to evaluate their attitudes and practices, in part at least, on the basis of friends' responses. The psychological and social significance of friends (in relation, for example, to loyalty, trust, respect and empathy [James and James, 2009]) can be measured indirectly by the amount of **time** they spend together. In this regard, Zuzanek's (2005) review of adolescent time-use internationally (including the United States, Canada, Australia and several countries in Europe) demonstrated that young people spend relatively large periods in the company of friends and peers and 'interacting with friends' was consistently top of adolescent's favourite daily activities.

Youth is also a period in which young people seek increased autonomy and independence. Nevertheless, because friendships and sociability are so important to them young people are keen to become independent in socially acceptable ways; that is to say, ways acceptable to their friends and peers. Their desire to feel as if they belong and are accepted means that friends, in particular, act as 'a form of reflected appraisal for a youngster' (Brustad et al., 2008: 360) and provide an influential setting for the validation of young people's tastes and identities (Jones, 2009). Friends are not only central to the processes of gaining independence and developing an identity but are also important to young people's well-being. Young people appreciate that being surrounded by likeminded people and being central to such networks is likely to make them happy and that such happiness can be contagious (Fowler and Christakis, 2008): Zuzanek (2005: 408) observes that 'the emotional correlates of socializing with friends' included a sense of happiness and less boredom.

Despite the significance of the company of their friends (whether intimate or passing acquaintances), young people have tended to report less **participation** in social **leisure** activities (for the most part, being with friends and peers) since the late 1990s (Zuzanek, 2005). In countries such as Australia, Finland, the Netherlands, Norway and the United States this appears due to a re-channelling of free time from social activities to television viewing, additional hours of paid **work** and, in particular, going 'online'. This latter use of time is noteworthy, because young people increasingly service their friendship groups in ways that do not require face-to-face contact. They engage with friends 'online' and join virtual communities of youngsters they may never meet in person – in other words, 'social networking'. In such virtual communities young people can, by degrees, make and remake their identities rather than simply take them as a given from their past (Roberts, 2009). Such uses of modern **technologies** are said by some to be changing the nature of friendship. In practice, however, 'communications technology (the Internet and the telephone) may simply add another dimension to relationships with other bases' (Roberts, 2009: 134) rather than fundamentally change the character of young people's networks.

In addition to lifestyle dimensions to friendship, there are structural dimensions, one of which is cultural differences. There are, for example, international differences in the amount of time adolescents spend socializing with their peers during leisure: 'Youth from the US spend the most amount of their free time socializing with peers and age mates, followed by European youth' (Staempfli, 2005: 680). In Zuzanek's (2005) study, however, adolescents in Norway and Canada appeared to have engaged in 'social leisure' (largely being with friends and peers) more actively than in other countries. 'Korean, Japanese and Indian youth', by contrast, had 'fewer opportunities to do so, partly due to time demands from school and domestic chores but also due to cultural constraints and context specific opportunities' (Staempfli, 2005: 680). Other structural dimensions to friendship include social class and gender effects: not only are 'the middle classes better than the working class at forming and maintaining circles of friends' but also 'women are better than men at maintaining close same-sex friendships' (Roberts, 2009: 103) and both of these things are true for young people.

Overall, it would be difficult to overestimate the significance for their lives in general of young people's relationships with friends and peers and this is particularly so in relation to their engagement with leisure and sport.

The significance of friends and peers for youth sport

As young people move towards and through the life-stage of youth, not only does the nature of their leisure activities begin to change so too does the company they keep (Feinstein et al., 2005). Family leisure activities give way to those initially of single-sex and, subsequently, mixed-sex friendship and peer groups (Feinstein et al., 2007). Because friends have pride of place in young people's leisure lives other leisure activities often tend to be subordinated to this priority. Consequently, young people spend a relatively large proportion of their time socializing, hence the popularity of cinema-going, virtual forms of socializing via the Internet and, for that matter, drinking alcohol. A similar process occurs in relation to sport: friends and peers become increasingly influential on young people's leisure and sporting involvement while the immediate (but not foundational – see **habitus**) significance of parents and family in leisure choices diminishes.

Evidently, the networks that are young people's friendship groups facilitate links with other young people sharing similar interests and situations. It is unsurprising, therefore, to find that friendship groups can influence the levels and forms of exercise in which young people engage. In the mid-1990s, De Knop et al. (1996) noted a trend across Western Europe for young people's own age group to become more significant as agents of **socialization** into sport than their parents did. More recently, a number of qualitative studies worldwide confirmed that youth's sporting involvement can be strongly influenced by their friends and peers (Brustad et al., 2008; Smith and McDonough, 2008). Youth view participation with friends as not only enabling but also motivational. Several studies indicate that 'participation of friends in physical activity is a reason why young people participate themselves, particularly in unstructured [lifestyle] forms of physical activity' (Smith and McDonough, 2008: 303). As with family socialization, the mechanisms by which friends enable or discourage sports participation involve not merely the transmission of attitudes and values but also modelling active or inactive pursuits and providing psychological support or reinforcement for certain behaviours (Smith and McDonough, 2008). All in all, in those studies that explore, empirically, the significance of friendship for youth sport, the leisure (and sporting) practices of young people appear heavily circumscribed, even conditioned, by their perceptions of their friends' likely or actual reactions to their choices (Smith, 2006).

It is not just what their friends think about sport and do or do not do in practice, however, that influences young people. It is also the opportunities that sport (and, for that matter, any leisure practice) provides for making and sustaining friendships and the ways in which young people's friendship groups facilitate links with other young people sharing similar interests and situations. Indeed, one of the main motives for engaging in sport among young people is the opportunity it provides for establishing and maintaining friendships (Brustad et al., 2008; Hendry et al., 1993) and 'best' friendships in particular. Sport is often a site for the generation of friendships that sport then becomes a means of sustaining. In their study of 800 14–15-year-olds in Perth, Western Australia, Carter, Bennetts and Carter (2003) found that it was often commonality of activity or interest that brought individuals together. Citing Carver et al. (2003), Smith and McDonough (2008: 305) note that, 'Having opportunities for socializing, characterized by having more friends in the neighbourhood and many same-age peers to hang out with, are predictors of walking and cycling in one's neighbourhood among adolescents'. Thus, social networks such as friendship groups are especially likely to affect the amount of physical **activity and exercise** in which young people engage (Fisher, 2002).

The concept of social **capital** has been coined to refer to the 'norm(s) and expectation(s) of ... trust and reciprocity' (Johnston and Percy-Smith, 2003: 323) involved in social relationships (Field, 2003) – such as networks of friends – that individuals can draw on for social and emotional support, not least in a sporting context. Young people can, and do, 'invest' in social capital 'by building up a circle of friends' (Roberts, 2001: 218) and associates. The capacity for young people to draw upon their social capital when they need to do so is especially useful in sporting and leisure contexts. This is what Collins (2003: 69) is hinting at when he observes that taking part in sport and physical activity may often require, among other things, 'a group of supportive friends and companions, including some who share the same desire to take part'. Indeed, it is probably why 'drop-out from teenage leisure activities [including sport] could be at least partly due to the break-up or loosening of peer groups after young people exit full-time education' (Roberts et al., 2009: 275).

Peer-group pressure and the influence of friends are particularly significant for gender identities. 'During early and middle adolescent years, most of adolescents' activities revolve around same-sex peer groups, in which boys and girls develop interest in "sex-appropriate" things' (Van Wel *et al.*, 2008: 337). Opportunities for 'social interaction with friends' (Rowe, 2005: 4) are an especially important consideration and **motivation** for girls (Hills, 2007; Smith, 2006) who 'are more likely to be attracted by the social aspects of [leisure and sporting] provision' (Coalter, 2007: 129) and, in particular, the company of friends (Holt *et al.*, 2008: 411). This is because girls' and young women's friendships are more likely to be close and dyadic compared with 'the larger and more dispersed nature of boys' friendship groups' (James and James, 2009: 61). These different forms of friendship are reflected in the different types of games that children play: 'Girls' close one-to-one friendships facilitate the more structured games they often play on the edges of the playground' while 'boys occupy the centre of the playground with large team-based games of football' (James and James, 2009: 61). Girls and young women are also much less likely than are boys and young men to base their friendship networks on sport (Mason, 1995) and girls' friendship groups are particularly likely to facilitate or, more often, hamper engagement with sport and PE. Coleman *et al.* (2008: 633), for example, highlighted the primacy of friends over other factors (such as self-perceptions of **ability**, motivation, self-consciousness and personal choice as well as family influence) in their study of the determinants of sports participation among 15–19-year-old young women. Nonetheless, where they do engage, participation with friends seems to provide not only a source of enjoyment for many girls but also 'protection against the emotional costs' (Hills, 2007: 351) of PE and sport. Along with their friends, peers more generally are also particularly significant for girls. Smith and McDonough (2008) cite research indicating that boys' attitudes towards, as well as their treatment of, girls in physical activity contexts can contribute to inactivity among the latter.

All in all, 'in all modern societies, around or after age 16, self-selected males and females become close friends and eventually partners and are likely to spend much of their leisure time together, increasing the likelihood that they will do similar things' (Roberts *et al.*, 2009a: 275). The significance of their friends to young people in both absolute and relative terms should not disguise the fact that parents and family can remain substantial and significant dimensions to their sporting lives both in terms of accessing sporting opportunities and participation itself. Albeit to a lesser extent in Western Europe and the developed world, this is true across many countries including China, where Xiong (2007) observes that participation tends to take place with friends and family as well as individually. Indeed, it would be a mistake to view friends and family in dichotomous terms vis-à-vis **youth lifestyles** and youth sport in particular. There is widespread continuity alongside the undoubted change. In other words, while youth is characterized by a shift away from parents and adults and towards friends and peers, many young people continue to take part in some sport and physical activity alongside their parents, at their parents' **clubs** or while in the company of their parents (e.g. on holidays).

GENDER

Sex is generally considered a straightforwardly biological term indicating distinct, genetically inherited, anatomical and physiological characteristics. Gender, on the other hand, is a more complex concept and one which refers, in broad terms, to learned masculine and feminine behaviours. It is a common mistake to use the term sex when what is actually being referred to are norms regarding 'appropriate' sex-specific behaviours – in other words, gender – and to talk of gender when distinguishing between the sexes. Sex is, of course, an aspect of gender. The latter cannot simply be 'read off' from the former, however. Nor, for that matter, should masculinity and femininity be treated as dichotomous terms: gender is a dynamic and fluid category. Rather than constituting rigid and unchanging characteristics, masculinity and femininity are more adequately viewed as poles on a continuum with each individual expressing (what are characteristically viewed as) both masculine and feminine attributes to varying degrees.

The significance of gender for youth sport

The gendered character – in terms of both **participation** and experiences – of sport has been amply demonstrated by researchers over the last 40 or so years. Males, whether young or old, participate in sport in greater numbers, more frequently, for longer periods and, usually, in more competitive and combative forms. The higher levels of male participation coupled with the manner in which sport serves to inculcate, perpetuate and celebrate 'a type of masculine **identity** based on physical dominance, aggression and competitiveness' (Malcolm, 2008: 116) has led to its depiction as a 'male preserve'.

The historical gendering of sports participation notwithstanding there have been some marked changes in (young) women's relationship with sport in recent decades, alongside the undoubted continuities. As far as school sport is concerned, girls often play as much sport, and as many sports, as boys in school lessons and in England, as in many developed countries, they are being offered an increasingly wide range of sports and physical activities encompassing those played mainly by girls and others undertaken by both sexes (Quick *et al.*, 2009; Sport England, 2003a, 2003b)[1]. It is out of lessons, during **leisure**, where sex differences in sport tend to be widest. Even here, though, there have been substantial increases in women's involvement in sport in all **age** groups over the last 30 years. Although they remain less likely to participate in sport than young men and are more likely to abandon involvement earlier, girls and young women are now playing far more sport than ever before and have been closing the gap on boys and men. Sabo and Veliz (2008) talk of an 'explosion' of girls' sports participation since the early 1970s in the United States, such that by the end of secondary schooling approximately two-thirds of girls (66 per cent) as well as boys (69 per cent) were playing sport. Within the upward trend in Finnish adolescents' leisure-**time** physical **activity**, Laakso *et al.* (2008) noted a bigger increase of activity among girls than boys and, in Portugal, the numbers of girls participating in organized ('formal') sport is reported to have 'increased threefold from 1996 to 2003' (Seabra *et al.*, 2007: 378). In addition to their increased levels and rates of participation, girls now tend to take part in a wider array of sports than boys overall and are more inclined to engage with several **clubs** and organizations outside sport whereas boys are more likely to 'focus singly on sports' (Sabo and Veliz, 2008: 3).

The increasing numbers of studies demonstrating a decline in sex differences in sports participation in recent decades notwithstanding, gendered patterns persist. As well as being less likely either to devote themselves to sports than boys or engage in competitive, physically intense and contact activities than their male counterparts (Koska, 2005; Smith, 2006; Sport England, 2003a, 2003b), girls tend to be more involved in indoor and solo as well as recreational and newly emerging sports such as cheerleading, swimming, gymnastics and dance (Scheerder *et al.*, 2005b). In addition, girls remain more likely to drop out of sport sooner and in greater numbers (Sabo and Veliz, 2008; Scheerder *et al.*, 2005; Seabra *et al.*, 2007; Staempfli, 2005). This tendency appears exacerbated by the manner in which **friends** and paid **work** compete more strongly for girls' sporting leisure time (McPhail *et al.*, 2009) than they do among boys.

The persistence of sex/gender patterns notwithstanding, our understanding of young women's sports participation needs to be more nuanced than the simple mantra 'boys do more'. Sabo and Veliz (2008: 2), for example, show how the gender gap in sports participation in the United States is far from uniform: 'In many communities [and specifically suburban and, therefore, more middle-class communities], girls show similar levels of athletic [sports] participation as boys' while, in other (specifically urban and rural areas) areas, girls' participation is narrower'. According to Clark (2008), the frequency of sports participation among Canadian youngsters aged 5–14 in recent years has been similar for both boys and girls, at 2.5 times per week for boys compared with 2.7 times per week for girls. The situation in Canada and the United States is likely to be reflected elsewhere in the world insofar as the changes in female participation in sport remain uneven with the poor and mainly urban girls often being the ones left behind (Sabo and Veliz, 2008).

As the gendered make-up of leisure changes and 'many girls and women embrace a myriad of potential leisure choices' (Henderson and Hickerson, 2007: 603), young women are increasingly involved in sporting activities once associated almost entirely with men such as football, martial arts and outdoor pursuits. Their rapidly growing involvement in football is illustrative of a trend towards greater involvement by girls and young women in traditionally male-dominated activities, including games. In England, levels of girls' frequent participation in football as an extra-curricular activity more than doubled (from 3–7 per cent) among girls between 1994 and 2002 (Sport England, 2003a). Indeed, in 2002, 18 per cent of school-aged girls participated in football out-of-lessons on a frequent basis (Sport England, 2003a).

The increasing similarities, not to say convergence, between boys' and girls' sporting lifestyles (and, for that matter, their lifestyles generally) may, in part, be explainable in terms of girls' and women's lives as a whole having come to resemble those of boys and men more and more in recent decades. In other words, it has been the general changes in the conditions of girls and women that have begun to impact upon their participation in sport more so than policies designed to encourage participation. Thus, developments in girls' sporting habits are partly explained in terms of changing technological (e.g. birth control and the tampon) and social (greater gender equality) preconditions for young women's engagement with various aspects of leisure including sport. Given that education and work are pivotal to the social situation of women (Abbott, 2006), the increasing numbers of them engaged in part-time work alongside their improved levels of education (Jones, 2009) seems likely to further enhance the independence of young women and, thus, convergence between the sexes in many if not all areas of social life.

Increased levels of participation notwithstanding, their experiences in sport can have a profound effect on young women and, for that matter, young men. Sport tends to be a very public and visible arena and offers numerous opportunities (not to say, pressures) to conform to, or even contradict, accepted stereotypes of feminine and masculine behaviour (Clarke, 2006). It does not, however, tend to offer the same avenue to orthodox femininity for girls, as it does in terms of orthodox masculinity for boys. Sport can still reinforce the construction of heterosexual femininity and masculinity (Flintoff and Scraton, 2006) and, in contributing to stereotypical perceptions of gender-appropriate and inappropriate behaviours, continue to influence whether (and which) young people choose to participate as well as how they are viewed by others if and when they do so (Alley and Hicks, 2005). Unsurprisingly, therefore, girls' relationship with sport and exercise is often intimately related to their perceptions of their own bodies and their 'look'. Indeed, in different ways, concerns about their **body** shape tend to be a major reason for either participation or non-participation among girls. A leitmotif of the abundant research on girls' experiences is the tendency for school PE to alienate many of them from sport and, in the process, exacerbate any unease they may feel with their bodies. More so than boys, girls seem to need more frequent and supportive extrinsic judgements from their teachers (Wallhead and Buckworth, 2004) as well as their **parents** – a situation that is not helped by the continued predominance among adults of stereotypical gender ideologies 'concerning expectations of women's physicality, their sexuality and their role as mothers and carers' (Scraton, 1993: 143). The traditional and stereotypical sporting rituals in PE and sport tend to contradict many girls' conceptions of an appropriate and desirable female and feminine appearance and, consequently, lead to conflicting and contradictory pressures on female self-identities (Cockburn and Clarke, 2002; Gorely *et al.*, 2003). Furthermore, many of the activities – and the 'traditional' behaviours associated with them (e.g. the demonstration of physical vigour and the associated likeliness of getting sweaty and dirty) – are performed in public, not just in front of other girls but often in front of boys and men. Unsurprisingly, many girls' feelings of bodily awkwardness tend to be exacerbated by being in the public (usually male) gaze and the frequently stereotypical perceptions of, and associated attitudes towards, girls of their parents, teachers and friends.

It is during the particularly sensitive years of adolescence, when young women are developing physically and sexually, that ideologies of women as sex-objects and mothers become the prevailing ones (Scraton, 1993). Indeed, it is suggested that some of the more popular activities among women, such as aerobics and dance, merely serve to sexualize the female body in conformity with male stereotypes of female attractiveness. In the process, these activities tend to alienate young women from each other along dividing lines between those who are fat and those who are fit and attractive (Harris, 2005). The potential, therefore, for PE and sport to not only highlight girls' self-consciousness (O'Donovan and Kay, 2005) but also to impact negatively on their self-esteem appears exacerbated during early adolescence (Cockburn and Clarke, 2002) and youth; embarrassment becomes viewed by teenage girls as a very real likelihood as well as a substantial cost of participation in sport. On the other hand, and in marked contrast to the young women who 'never' participated in sport, those in Cox *et al.*'s (2005) study who 'always' participated reported very low levels of self-consciousness and claimed to rarely get embarrassed when taking part in sport – deeply involved in their activities, they appeared not to care what other people might think about them. It remains the case, nonetheless, that girls who resist gender-stereotypes – especially during adolescence – run the very real risk of 'alienation from the people around them and those most important to them' such as friends and family (Cockburn and Clarke, 2002: 659).

While girls who either 'hate' or 'love' sport are situated at either end of the continuum of engagement with sport, the vast majority lie somewhere between the two poles – they are biddable but not at any cost to their self-esteem. Consequently, many girls find themselves in a 'no-win' situation: damned if they do sport and damned if they do not. It is often said that because, 'It is highly unlikely that girls can achieve being both physically active *and* (heterosexually) desirable … they are often obliged to choose *between* these images' (Cockburn and Clarke, 2002: 665; emphasis in the original).

'The result', Cockburn and Clarke (2002: 665) conclude, 'is a paradox, a double standard to which teenage girls and young women are subjected … and most girls compromise'. It is perhaps unsurprising that, as a result, many girls appear to feel constrained to appear disinterested in sport.

Over the years gender-related research has broadened to encompass the significance of gender for boys' experiences of sport and, in particular, the **socialization** of boys therein. Whitson (1990) articulated a common-place view that sport acts as 'one of the central sites in the social production of masculinity' (p. 19) and that the kinds of sports conventionally prioritized in school PE are ones that 'naturalize' the idea that masculinity involves aggressiveness and a desire to compete with and overcome others. Assertive masculinity, with a focus on aggression and intolerance, is a particular characteristic of working-class youth (Jones, 2009) and working-class male sporting tendencies. An incidental expression of this dominant ideology of masculinity is the prevalence of the view among boys that activities such as dance are not only pointless but also 'gay' (homosexual) or 'unmasculine'. Dissatisfaction with one's body is not, then, solely the preserve of girls. Sport is an arena in which the demanding nature of living up to masculine norms for boys (Martino and Pallotta-Chiarolli, 2003; Wright, 1999), as well as feminine norms for girls, is thrown into sharp relief. Young men's anxieties regarding their masculinity is reflected in their concern for physical strength and muscularity – around a quarter or more of the 15–16-year-old boys in Smith's (2006) study reported participating regularly in their spare time in gym/weight training activities. The manner in which boys feel compelled to negotiate ways through the demands of masculinity (Bramham, 2003) resembles girls' attempts to compromise between sporting and heterosexual images. It seems that there are established and outsider groups within as well as between the sexes.

Although they have lessened, sex differences remain wider in sport than in any other area of leisure and remain stark. Indeed, 'sport illustrates a general leisure tendency; sex differences that are evident in the primary school years become wider with age' (Roberts, 1996a: 55). There is an argument that the sexes' different propensities to participate in sport are fixed in childhood via socialization: 'in most countries, adolescent girls experience more restrictions than boys in choosing the level and the place of leisure involvement, as well as the type of activities they engage in, or with whom they are permitted to spend their leisure. Typically, they are encouraged to spend their leisure close to home with family or pursuing custom-oriented activities' (Staempfli, 2005: 680). This is particularly true for young women from groups in which levels of religiosity are high. Nevertheless, even though young women will have learned (with their mothers serving as **role models**) that as adults they are unlikely to be active in sport (and certainly not as active as they have been at school), there is evidence to suggest that they are no more likely to be forced out of sport by marriage and parenthood and other such life events in young adulthood than young males (Birchwood et al., 2008). The crucial issue is whether or not they have developed a sporting **habitus** in their early lives; and that is related to **gender socialization**.

Note

1 This may not be the case, however, in single-sex girls' schools. A recent study of *PE and School Sport* among 5–18-year-olds in England (Quick *et al.*, 2009) revealed that among the 2 and 3 per cent of boys and girls, respectively, in single-sex schools only 33 per cent of those in girls-only schools participated in at least three hours of PE and out-of-hours school sport compared with 49 per cent of boys in single-sex schools and an overall average of 50 per cent in mixed-sex schools.

GENDER SOCIALIZATION

Gender socialization refers to the ways in which boys and girls are introduced to and more-or-less steeped in what are seen as male- and female-appropriate values, attitudes, behaviours and practices. It is, in other words, the process by which boys learn to be boys and girls learn to be girls in relation to the norms of femininity and masculinity. Although what it means to be a boy or a girl varies between cultures, distinguishing between male and female children is a common feature of everyday social practices in most societies (James and James, 2009). In short, from birth, 'biological sex differences are noted and ascriptions of the child as male or female follow' (p. 65).

The significance of gender socialization for youth sport

In sporting terms, gender **socialization** refers to the ways in which boys and girls are introduced to what are viewed as male- and female-appropriate activities (contact or non-contact play and games, for example), behaviours and practices (such as aggressiveness and competitiveness) – including those that might be seen as forming the initial preparation for later engagement with, and adherence to, sport.

Leisure in general and sport in particular are sites where gendered dispositions and behaviours are not only expressed but also reinforced and/or challenged. Consequently, sports have the potential to reinforce and/or challenge young people's gendered self-**identities**, because they place young people in situations, and involve experiences, that tend to evoke strong emotional responses. Thus, sport is particularly susceptible to serving as a subconscious vehicle for messages about appropriate gender-related attitudes and practices. In terms of the reinforcement of gender stereotypes, sport – especially in the form of school **physical education** – has long displayed a tendency to normalize (in the sense of becoming widely accepted and taken-for-granted) particular views of gender-appropriate behaviours among boys and girls (Hargreaves, 1994; Scraton, 1992); including, for example, appropriate attitudes (e.g. cooperative or competitive) and skills (such as dancing and fighting). Similarly, gendered practices and experiences in sport reinforce boys' and girls' common-sense assumptions regarding what constitute appropriate activities for each to engage in. In the process the 'gender order' comes to appear quite normal, even natural, to those involved and taken-for-granted assumptions 'about what it means "to be a girl" or "to be a boy"' (Scraton, 1992: 9) are bolstered. In this vein, a study of 357 secondary-school students in Norway revealed that boys rated appearance of strength, competence in sport and masculinity as particularly important whereas the girls were more concerned with looking good and being feminine (Klomsten *et al.*, 2005). This, the authors suggested, resulted in more boys participating in traditionally male sports and girls in traditionally female sports. More often, we might add, it results in girls simply eschewing sport.

Motivation is a particularly interesting aspect of gender socialization. Girls, it seems, are more likely to approach PE and sport with a task-orientation and boys with an ego-orientation – attributable to their socialization into masculine norms of achievement. Lenskyj and van Daalen (2006) found that Canadian high school girls' confidence and competence were enhanced when they had participated regularly in enjoyable sport and physical **activity** from an early age. Unsurprisingly, it seems that frequent **participation** and motivation go hand-in-hand. In their study of 75 young women (aged 15–19 years) who 'always' and 'never' participated in sport and physical activity, Coleman *et al.* (2008) found that the main differences lay with the former in relation to the latter; that is, the 'always' participated reported 'more positive images of "sport", positive perceptions of their own **ability**, low self-consciousness, firm motivation and personal choice to engage in activities and the supporting influence of their **friends** and family' (p. 633).

Because **habituses** develop most rapidly during childhood and youth, sports participation during this period has the potential to go some way towards challenging (sometimes at the same time as reinforcing) certain dimensions of gender-stereotypes. The dramatic growth in popularity of girls' and women's football in recent years amid a range of hitherto exclusively male sporting and leisure activities points to the socially constructed, processual and, therefore, changeable character of gendered identities. Cox *et al.*'s (2005) study suggested that young women aged 15–19 years who, as they put it, 'always' participated in sport – and often increased participation as they got older – reported regular participation in and positive experiences of sport from an early age. Interestingly, some young women in the 'never' participate group also reported positive experiences of sport from an early age. It was the move to secondary school – where sport involved more **competition** – that was associated, among other things, with sport becoming less enjoyable among this group.

Although friends become increasingly significant in relation to gender sociali-zation during adolescence and youth, **parents and family** are especially important in passing on common-sense notions regarding the (supposed) appropriateness of particular activities for each of the sexes. Children typically take on gender roles by observing and then imitating the behaviour of their parents in particular. By providing **role models** as well as gendered play equipment and opportunities, adults are continually and persistently, wittingly and unwittingly socializing boys and girls into masculine and feminine activities (James and James, 2009). Research by Armstrong (1991) among others in paediatric exercise and fitness patterns points up the significance of parental behaviours in encouraging differential rates and frequencies of exercise among boys and girls. Common-place sex-stereotyped assumptions regarding exercise and sport manifest themselves in, among other things, boys receiving more parental reinforcement towards sports and exercise than girls receive: 'Girls are still being given dolls and prams and are instructed to be neat and tidy. Boys are still being sent to play with footballs and soldiers and are excused if they are rough and dirty' (Roberts, 2006: 120). Thus, boys appear particularly advantaged and girls disadvantaged in relation to early engagement with physical activity in general and sport in particular. Despite very often feeling that 'their daughters and sons have similar interest in sports, especially when their children are younger' (Sabo and Veliz, 2008: 3), parents in the United States tend to introduce boys to games and sports earlier than girls. Consequently, many boys in the United States 'get a head start entering a lifestyle that includes athletic [sports] participation' (Sabo and Veliz, 2008: 131). Girls' later entry into sport in the United States (7.4 years of age compared with 6.8 years for boys) is said to hinder their development of basic physical skills and cultural values and this may, in turn, 'be setting girls up for failure and drop-out' (Sabo and Veliz, 2008: 168). Parents are likely to elicit more gross-motor behaviour at a young age from their sons than their daughters. In addition, the games boys play tend to be of longer duration and incorporate a higher ceiling of skill than those of girls and the types of games adopted by boys can be played in more simple versions at younger ages, becoming more challenging with age as higher levels of skill and strategy are incorporated (Armstrong, 1991). Parents are likely to elicit more gross-motor behaviour at a young age from their sons than their daughters. In contrast, the kinds of games that girls tend to be introduced to and consequently come to favour 'seem to be less challenging with increasing age because the ceiling of skill was achieved at an earlier age' (Armstrong, 1991: 9–10). To compound the constraints on girls' physical activity experiences, teenage boys tend to enjoy a greater 'right to roam' than girls – for reasons largely related to safety concerns – and, as a result, their freedom tends to be curtailed.

Despite the evident changes in recent decades in girls' socialization towards active uses of leisure, boys continue to be given greater encouragement to engage in sport by parents and teachers and, consequently, tend to play more sport than girls (Balding, 2001; SCW, 2001, 2003; Sport England, 2003b), and this tendency increases as youngsters grow older. This is hardly surprising in the light of research demonstrating the central position of not only the family (Biddle *et al.*, 2005) but fathers in particular in their children's leisure and sporting socialization (Harrington, 2006). 'Men', it seems, 'are typically more likely to spend **time** with their children in playful activities than routine caring tasks' (Kay, 2006: 126) and 'fathers are more likely than mothers to have or claim expertise in sport' (p. 127). For all of these reasons, it remains far more likely that fathers will be the ones to get involved in this aspect of children's socialization. Despite the fact that boys continue to be the ones 'better supported and more influenced by parent physical activity' (Saelens and Kerr, 2008: 281), it has become increasingly apparent that parental and family support is strongly correlated with girls' and young women's involvement in physical activity and sport (Biddle *et al.*, 2004; Saelens and Kerr, 2008). Saelens and Kerr (2008) pointed to positive correlations between mothers' and daughters' levels of physical activity as well as that of fathers and sons. Family support appears especially strongly correlated with girls' involvement in team sports not only in the form of 'modelling' participation but also in terms of transportation to and from sports locations – something which is particularly positively related to girls' participation (Saelens and Kerr, 2008).

Overall, the impact of gender on young people's leisure and sporting lifestyles has become blurred in recent decades as males and females from all social classes have tended to experience 'more free time than previously and engage in a greater range of leisure pursuits which, on the surface, appear to display greater similarities than differences' (Furlong and Cartmel, 2007: 71). Nonetheless, while young people as a whole are experiencing a broader diet of sports and physical activities at school than previous generations, they frequently continue to be introduced to various sports and physical activities according to their sex. The upshot is that there remains a great deal of continuity alongside the evident change in the sporting socialization of girls and young women.

GLOBALIZATION

Globalization refers to the process whereby national boundaries become less significant as the interconnectedness and interdependencies between people and countries across the globe 'intensifies and grows stronger' (Malcolm, 2008: 119), particularly in economic and cultural terms. The pace of globalization intensified during the latter decades of the twentieth century 'due to developments in electronic communications, the globalization of the market economy ... the rise of transnational businesses and financial institutions, and the creation or enlarged role of international organisations' (Roberts, 2008: 14).

A feature of globalization has been increasingly cosmopolitan cultures, especially in the developed world. Thus, while the study of youth in the twentieth century confirmed the relatively different conditions of young people in each country, in the early years of the twenty-first century, it makes sense to talk of 'global youth' insofar as **youth cultures** around the world have begun to converge. Based on a review of surveys of adolescents in Europe, North America and Australia, Zuzanek (2005) concluded that comparisons of adolescent **time** use over the past 20 years revealed strongly converging trends. Thus, if one dimension of globalization is the 'presence of common trends in the development of geographically and socio-historically distant societies' (p. 396) then talk of global youth cultures cannot be disputed. Advances in mass media, computer **technology** and electronic communication and their global spread have provided the preconditions for some of the increasingly common features found in youth lives and lifestyles. In most of the countries Zuzanek reviewed, adolescents gained additional free time and mass media consumption and the use of electronic media expanded. In addition, teenagers went to bed later on school days, and read and ate at home less. In South Africa, research conducted for the *Sunday Times Generation Next* (2006) reflected the kinds of tastes and styles also to be found on the streets of Britain, the United States and Australia. The report noted that South Africa's 'kids, teens and young adults (aged 8–22 years) indicated that Billabong was the outright coolest brand followed by Adidas, Levi's, Coke and Nokia', their 'coolest' TV channel was MTV, they all liked iPods and, if given a choice, would eat at KFC!

Ironically, however, globalization has also brought with it 'a resurgence of localism and a strengthening of local **identity** (Malcolm, 2008: 119). Consequently, 'while some life-style patterns are readily "universalized" others resist change and remain "country" or "culture" specific' (Zuzanek, 2005: 396). Put another way, universal and particular aspects of cultures co-exist in youth cultures and in youth sport (e.g. tennis and pelota in Spain, downhill and cross-country skiing in Scandinavia, and soccer and American football in the United States). From his analysis of time-use data and experience sampling, Zuzanek (2005) concluded that, in terms of globalization, countries could be placed on a continuum with North America, Australia and the United Kingdom occupying the convergent pole and France and Belgium the more traditional country or culture specific one. While there were some similarities between Germany, Finland and Norway, adolescents' time-use in these countries differed considerably from that of teenagers in the Netherlands, France and Belgium with the lifestyles of French and Belgium youth the most dissimilar to those of teenagers in North America, Australia and other European countries. All in all, comparisons of adolescent time-use in developed countries 'shows many common trends and life-style similarities, as well as some distinct national and cultural differences' (Zuzanek, 2005: 397). Youth in North America and Australia, for example, spent 'less time attending movies and cultural events, and more time in sports and outdoor activities than their counterparts in continental Europe (save Finland)' (p. 397). Hence the claim that processes of globalization involve degrees of continuity interspersed with, and sometimes reinforced by, change.

Difference and continuity notwithstanding, global trends in education, labour markets, housing and family arrangements are said to be 'creating a common, global, twenty-first century youth condition' (Roberts, 2008: 203). There is, however, a view that rather than being described simply as globalization, the future of youth might best be seen as American; not so much because of American power or hegemony but rather because the commonalities in global youth culture tend to be first seen in America. In other words, most of the emergent global similarities in youths' situations and responses 'became common features of youth's condition in America prior to their internation-alization'; that is, prior to their becoming 'increasingly common features of global youth's condition' (Roberts, 2008: 197). The commonalities have their roots in the market economy, democracy, the nuclear family and processes of globalization (Roberts, 2008). The upshot is that while America can be seen as prototypical, the future of youth cultures is global Americanization. Even though it is losing its once central position in cultural production, America's youth **leisure** scenes are likely to become even clearer examples of American exceptionalism. Its usefulness notwithstanding, a caveat needs to be added to the notion of global youth. Young people in the developed world experience globalization in full flood, so to speak. This is one of the reasons why it is easy to be convinced of the plausibility of post-modernist theories. It is important to bear in mind, however, that in large stretches of the relatively less-developed world, globalization is a relatively weaker process.

The significance of globalization for youth sport

Across the world, young people share some tastes and habits, and there are substantial similarities in how young people around the world spend their leis-ure time and money – in terms of fashions in clothing, music and media and many other things including sport. Nevertheless, increased interdependence does not automatically lead to homogenization – everywhere becoming more similar – and there are always aspects of culture specific to particular countries that contrast with other countries even in the same region. 'The global is', in other words, 'always interwoven with local features thereby producing myriad examples of "glocalisation"' (Roberts, 2008: 12) – 'mixtures of the global and the local' (p. 14).

The obvious question is, then, what are the similarities and differences in the sporting behaviours of youth? In terms of similarities, the most global of sports among young people is, unsurprisingly, football, which originated in England. At the same time, increasing numbers of young people play sports that either originated in the United States, such as basketball or were given a tremendous fillip by their rapid growth there, such as golf (Wheeler and Nauright, 2006). On top of this, there are games that merge the characteristics of **lifestyle activities** with conventional sports, such as Ultimate Frisbee (Frisbee, played according to the rules of American Football). Like international cultural products generally, many international sports have been given localized meanings in particular local contexts (Roberts, 2008). Rugby union, for example, was transformed into American football in the United States and 'Aussie rules' in Australia. Similarly rounders became baseball in the United States. Fusions between the global and the local are also illustrated in the more-or-less popular variants of snow sports across the world ranging from the pre-eminence of cross-country skiing in Scandinavia to that of downhill skiing in the alpine countries of Europe. The tendency for local resistance can be illustrated by examining the globalization of various countries' sports. While some American sports have globalized (such as basketball and various forms of popular dancing) others have not or, at least, not to the extent where they can be said to be truly international (e.g. baseball and American football).

The most significant global developments in youth sporting culture, however, have come in lifestyle and adventurous sports such as skateboarding, mountain-biking and surfing (many of which also originated in the United States). In this regard, contemporary youth cultures, including sporting cultures associated with lifestyle activities, are very mobile. Even though cultural products flow globally irrespective of travel (e.g. the Internet hosts many thousands of cross-national virtual communities), this has been due, in no small part, to the rapid spread of youth travel (Roberts, 2008).

HEALTH, WELL-BEING AND PHYSICAL ACTIVITY

In the world of sport there are probably few ideas which are as widely and uncritically accepted as that linking sport and exercise with good health (Waddington, 2000) – where health is defined not merely as the absence of disease but also 'the maximization of physical and socio-psychological well-being' (Roberts and Brodie, 1992: 96). There are a number of reasons for viewing sport as a suitable vehicle for the promotion of health, not least of which is that it confers health benefits which can be experienced not only by 'ordinary' participants but also across all socio-demographic groups (male/female; young/old; employed/unemployed; rich/poor) (Boreham and Riddoch, 2001; Roberts and Brodie, 1992). Central to claims regarding the health-related benefits of sport are issues to do with **activity and exercise** as well as health-related fitness. Among other things, physical activity and exercise can reduce **body** fatness, lower high blood pressure, increase bone mineral density and enhance psychological well-being (Winsley and Armstrong, 2005). Fitness (the capacity to perform particular physical tasks such as walk up stairs or play sports) – and, in particular, certain dimensions of fitness (such as aerobic endurance and body composition) – is referred to as health-related fitness when it results in reductions in the incidence of certain diseases such as coronary heart disease, forms of cancer and type 2 diabetes, for example (Butterly, 2008).

The significance of health, well-being and physical activity for youth sport

The particular significance of youth and youth sport in relation to health is twofold. First, it is childhood and youth where predispositions towards, on the one hand, lifestyle diseases (associated with **sedentariness**) and, on the other, sport and physical activity are laid. Second, young people of school **age** experience sport (in the form of school **PE**) on an almost weekly basis throughout their young lives and are the group most likely to engage with sport in their **leisure**. They are, therefore, a captive audience for health-related exercise and health education.

Despite the seemingly straightforward case for the health-related benefits of youth sport there are several important caveats. First, sport per se tends to have little impact upon the general levels of health and fitness of young people (see activity and exercise). Indeed, somewhat ironically, sport can have health-damaging side effects among regular participants. In the first instance, most young people simply do not (and probably cannot) do enough sport to improve their health-related fitness (i.e. on most days each week, pretty intensively) or even sufficient physical activity of the right kind (moderate, regular and rhythmical) to significantly improve their health. Getting young people to participate in sport is not an issue – getting them to participate often enough and at sufficient intensity to improve their fitness and health is, however. Despite the high **participation** rates in sport and physical activity recorded among children and young people in Wales, for example, levels of energetic physical activity remain 'below what might be desired': 'Only 24 per cent of secondary pupils and 41 per cent of primary school pupils are physically active for 60 minutes on at least five days of the week' (SCW, 2006: 6). On top of this, the very nature of much sport as well as the kinds of **lifestyle activities** that youngsters increasingly favour is such that levels of physical activity are inevitably sporadic and intermittent.

In relation to the contribution of sport and physical activity to health overall, it is apparent that in order to improve normal day-to-day health (in terms of lowering body fat, lowering cholesterol and improving physiological functioning generally) people need to raise their heart rate by exercising regularly and continue to do so throughout the life-course. This is the problem of persistence: for benefits to be lifelong it is necessary to be a lifelong participant (the same is true in relation to healthy diets and limiting tobacco and alcohol consumption). In addition, not only do people tend not to do enough physical activity to benefit their health, but they also tend not to do it in the right way. While the health-related arguments in favour of regular, rhythmic and moderate exercise may be very persuasive, the health-promoting case for energetic and competitive sport deserves only qualified support. Waddington, Malcolm and Green (1997: 169) point up the fallacy of assuming that sport and physical activity are necessarily beneficial to health:

> one cannot assume that the health benefits associated with moderate exercise will simply be duplicated – still less can one assume that they will be

increased – by exercise which is more frequent, of longer duration and of greater intensity, for exercise of this kind ... may generate health 'costs' in terms of additional stresses or injuries, for example those associated with overuse.

In general, it is reasonable to suggest that in the case of rhythmic, non-competitive exercise – where bodily movements are to a large extent under the control of the individual participant – the health benefits substantially out-weigh the health costs. However, as participants move from non-competitive exercise to competitive sport and from non-contact to contact sport, so the health costs, in the form of injuries, begin to mount (Waddington *et al.*, 1997). Indeed, while the kinds of specific training associated with competitive sport do not necessarily lead to generalized health benefits, they do make sports players more susceptible to sports injuries. Whyte (2006: 14) argues that the commonly held belief that 'if a little is good a lot must be better' is mistaken: sports participation, he observes, 'is associated with injuries that have both acute and chronic implications for health and well-being. Exercise can result in injury to all systems associated with an acute or chronic insult' (Whyte, 2006: 14). Forty years ago, sports injuries comprised 1–2 per cent of all injuries presented in the emergency rooms of hospitals whereas nowadays 'about 10 percent of all hospital-admitted injuries are sustained in sports' (p. 14). This only represents the most severe tip of the injury iceberg according to Whyte (2006). As if to compound the potential health costs of sports participation, some would argue that participation in sport might, itself, be viewed as a kind of drug; not least insofar as it elicits withdrawal symptoms from those who feel themselves to be 'addicted' to it (Dunning and Waddington, 2003; Koska, 2005) – as harmless as this form of addiction may well turn out to be. In short, sport makes more of a net contribution to health if and when people engage in moderate regular and rhythmic activities – usually as they get older. Competitive, physically vig-orous and contact-based sports often popular among young people frequently result in a net cost to their health either at the time or as they get older.

The second caveat is that whatever health benefits sport may confer on young people these are often overridden by other lifestyle behaviours. Indeed, although sports participation is rising among school-age youngsters, it is not *the*, or in many cases even *a*, typical use of leisure for young people. At the same time as undertaking a lot of sport, young people as a whole are more sedentary overall. Thus, far from being irreconcilable, co-occurring increases in sports par-ticipation and **obesity** and/or negative health practices among young people are often the reality. Over the longer term, other aspects of individual lifestyles – such as diet, alcohol and tobacco and, for that matter, other forms of exercise – can be, and often are, more influential in determining young people's health status than levels of sporting participation. According to Zuzanek (2005), important determinants of adolescents' physical and mental health are embed-ded in their daily behaviours. He argues that those concerned with adolescents' health need to pay attention not only to their physically active leisure but also to their overall patterns of daily life, including sleep, eating habits, and mass media consumption: 'both "over" and "under" structured patterns of daily life and leisure may contribute to stress and emotional imbalance' (p. 413).

Third, it seems that even though very many young people are cognizant of the relationship between health and, among other things, physical activity, legal and illegal **drugs** and diet, very few show signs of acting upon this evidence. There appear to be two main reasons for this apparent paradox: first, (young) people generally tend not to act until they are bound to (e.g. following a substantial health crisis), and second, they are unable to sustain the levels of involvement they have in sport and physical activity during youth, either because a lack of breadth and depth to their **sporting repertoires** or because of '**life-stage** squeeze' (see **transitions**).

Fourth, it is noticeable that very many young people already view themselves as 'sporty' (Sport England, 2003) and 'healthy' (Zuzanek, 2005): the vast majority of young people in the SHEU (2007) surveys and Philo et al.'s (2009) study 'felt happy about their lives' (p. 331) including their health. On top of this, health promotion is not the main motive for participation in sport among young people, pleasure is. There is, nevertheless, evidence that the more involved in sport and exercise youth become the more satisfied they are with their lives (Brustad et al., 2008). The two nationwide surveys in the United States on which Sabo and Veliz's (2008) report was based revealed associations between sports and physical activity and improvements in physical and emotional health as well as academic achievement and quality of life. Physical activity appears to have a particularly beneficial impact on young people's psychological health in relation to such psychosocial outcomes as self-esteem, mental health and cognitive functioning and 'emotional well-being is positively associated with participation in vigorous recreation and sport' (Stensel et al., 2008: 46). Conversely, there is an elevated **risk** of depressive symptoms among physically inactive youngsters. This is pertinent because despite generally positive self-perceptions of their health status and levels of physical activity, 'sizeable groups' of youngsters in Zuzanek's (2005: 379–380) study reported 'a variety of health difficulties and negative mental health symptoms'. In this regard, Robb (2007b: 202) observes that, 'While mental and emotional difficulties can be viewed as a feature of "normal" adolescent development, there is evidence that some groups of young people are more vulnerable than others are and that the experience of mental health is influenced by factors such as **gender, social class** and **ethnicity**': 'Young people's experience of mental health is strongly gendered, with young women at greater risk of eating disorders and self-harm, and young men have higher rates of suicide' (Robb, 2007b: 202). Levels of perceived stress (especially anxiety, fear, worries and loneliness) appear to be especially high among late (18–20-year-old) adolescents in most industrialized countries (Zuzanek, 2005) and young black men, in particular, experience a disproportionately high rate of mental health problems.

All in all, 'sport *may* assist a health life-style, but it *may not*' (Parry, 1988: 108; emphases in the original). Far more important to health status are social dynamics (sport cannot eliminate or even reduce health inequalities associated with age, sex and socio-economic status) and other lifestyle practices (such as diet and consumption of tobacco and alcohol). Sport and physical activity are useful in health promotion alongside, but not as a substitute for, other healthy lifestyle practices (Roberts and Brodie, 1992). Thus, the 'great health expectations of sport need to deflated on scientific and health grounds' (Roberts and Brodie, 1992: 142): 'sport deserves a niche, but no more, in health **policy** ... [and] health objectives merit only a niche in sports promotion' (p. 143).

Despite the many caveats to naive faith in the potential of sport as a 'silver bullet' for health issues – and the fact that sport is only one of a number of active leisure pursuits that can make people feel better and serve as a vehicle for positive relationships (with friends and family, for example) – it is worthy of note that sport does appear particularly well placed to provide people with peak experiences (or 'flow'), through activities where the skill required meets the challenge of the activity and the participant becomes absorbed (Csikzentmihalyi, 1990). This is, of course, where and why so many youngsters find **motivation** for sport.

IDENTITY (SELF-)

The period leading up to and including youth is one characterized by a desire among young people to establish a personal (or self-)identity beyond that ascribed via primary (the family) and secondary (school, in particular) **social-ization** (Coalter, 2007). The concept of self-identity refers to an individual's sense of self; in other words, the kind of person they see themselves as being – who they feel they are – and what marks them out in their own minds as well as that of (generalized) others. Thus, self-identity has two dimensions: 'a desired self (how I would like to be), and a presented self (how I try to appear to others)' (Roberts, 2009: 251).

Self-identity is not a straightforwardly personal matter, however. It is strongly associated with social identity in terms of the groups young people choose to be a part of (such as fellow skaters or rugby **clubs**) as well as those they are inevitably part of (families, schools, ethnic and gender groupings, for instance). Whether acquired or ascribed, young people's identities are grounded in their routine interactions with members of the various networks they inhabit. In other words, because they lead their lives in social groups (at school, with friends and in sport, for example), young people's social identities are shaped by what they have in common with these groups (such as sporting and musical tastes). The common bond of a social or group identity is not, however, 'exclusively dependent on direct interpersonal interaction with other members of the category' (Payne, 2006: 9) – young people's identities are also circumscribed by groups they are part of but might not closely or consciously interact with in the same way they might a group of surf 'buddies' or friends. Such common bonds take the form of looser, less immediate social categories such as **social class**, **gender** and **ethnicity**, nationality and **age** cohorts. Although more abstract than the immediacy of family and friends, these 'imagined communities' (Payne, 2006: 9) can be no less significant in their effects. In addition to such overarching social categories, some aspects of young people's personal identities are situation specific in the sense that they depend upon where they are, who they are with and what they are doing – for example, as religious worshippers, joggers, skaters and climbers – and some of these situations are more significant in their ramifications for personal identity than others. Indeed, because young people are inevitably members of multiple groups from family through schools, regions, nations, ethnicity, sexes and clubs, identities tend to be multifaceted. Consequently, young people develop differing, if sometimes overlapping and mutually reinforcing, identities in different areas of their lives. Identities are, therefore, multidimensional – incorporating some or all of age, kin, nationality, ethnicity, sex and gender, peers and friendship groups and so on (Jones, 2009) – and youngster's freedom to achieve desired identities is inevitably circumscribed by their ascribed identities.

Although not interactions of the face-to-face variety, membership of wider social groupings still impose constraints on individual tastes and behaviours. This is why individual identities can only be achieved by young people comparing and defining themselves in relation to others in their groups or networks (see **friends and peers**) and why young people's links with people in one particular category (an ethnic grouping such as British Muslims, for instance) may sometimes be at odds with their differences from them, owing to membership of some other category (such as a girls' football team). Although ethnicity remains a significant aspect of many young people's self-identities, the contingent and complex nature of self-identity is reflected in the multiple and diverse identities of ethnic minority youngsters. Warikoo (2005), for example, found that Indo-Caribbean young men and women in London and New York drew from multiple influences on their identities and, in the case of boys, often chose to distance themselves from an Indian identity. In such cases, where young people inhabit an ethnically diverse society, ethnicity can serve as an important signifier of difference which they may seek to downplay or emphasize in order to fit in with their peer groups. The particular mix of identities – Muslim, sportswomen and trainee PE teachers – experienced by young South Asian Muslim men and women in Dagkas and Benn's (2006: 22) study, by contrast, resulted in 'cultures of hybridity'. The complex nature of personal identity encourages social scientists to talk of identities in the plural as a means of acknowledging the different facets of people's global identity, such as Muslim, footballer, daughter, girlfriend, student and so forth.

In Western societies, in particular, many young people absorb the general pressure to express their individuality by seeking to stand out but only in socially acceptable ways that cement particular group identities – in other words, to simultaneously belong to specific groups while maintaining a degree of individuality. The greater range of consumption available in twenty-first century global economies enables young people to express their individuality (Furlong and Cartmel, 1997) in ways acceptable to their peers. Young people can choose from an ever-burgeoning range of identities (many available for purchase) in the form of music, dress, hairstyle, sports, **leisure** activities and so on and utilize these to present and project a particular image and identity. They can, in effect, 'pick and mix', refine and even change their identities – in line with 'Sought-after and acceptable styles that change periodically' (Roberts, 2009: 95) – within the confines of available and realistically achievable (as well as ascribed) identities. While young people report being under a good deal of peer pressure to appear independent, to be recognized, to appear grown up and to have fun (Carter *et al.*, 2003), Van Wel *et al.* (2008: 33) study of Dutch youth led them to conclude that the majority of adolescents simply want to belong to 'mainstream youth' rather than stand out – or, at least, only stand out in ways acceptable to their friends and peers. In fact, many young people appear not to identify with distinctive **youth cultures**. Indeed, they are inclined to report their social identity as 'normal' and remain fundamentally conformist (Jones, 2009).

There is, it seems, a downside to the relative freedom to 'create' individual identities. Because young people's lives in (post-) modern societies are so fluid and fragmented, it is said that they lose any sense of who they really are – young people find it more difficult than previously to 'develop and maintain a stable and coherent self-concept' (Roberts, 2009: 251). This situation is believed to be exacerbated by, first, the constant change and revision to their identities that youngsters may deliberately choose to make and display via clothing, musical and even sporting (e.g. surfing and skateboarding) tastes and, second, the manner in which young people interact with different sets of people in different places with the upshot that their identities are inevitably more compartmentalized and fragmented (Roberts, 2009). This is the reason that personal identities are not tantamount to social identities – young people tend not to mix exclusively with one group and can be members of multiple groups (based, for example, on musical, sporting and gender bases). In fact, they often mix with different people at different times in what are sometimes referred to as 'proto-communities'. It is also the reason why post-modernists view self-identities as choosable and plastic, insofar as young people's identities represent their own particular mix of social identities which shift as individual tastes shift. Indeed, post-structuralists claim that in contemporary society (in contrast to twentieth century 'modern' societies) there are no core or central dimensions to young people's identities, based, for example, on social class, gender or ethnicity; identities are no longer anchored in such structures, being chosen from a range of lifestyles and consequently 'fluid' and unique to individuals. For most academic commentators on youth cultures, however, post-modernists and post-structuralists overstate the nature and impact of those economic and social developments labelled as post-modern. In other words, while **youth's new condition** has, indeed, impacted upon young people's identities, it has only blurred rather than obliterated the impact of structural factors and young people have no trouble recognizing their gender, ethnic and even social class identities. Put another way, 'despite young people's heightened self-awareness, structural determinants of their futures remain as powerful as ever' (Roberts, 2008: 196) – the 'post-' perspectives simply exaggerate the scope for individuality: style groups and neo-tribes are too fluid and transitory to form a basis for identity (Jones, 2009).

The significance of (self-)identity for youth sport

Physical and sporting domains feature prominently in the cultural practices and value systems of societies worldwide and especially in the West. Consequently, physical and sporting prowess is a salient features of young people's identities as either positive or negative referents and sometimes both. Physical and sporting skills and competencies and levels of strength and fitness are evidently important to many young people and are central to their self-esteem (Fox, 2000; cited in Coalter, 2007) as well as their more enduring identities. Indeed, achievement in and through sport is often viewed by young people 'as a sort of "functional alternative", an alternative way of feeling a sense of achievement and developing self-esteem' (Coalter, 2007: 125). Hence, acquiring and developing sporting skills can be important for self-image and identity as well as in gaining acceptance among peers (Brustad *et al.*, 2008: 355). Infact, they often appear interrelated in the sense that more favourable perceptions of peer acceptance tend to be associated with stronger perceptions of physical self-worth and this, in turn, seems to result in higher levels of attachment to sport.

One aspect of self-identity of particular significance for sports **participation** (and, consequently for young people's self-esteem – the ways and extent to which they value themselves) is what social psychologists refer to as self-efficacy. Self-efficacy is a person's belief that s/he 'can execute a course of action and achieve a desired outcome' (Roberts, 2009: 75). It is related to willingness 'to take on a challenging task, to expend effort and to persist, and to a belief that one can control and shape one's own life' (p. 75). Nonetheless, although 'Physical self-efficacy and physical self-worth, feelings of self-determination and personal control can be developed via improved sporting competence' (Coalter, 2007: 125–26), their relative importance varies between individuals and, in particular, between ages and genders.

As an area of their lives where young people can decide for themselves not only what they will do and how they will do it but also crucially who they will do it with (DCMS/Strategy Unit, 2002; Roberts, 1999), sport (as with leisure as a whole) serves as a key site for young people to become more independent and to establish self-identities. Young people often choose leisure activities that are not tightly controlled by adults (Coakley and White, 1999). Hence, the steady trend away from organized, supervised leisure 'towards spending **time** with groups of friends in unsupervised situations' (Roberts, 1999: 118). In the process of asserting their independence young people increasingly engage in activities that 'prepare them for adulthood or enable them to do adult things' (Coakley and White, 1999: 80). Young people's leisure (and leisure-sport) activities can be identity-conferring insofar as they help them to recognize and to some extent construct who they 'are' (Roberts, 2003) through the things they (like to) do (a lot of) in their free time: for example, climb, bike, dance and surf. Thus, leisure provides opportunities (times, places and activities) for young people to express and, in the process, reinforce and embellish their more-or-less individual identities. Such identities may be expressed in musical tastes and dress styles, for example, and also in active leisure forms such as sport.

Young people's self-identity and predispositions (**habitus**) develop rapidly and profoundly during childhood and youth and the teenage years are especially important. To the extent that they can access sports such as tennis, golf, martial arts, soccer, horse-riding, sailing and skiing, middle and working-class youth may challenge and/or reinforce the socio-economic dimensions of their personal identities. Similarly, through games like basketball, soccer and rugby some girls evidently challenge stereotypical female identities while others, through activities such as dance and aerobics, bolster their preferred perceptions of themselves as quintessentially female and feminine.

Youth are particularly concerned with developing stable self-identities in the light of the changes associated with physical maturation, gaining relative independence from parents, determining which parental and adult values to accept or reject, developing and extending friendships and preparing for an occupational role (Feinstein *et al.*, 2007). Changes to the **body** during puberty, in particular, can have a substantial affect upon young people's self-perceptions, especially among young women – the way they look remains the principal worry of female adolescents (SHEU, 2007). Girls and young women quickly develop views of themselves as more-or-less suited to sport (in terms, for example, of their physical stature and prowess and their coordination and skills). Approximately a third of girls in a *SportScotland* study (Biddle *et al.*, 2005) reported not liking to see how they looked when they were exercising. Consequently, leisure in general and sport in particular are processes through which young people are likely to have their developing views of themselves as more-or-less masculine or feminine reinforced or challenged. Several young 15–16-year-old women in Smith *et al.'s* (2009) study expressed the view that increasing the choice of activities available to them in school PE had the potential to impact positively upon their confidence and self-esteem as well as their identities. They suggested that choice might enable them, as young women, to avoid the kinds of activities that might undermine their self-confidence – sensitive as they were to the views of other people – and to choose activities that might help enhance their self-perceptions. It seems that where schools fail to offer young women a broader range of activities than the conventional **PE** diet, they may be missing a substantial opportunity not only to increase participation rates among young women but also to enhance their self-esteem and identities.

So far, it has been argued that sport can make a substantial contribution to young people's self-esteem and more generally their self-identities (and it is interesting to note in this regard that over 70 per cent of young people surveyed by Sport England [2003a] considered themselves to be 'a sporty type of person'). As previously indicated, however, there is an inevitable limit to the role of leisure and sport in young people's construction of identity, and it would be a mistake to assume that young people's leisure-based identities are especially deep-seated. Although sporting prowess can undoubtedly form an important aspect of young people's self-identities and can, indeed, make them feel more satisfied with their lives, it does not tell them who they fundamentally are – it does not, in other words, form the basis for young people's 'core views and feelings about their society and their own positions within it' (Roberts, 2003: 22). While young people tend nowadays to be more aware of their personal identities and how they, as 'individuals', stand out from others, they tend to be less consciously aware of some of those things they have in common with their peers and others around them. At the same time, however, they continue to recognize themselves and others as male or female, black or white and to some extent middle or working-class and their leisure and sporting lives are not indicating an end to the significance for youth identities of these structural dynamics. Thus, while they have the potential to make a significant contribution to youth identities, the typical effects of leisure and sport pale in comparison with the broader social categories in generating and establishing identities. Indeed, young people often experience their membership of larger age, national, class, gender and ethnicity groups via the local groups they are directly involved with (e.g. football, rugby league, cricket clubs, kabbadi and handball teams, and dance groups). This is partly because young people are most likely to select those with whom they wish to take part in leisure activities (such as sport) from those they are most likely to meet and meet most easily and most often through, for example, family, neighbourhood and school. This is where economic, social and cultural **capital** (often mediated by **parents and family**) can broaden or restrict the networks youngsters become a part of and, as a consequence, their emerging and developing self-identities.

INDIVIDUALIZATION

Changes in national and global economies in the last 50 years or more (see **globalization**) have exacerbated a number of trends present in Western societies over a much longer time-frame. One such trend has been towards social relations becoming increasingly individualized and privatized (Elias, 2001; Rojek, 1985). Individualization refers to a trend towards each person having a unique biography in the sense that 'each individual's chain of experiences is a unique series' (Roberts, 2008: 75). This trend has been more rapid and even in more complex societies (European countries, for example) and slower and more uneven in comparatively simpler societies (Elias, 2001). Thus, the individualization of youth biographies has been especially marked not only in Europe (Iacovou and Berthoud, 2001) – and Northern and Western European regions (such as Scandinavia and the United Kingdom) in particular (Schizzerotto and Lucchini, 2002) – but across the Western world in general (Shanahan, 2000). The upshot has been that there are, in effect, no longer normal biographies for young people in the sense of typical sequences in their **transitions** from youth to adulthood (Schizzerotto and Lucchini, 2002) – young people have more varied experiences in schooling, post-compulsory education, the workplace and **leisure** and within the social networks to be found in all these places. Consequently, in contemporary societies, **youth's new condition** means that young people each have their own (more or less) highly individualized lives.

The growth of individualization – and corresponding new forms of self-consciousness (Elias, 2001), including a 'heightened awareness of the self' (Roberts, 2009: 131) – exacerbates 'the growing autonomy which tends to accompany the physical and social maturation of the young' (Dunning, 1999: 4) in the modern, developed, capitalist economies of the Western world. It also exacerbates young people's feelings of agency as well as responsibility for their own situations (Jones, 2009: 102). In the **'risk'** society' individuals have been freed from clear socially structured social roles while at the same time confronted with 'an infinite range of potential courses of action (and attendant risks)' (Jones, 2009: 26), resulting in their forced individualization.

One way in which this individualized self-consciousness manifests itself is in young people's relatively weak awareness of the common bonds they share with other youngsters – on the basis of **social class**, for example (see **identity** and **youth culture and lifestyles**). They tend, nonetheless, to be acutely aware of group identities shared around dress styles, musical tastes and so forth and, in establishing their own identities, young people seek to assert their independence from others in a manner that marks them out as individuals without compromising any group identity they may covet.

The process of individualization is significant for young people's psychological well-being. On the one hand, highly individualized people often place considerable value on their perceived differentness to other people and their 'freedom' to go their own way – associated with the apparent spread of individualization has been the supposed growth in significance of the reflexive self; that is, the tendency for (not to say, obligation on) individuals to reflect upon and consider their abilities, inclinations and opportunities and plan their futures accordingly (Roberts, 2008). On the other hand, however, there is a

99

simultaneous tendency for people to experience a whole range of emotions including feelings of not living their own lives, greater isolation from others and corresponding feelings of solitude (Elias, 2001). In other words, while it is frequently 'a personal ideal of young people and adults to differ from others in one way or another ... in short, to be different' (Elias, 2001: 140), the individualization of social life has generated corresponding feelings of 'separateness and encapsulation of individuals in their relations to each other' (Elias, 2001: 121).

Among other things, the individualization of their biographies has resulted in major changes in young people's leisure lives, including the fragmentation of youth leisure tastes and styles (Hendry *et al.*, 2002): 'the trend is towards every individual having a particular combination of leisure interests and activities, and a unique leisure career' with individuals developing 'personal stocks of leisure skills and interests' (Roberts, 1999: 43). This, in turn, has led to corresponding changes in the ways in which young people participate in sport.

The significance of individualization for youth sport

Leisure in general and sport in particular provide opportunities for young people to establish and assert their independence (DCMS/Strategy Unit, 2002; Roberts, 1999). A significant corollary of the process of individualization has been a gradual trend among youth 'away from spending leisure in organized and supervised settings' (Roberts, 1999: 118) and as leisure activities have become more informal (and, in particular, less organized) across Europe so too has participation in sport. A tendency towards more individualized forms of **participation** has corresponded with the increased appeal of informal, casual, recreational or **lifestyle activities** as young people become increasingly inclined to adopt leisure and sporting styles which highlight their individuality; including greater scope for choice and informality (see **informalization**). In this vein, sport is a leisure site in which young people can decide for themselves what they will do and how and where they will do it, as well as who they will do it with. The **commercialization** of leisure has added impetus to individualized leisure lifestyles as an increasing variety of commercial enterprises have sought to cash in on the new forms of popular leisure and sport. Indeed, young people's desire to highlight their individuality while standing out in socially acceptable ways has been encouraged by the greater and more diverse range of (sporting and leisure) consumption available to them (Furlong and Cartmel, 1997).

Unsurprisingly, the process of individualization has had inevitable repercussions for team sports (De Knop *et al.*, 1996) and, for that matter, sports **clubs** and organizations – and sporting **competition**. Lower levels of participation in team sports alongside higher rates in individual activities and increased provision by the private sector have reflected trends towards individualization (Coalter, 1999). This individualization of sports participation among youth has been reinforced by the **time** pressures felt by those most likely to be active in sport (16–34-year-olds) and those in the higher social classes (Coalter, 1999). Taken together, these twin processes go a long way to explaining the increased popularity of more individual, more informal activities alongside institutionalized sports across Europe over the course of the last four decades or more (Brettschneider, 1992; De Knop and De Martelaer, 2001).

Furlong and Cartmel (2007) recite Beck's (1992) claim that (young) people are constrained to demonstrate their independence through their leisure lifestyles and, in particular, their patterns of consumption. Although young people may actively seek to 'pick and mix' from a wide repertoire of possible sport and leisure activities (Roberts, 1997) – and consume particular styles of clothing, music and such like as a means of expressing their individuality and establishing, maintaining and experimenting with their highly individualized identities and lifestyles (Miles, 2000, 2003) – such behaviours always occur in the context of their relations with others and especially their **friends and peers**. Thus, throughout their young lives young people seek to strike 'a delicate balancing act between the construction of individuality and relationships constructed in groups' (Miles, 2000: 24). Indeed, young people often use sport and leisure as a means of coping simultaneously with the felt need to 'fit in' within those around them (including their **gender** and **ethnic** affiliations) and, at the same time, 'stick out' in terms of individual identity and self-expression.

All in all, the double-edged character of individualization that has developed over the course of several centuries has involved a gradual shift in the balance between the we- and I-identity (both of which are integral to the social **habitus** of a person) towards the I-identity. Put another way, greater emphasis has come to be placed on 'the I-identity of the individual person, and the detachment of that person from the traditional groupings' of people (Elias, 2001: 179).

The increasing individualization of young people's biographies, lifestyles and identities alongside the growing emphasis that has come to be placed upon the significance of the 'I-identity' in their lives has had ramifications for youth sport and leisure. Young people's individuality is, nevertheless, an expression of structured individualization in the sense that their sporting, leisure and general lifestyle decisions (and corresponding **identities**) are inevitably and always circumscribed by their own personal contexts in relation to physical capacities and abilities as well as their gender, position in the social hierarchy and ethnic affiliations. In addition, very many young people remain, by degrees, more-or-less dependent upon adults (**parents**, siblings, teachers, employers and so forth) for their sporting involvement, not least in terms of financial resources, transport and social and cultural **capital**. In other words, 'children's participation in constructing their own everyday world takes place within the constraints set by their subordinate location in relation to adults' (Jackson and Scott, 2006: 218).

While being excluded from many adult activities, young people are, at the same time, expected to behave like adults in several respects, and it is hardly surprising that they 'are often confused and resentful' (Jackson and Scott, 2006: 222). Consequently, while excluded from full participation in adult society (Jackson and Scott, 2006), youth very often refuse to remain childlike in their outlook and leisure activities, and the adult-like activities they become involved within tend to provoke disquiet, not to say **moral panic**, among adults. Nonetheless, in an age when very many branches of leisure (and especially those seen as fashionable or 'cool' among young people, such as music and health and fitness gyms) have become heavily commercialized, young people's independence is inevitably circumscribed by their economic dependence upon their parents: they can only 'exercise consumer choice if their parents permit it' (Jackson and Scott, 2006: 223). Hence, the popularity not to say necessity among youth of part-time paid **work**.

INFORMALIZATION

Informalization refers to the changes in human relationships (over the past century or more) as a consequence of shifts in the balance of power between, and integration among, the **social classes**, sexes and generations. In this sense, informalization is associated with a narrowing of power differentials and a process of social equalization (or levelling) as hierarchies of rank gradually diminish and attitudes are softened where social conditions become more equal (Kilminster, 1998). In the second half of the twentieth century, in particular, social life became increasingly characterized by a 'democratization of relations between adults and children and a decline in inequality between them' alongside 'a more general informalization of relations between adults and children' (van Krieken, 1998: 156). This incorporated an increased emphasis on informal, relaxed behaviours among young people as well as between them and adults. This is best illustrated, perhaps, by the manner in which, 'The expectation that teenagers submit unprotestingly to their parents' wishes ... diminished dramatically between the 1950s and the 1970s (Mennell, 1998: 242). In short, informalization is an expression of the ways in which many power ratios have become more equal over time (Mennell, 1998), tying people more closely together than hitherto. The upshot has been that power relationships between generations (and, for that matter, the sexes) have become less uneven and 'the imposed sense of inferiority' felt by young people (and girls and young women in particular) has been 'weakened' (Mennell, 1998: 123).

As young people have sought to emancipate themselves from the dominance of established groups (such as adults) and struggled to reject old behavioural codes while developing new ones, a trend has emerged towards increasing varieties in permissible behaviour (Kilminster, 1998; Mennell, 1998). Thus, the reduction in the power differentials and social distance between groups – and between young people and adults in particular – has found expression in 'less formal regulation of the spoken and written language, clothing, music, dancing and hair styles' (Kilminster, 1998: 151). The diminishing social distance between adults and younger people is expressed not only at the relatively superficial level of more frequent use of Christian names and informal language (Wouters, 2007) but also at a more profound level in terms of more frequent occurrences of negotiation rather than prohibition (Kilminster, 1998) – in relation to **leisure** lifestyles, for example.

Among other things, informalization has involved an emancipation of the emotions (Wouters, 2007) and the repositioning of emotions at the centre of personality – including an increasing permissiveness and informality in public and private relationships (exemplified in the prevalence of social kissing, the use of personal pronouns, more 'relaxed' and expressive forms of dancing and so forth). The diminishing power relationships between adults and young people have made relationships more lenient, more varied and differentiated and some of the behaviours of these groups have grown closer to each other. Thus, some of the cultural and behavioural developments witnessed contemporarily are explicable as an expression of the balance of power tilting more in favour of young people. Hence, the prevalence of what would once have been viewed as youth dress-codes and lifestyles, musical tastes and sporting involvement (e.g. in surfing and mountain-biking) among older generations.

Increases in informality between adults and children have enabled the latter greater freedom of self-expression and resulted in a diminution of the so-called 'generation gap'. With shifts in the power balance between older and younger generations, it becomes inevitable that the more established group feels compelled to change their stance and become more accommodating towards the younger generation's attitudes and behaviours. Consequently, negotiation rather than direction and prohibition become more prominent in relations between adults and young people over issues (such as teenage sex and **drugs**) that the established adult groups previously refused to consider acceptable.

Unsurprisingly, given the organized and formal nature of much sport and the centrality of adults therein (e.g. as **parents**, spectators, coaches, **club** and **competition** officials), informalization processes have significant ramifications for youth sport.

The significance of informalization for youth sport

In the latter decades of the twentieth century, informalization became not only an increasingly significant aspect of **youth cultures** generally but also a feature of their leisure and sporting lives in particular. Consequently, over the last 40 years, there have been major changes in young people's leisure styles (Roberts, 2006) and corresponding changes in their sports **participation**. Particularly noticeable has been the tendency for young people to spend less **time** in organized and supervised sport and leisure settings. As young people, youth and adults have all been drawn increasingly towards less formal, less rigidly organized leisure activities so participation in sport has been marked by a shift towards informal and recreational forms and styles. Inevitably, the processes of informalization and **individualization** have had repercussions for team sports and, for that matter, sports **clubs and organizations**, Europe-wide (De Knop *et al.*, 1996; Telama *et al.*, 2002).

In its stronger sense, the concept of informalized sport describes those activities which take place outside the conventional sporting environments of sports clubs, public leisure centres and commercial venues: for example, skateboarding, surfing, free-running and mountain biking. In a weaker, more general, and perhaps more useful sense, informalized sport refers to the manner in which sport is undertaken rather than the venue and/or degree of organiza-tion. In this sense, informal sport refers to more recreational (less- or non-competitive) forms of participation as well as **lifestyle activities** such as aerobics, dance, jogging and walking (in addition to those activities mentioned earlier). Shooting basketball against a garage backboard, playing 'kickabout' football, cross-country skiing, and canoeing are examples that fit both senses of informalized sport. These activities can, of course, become more formal in the competitive, organized sense and can take place in conventional sporting venues but still be undertaken in a recreational manner. The informalization of sport among young people in recent decades is perhaps most clearly manifested in the substantial growth of lifestyle sports. Indeed, informalization is one of the central features of lifestyle sports.

All in all, it pays to keep both senses of the term informal in mind when making sense of youth sport. Indeed, the notion of a formal–informal con-tinuum – with set venues and a competitive, organized structure at one end and a variety of alternative venues and a more recreational ethos at the other – is crucial in understanding developments in youth sport in recent decades. In more democratized, individualized, informalized societies school **PE** teachers, club coaches and adults working in sport generally have been obliged to respond (wittingly or otherwise) to developments in youth cultures and, in particular, their preferences for more informal relationships, behaviours and activities. As young people increasingly view 'leisure activities as a social enclave within which restraints may be loosened' (Mennell, 1998: 143) control over content as well as teaching and coaching styles – previously taken largely for granted by teachers and coaches – has been increasingly challenged explicitly and implicitly, directly and indirectly. In a similar manner, the sporting provi-sion of local authorities has necessarily developed to include, for example, skateboarding and BMX **facilities** and mountain-bike trails.

LEISURE

There are two broad ways of defining leisure: either as a residue (of **time**) or as an experience. The first definition is commonplace in government and commercial surveys as well as academic studies of the topic and conceptualizes leisure as

time left over after **work** and obligatory activities (such as domestic responsibilities, family commitments and personal hygiene) in which people are relatively free to choose what they do as well as how they do it (Roberts, 2006).
Defining leisure in terms of free time and free choice has the obvious benefit
of coinciding with ordinary, everyday uses of the term while allowing for
measurement of what people actually do with their time when they are free to
choose – for example, at the end of the school day, when homework and
chores have been completed and during weekends and holidays. The second
approach (and one associated with social psychologists' views of leisure in the
1960s and 1970s in particular) defines leisure in terms of the quality of experiences: in effect, whether or not leisure involves intrinsic satisfaction and self-
realization. The problem with this kind of subjective definition is that it is
pretty-much immeasurable; not least because the notion of leisure as a 'quality
experience' does not match the general public's everyday understanding of
what is meant by the term – as illustrated by the commonplace tendency for
people to refer to 'just killing time' in their leisure. As we shall see, the nature
and quality of leisure and sporting experiences is, nevertheless, an important
dimension to understanding developments in youth sport.

In terms of the more objective, residual definition of leisure (as time left
over), **participation** tends to be measured against one or all of three criteria:
rates (of participation), time (given over to various leisure activities) and money
(spent on leisure activities). Some popular leisure activities (such as watching
TV) take up a good deal of spare time and involve large numbers of people of
all ages and from all social groups but are relatively inexpensive to undertake.
Others, such as (sporting) holidays require relatively little time but are usually
quite expensive. Against some or all these measures growth has been a prominent feature of leisure (in both the twentieth century and the early years of
the twenty-first century) as more and more people become involved in most
types of leisure activity, participate more often and spend more on them
(Roberts, 2005).

There have been two major trends within the general growth of leisure:
(i) privatism (treating the home as the primary site for leisure) – 'for most
people, most of the time, leisure takes place within and around the home and
usually occurs with members of their family and close friends' (Harrington,
2006: 417) – and (ii) **commercialization**. As with adults, the vast majority of
young people 'spend some time engaged with core activities such as watching
TV, socializing with **friends**, shopping, playing computer games and so on'
(Furlong and Cartmel, 2007: 73) and substantial elements of these are both
privatized and commercialized experiences. Where differences occur, these
tend to be a matter of emphasis and degree as various groups of young people
place more or less emphasis upon particular activities due to differences in
resources and preferences.

Only time will tell whether or not recent developments with ramifications
for leisure – the electronic media (the Internet, mobile phones, iPods and so forth),

for example – will prove to be as significant in terms of changing people's ways of life as the genuinely revolutionary developments (especially for leisure, sport and physical recreation) between the latter years of nineteenth century and the early years of the twentieth century: radio, cinema, television, motor car, mains electricity and central heating to homes (Roberts, 2006). Either way, in terms of the quality of people's leisure it is interesting to note that the relationship between leisure and well-being is not as straightforward as might be expected. Despite the continued growth of leisure, people today 'are no more satisfied with their lives than they were 50 years ago' (Roberts, 2005: 3) – it seems that 'the growth of leisure time and spending has inflated types of leisure activity that are far less likely to leave people feeling fulfilled and satisfied with their lives' (p. 5).

The significance of leisure for youth sport

A good deal of young people's lives is technically leisure. The time use of 15–24-year-olds in various countries in a European Commission (2003) study revealed that, after 'personal care' (including eating and sleeping), leisure accounted for the next biggest block of time for young people – greater than study, employment and domestic work (Furlong and Cartmel, 2007). According to Fredricks and Eccles (2005: 507), adolescents in the United States 'spend more than half of their waking hours in leisure activities'. In addition to spare time, youth have a wider range of leisure and sporting activities available to them than previous generations – if they can afford them.

Through the teenage years leisure activity becomes an increasing significant aspect of young people's lives (Feinstein et al., 2005) and many participate in a variety of leisure forms and settings. On the face of it all those young people still in education have to do with their leisure is enjoy themselves! In principle, at least, they could play more sport – assuming they have sufficient **motivation** to do so. This is significant in sporting terms, because childhood and youth are the **age and life-stages** where the foundations for long-term uses of leisure are laid and, during their teenage years, young people 'typically dabble and experiment with a wide range of leisure interests' (Roberts and Brodie, 1992: 39). They are, as Roberts (1997: 3) observes, 'the section of the population with highest levels and most diverse patterns of cultural consumption'. In part because young people are the age group most receptive to 'doing new things', their leisure interests and lifestyles are characterized by changeability and insta- bility (Iacovou and Berthoud, 2001; Schizzerotto and Lucchini, 2002). Although, during adulthood, leisure tastes and behaviours tend to stabilize (Roberts et al., 2009: 262), young people's leisure is chronically unstable and more so than the leisure of any other age group. Consequently, many of their leisure interests are soon dropped or replaced – although as a group they have the highest parti- cipation rates 'across out-of-home leisure in general' (Roberts, 1999: 114), and sport in particular, young people also have the highest drop-out rates.

Nevertheless, the tendency towards changeability and instability does not necessarily mean a tendency towards disengagement with active uses of leisure. Teenagers do not just lapse (e.g. from sport), they move to other activities in their relatively busy leisure lives – they do something else, something they enjoy more. In this regard, the UK Government – concerned as it has been with promoting youth sport – has felt compelled to acknowledge that 'Most young people stop [sport] because of interest in other activities' (DCMS/ Strategy Unit, 2002: 96) rather than merely because they cannot be bothered. While sport is a significant aspect of youth leisure – in Brettschneider and Naul's (2004) study of out of home leisure in six European countries, 'recreational sport was the sixth most popular activity while organized sport was ninth' (Furlong and Cartmel, 2007: 75) – the constraints on sports participation tend to be other uses of leisure-time. Indeed, in any discussion of active leisure, it is important to bear in mind that informal leisure – 'time spent doing nothing, just relaxing, hanging about' (Roberts, 2008: 136) – accounts for a great deal of young people's leisure time as they watch TV, surf the Internet, listen to music, 'hang out' with friends and so forth. In fact, recreational forms of sport (e.g. kickabout football or one-on-one basketball outside a friend's home) can often be secondary activities that facilitate socializing with friends. Thus, leisure provides an important arena for **individualized** youth to come together and 'leisure contexts' have become 'crucial spaces' for **identity** construction (Arai and Pedlar, 2003: 194) – leisure has come to be viewed by young people as 'the pre-eminent domain' in which they can 'develop individual preferences and try out social roles through experimentation' (Zeijl *et al.*, 2001: 380).

The degrees of freedom young people have in choosing how to use their spare time notwithstanding, their uses of leisure tend to be patterned by age and form. Youngsters move through three age-related phases from organized through casual to commercial leisure (Hendry *et al.*, 1993; Roberts, 2006). Organized leisure includes sports participation 'which tends to decline from the ages 13 to 14' (Furlong and Cartmel, 2007: 75) to be replaced by casual leisure including 'hanging around' with friends. After age 16, commercial leisure (e.g. cinema and pubs and bars) becomes the predominant form of leisure for young people. Youth leisure is also shaped by social structures. Although times have changed quite markedly in recent decades, young people's uses of leisure continue, to varying degrees, to be patterned according to age, **ethnicity**, **gender** and **social class**, in particular. For example, while 14–16-year-old males in the *Longitudinal Study of Young People in England* reported participation in sport more often than the girls the latter reported going to a cinema, theatre or concert more frequently (DCSF, 2008).

It remains an open, empirical question whether or not the types of leisure young people increasingly engage in (e.g. the Internet and computer games) are more or less likely to leave them feeling fulfilled and satisfied with their lives when compared with active forms of leisure such as sport. Existing research

107

suggests, nevertheless, that active leisure tends to be most associated with higher levels of intrinsic satisfaction and psychosocial well-being; hence, the continued popularity of sport (among other active leisure pursuits such as playing a musical instrument) for many young people (see participation).

LIFELONG PARTICIPATION

People tend to reduce their levels of **participation** in a wide variety of **leisure** activities as they get older (Roberts, 2006). **Age** has a particularly deleterious effect on active forms of leisure, such as sport. When compared with other uses of leisure, loyalty rates (the likelihood that participants will continue) in sport are not good and drop-out rates from sport in youth and young adulthood are notoriously heavy (Birchwood *et al.*, 2008). Nevertheless, there is a wealth of research – exploring among other things the so-called 'determinants' and 'correlates' of participation in sport over the life course – providing support for the argument that active participation in sport during childhood and youth is an important prerequisite for involvement in later life (Scheerder *et al.*, 2006). Indeed, it seems that those who remain engaged in sport throughout the life events and **transitions** that accompany youth and young adulthood are then likely to remain sports active for many more years to come (Roberts and Brodie, 1992).

The significance of lifelong participation for youth sport

So what do we know about the recipe for lifelong participation? In particular, what, if anything, can be learned from the substantial growth in sports participation (across all age groups and throughout the developed world) over the last half century? Scheerder *et al.*'s (2006) longitudinal study of sports participation in late adolescence in Belgium provided support for the intuitive view that the longer an individual is involved in sport the less likely s/he is to drop out in later life. Scheerder *et al.* (2006) observed that sports participation in 'late adolescence' (or youth) correlated with adult participation while non-participation in leisure-**time** sport during adolescence was a relatively strong determinant of non-participation during adulthood. Similarly, in their study of men and women who had become 'committed' to sport as adults in seven major cities in the United Kingdom, Roberts and Brodie (1992) found that virtually all those who played regularly between the ages of 16 and 30 became, as it were, 'locked-in' to sport and were frequently 'established on continuous sports careers which ... [were] unlikely to be disrupted for many more years' (p. 37).

These and other similar studies suggest, however, that the recipe for lifelong participation involves more than the single ingredient of participation (at whatever age). Taking part in sport during childhood and youth may be a crucial prerequisite for ongoing adherence to sport for very many but it appears insufficient in itself. Scheerder *et al.*'s (2006: 427) study noted, for example, that 'a highly diverse sports pattern during late adolescence' carried 'better opportunities for active participation in sport as adults'. In a similar vein, Engstrom's (2008) follow-up study of 1518 53-year-old Swedish adults (aged 15 at the time of the original study in 1968) revealed that whereas neither amount of time spent on sport nor sports club membership at the age 15 showed any significant association with the exercise habits displayed in middle-age, the breadth of sporting experience while young did. Both studies lend support to the findings from Roberts and Brodie's (1992) seminal study in which the chief characteristic of the committed minority who became 'locked-in' to sport was that they had been 'active in several (usually three or more) games (or activities) throughout their sports careers' (p. 37). They tended, in other words, to possess what Roberts and Brodie (1992) referred to as 'wide **sporting repertoires**' and others label skill or activity 'portfolios' (SCW, 2000) or 'sports literacy' (DCMS/Strategy Unit, 2002). It was not so much the sheer *amount* as the *number of different* sports that young people learned to play that appeared crucial in determining whether people remained sports active into adulthood, according to Roberts and Brodie (1992). The point about wide sporting repertoires was that 'whatever their reasons for dropping out of particular sports, where the individuals played several games, their entire sports careers were less vulnerable' (p. 44). Findings such as these led Roberts (1996a) to conclude that the rise in sports participation in the United Kingdom over the course of the last few decades of the twentieth century was primarily explainable in terms of the introduction of 'higher proportions of young people to a wide range of sports' (Roberts and Brodie, 1992: 81) which brought with it higher degrees of 'sports literacy' among young people and concomitant generational shifts in attitudes towards physical recreation and sport (Coalter, 1999).

It is important to bear in mind that 'sports literacy' is not, however, simply a matter of playing, enjoying or being good at several sports. Neither, as Fairclough, Stratton and Baldwin (2002) intimate, is it the case that exposure to a range of activities constitutes a sufficient as well as a necessary condition for lifelong participation. Rather, as Roberts and Brodie (1992: 42) argue, it is the 'richness' of activities that is the chief characteristic marking out the sport and exercise **socialization** of those adults who become 'locked-in' to sport. Roberts (1999) describes richness not only in terms of a variety of activities but also as the satisfactions and skills that are generated and developed through particular activities, especially **lifestyle activities**, which individuals wish to repeat. Regular, voluntary and enjoyable participation tends to lead to the development of habitual, routinized behaviour (see socialization), underpinned and reinforced by organizational membership and social commitments that bind individuals into social networks in which sport and physical **activity** is customary (Roberts, 2006; Roberts and Brodie, 1992). In this manner, regular participation is mutually reinforcing in the sense that those who are active are exposed to, and are liable to absorb, **health** and fitness values which can be expected to strengthen their **motivation** to remain active (Roberts and Brodie, 1992). This, then, is the critical issue about motivation: very many individuals become motivated *because* they come to value physical activity, in part because they wish to repeat satisfying experiences. Thus, becoming motivated is often not so much a precursor to engagement with physical activity but, rather, a consequence of positive engagement and the resultant satisfactions associated with activities themselves.

In terms of the contribution of school **PE** to facilitating wide sporting repertoires, it seems that what matters is not so much what PE teachers might anticipate young people doing as adults, or even what they are currently doing. Whether youngsters experience, precisely the same activities at school as those they appear likely to engage in as adults, does not appear crucial. What seems to matter more is providing young people with a repertoire or portfolio of sports and physical activities. Some of these will endure while others will be replaced, supplemented or even dropped as their lives unfold; not least because the particular forms of activity in which young people find pleasurable excitement often develop and/or change as they grow older (Roberts and Brodie, 1992).

All in all, the arguments for the significance of youth sport for lifelong participation are well-established. So too are claims that barriers to participation – associated, for example, with adult transitions (and, in particular, responsibilities such as marrying and becoming a parent or being unemployed) have direct effects on sport participation rates. Nevertheless, a recent study casts doubt on assumptions that some of these barriers are as crucial as is commonly assumed. From their analysis of the sports careers of representative samples of 31–37-year-olds from three South Caucasus countries – Armenia, Azerbaijan and Georgia – Birchwood *et al.* (2008) conclude that many differences in sport participation rates commonly attributed to circumstances and experiences after age 16 (commencing higher education, for example) already exist at age 16 and that family cultures are the source of the crucial predispositions to participate which tend to have lasting effects. Birchwood *et al.* (2008: 283) observe that 'all the major, recognized differences in adult rates of sports participation between socio-demographic groups' appear to be generated during childhood 'via cultures that are transmitted through families' and that 'post-childhood experiences play a relatively minor direct part in generating these differences'. On this view, whether or not young people start or stop participating in sport – or, for that matter, increase or decrease their levels of participation as they approach and negotiate adolescence and adulthood – may very well depend upon predispositions formed earlier in life (Birchwood *et al.*, 2008). Consequently, any changes in the overall rates of participation (whether up or down, overall) among particular age groups (such as the general increases witnessed in the 1970s and 1980s) are probably best explained in terms of 'the standard pre-disposition within a socio-demographic group' (Birchwood *et al.*, 2008: 284) towards participation in sport and, for that matter, all other forms of leisure. Although, especially as adults, people are most likely to change their levels and, to some extent, forms of leisure participation alongside or following major life events and major life-stage transitions (Birchwood *et al.*, 2008; Gershuny, 2003), the crucial point is that 'life events and life-stage transitions can be accompanied or followed by increases or decreases in participation in particular activities' (Birchwood *et al.*, 2008: 284) and whether they are or not is highly likely to depend upon the predispositions to sport acquired during childhood socialization.

Birchwood *et al.'s* (2008) study also casts doubt on claims regarding the likely impact of school PE on adherence to sport in later life as well as the supposedly strong correlation between length of time in education and participation (in other words, that young people who undertake some form of post-secondary education are most likely to participate in sport in their adult lives). In this regard, Fraser and Ziff (2009: 2) observe that of the 16–19-year-olds in their survey, 'those who are currently in sixth form college (26 per cent) or at school (23 per cent) are significantly more likely to have done at least three hours of organized sport than those in higher education (21 per cent), working (19 per cent) or unemployed (12 per cent)'. If Birchwood *et al.* (2008) are correct, spending longer in education – as with sports participation – may simply be an artefact of early life (family) experiences. Young people's sporting routes are, it seems, best understood as trajectories and, therefore, subject – as with their lives generally – to 'the operation of push–pull forces' (Roberts, 2003: 23). In sporting terms, the push might come from **parents and families** who encourage their children towards sport and enable their continued involvement in it, while the pull effect might come from PE teachers, sports **clubs** and even **friends** who maintain the interest of those already predisposed, by degrees, towards active leisure in the form of sport.

All told, studies of adherence to sport through the life-course send one pretty clear message: it is much easier to keep people in sport – to stop them dropping out in the first place – than to bring them back. In many kinds of leisure, 'the people who continue to take part throughout adulthood were usually introduced and became committed when they were children. Sport is no different from many other leisure activities in this respect' (Birchwood *et al.*, 2008: 284). The **policy** implication of all this is that 'the best strategy for boosting adult participation in sport is not to try to reclaim the lapsed but to maximize participation among children and then minimize drop-out during the next life-stage' (p. 284). There are, nevertheless, grounds for optimism if policymakers and physical educationalists take on board the lessons to be learned about the centrality of enjoyment, competence (see motivation) and sporting repertoires as well as the significance of lifestyle activities and more recreational versions of traditional sport in encouraging adherence to sport. After all, later-life involvement in any leisure activity depends largely on the 'skills and interests that individuals carry with them from earlier life-stages' (Roberts, 1999: 140); hence, the significance for lifelong participation of childhood as a building up sporting **capital**.

111

LIFESTYLE SPORTS AND ACTIVITIES

In relation to youth sport the terms 'lifestyle sports' and 'lifestyle activities' tend to be used in one of two (overlapping) ways. For those charting allegedly post-modern trends in **youth cultures**, lifestyle sports are defined as 'a specific type of alternative sport, including both established activities like surfing and skate-boarding through to newly emergent sports like kitesurfng' (Wheaton, 2008: 155). In this 'alternative' sense, the term lifestyle 'encapsulates the cultures that surround the activities' (p. 155) as much as the activities themselves. Thus, according to Tomlinson, Ravenscroft, Wheaton and Gilchrist (2005), there are three ideas central to the concept of lifestyle sports. First, they are *alternative* in the sense of being different from conventional sporting forms (such as team games) and, unlike some sports, are fundamentally about **participation** rather than spectating – either live or via the media (Wheaton, 2008). In addition, and in contrast to conventional sports, 'alternative or lifestyle sports are char-acterized by a relative lack of regulation and a customary refusal by participants to follow regulatory codes' (p. 2). Second, the meanings attached to lifestyle sports often have a *personal* dimension beyond success in **competition**. Finally, they have a tendency towards being *extreme* insofar as they involve **risk**-taking, 'including extreme locations, extreme emotions, transgression and extreme skills' (Tomlinson *et al.*, 2005: 2).

There are a number of issues with this conception of lifestyle sports. First, it seems to over-exaggerate the distinction between lifestyle and conventional sports. Many sports are primarily 'about participation' in the sense that very many of those interested are either participating currently or have participated in them. Similarly, increasing numbers of young people are engaging with less formal and competitive, in other words less regulated, versions of conventional sports such as football. At the same time, sizeable minorities of those taking part in lifestyle sports not only participate but also watch and take part in demon-strations, exhibitions and competitions in, for example, surfing, climbing, skate-boarding, BMX, mountain-biking and snowboarding. Second, as portrayed in post-modern terms, the concept of lifestyle sports tends towards a dichoto-mous representation of what is better understood as a continuum. Put another way, young people – some of whom are involved not only in both established (such as climbing and surfing) and emergent (skateboarding, blading, free run-ning, street surfing, rock-it-ball and ultimate Frisbee, for instance) lifestyle activities but also more conventional sports (such as running and football) – differ, by degree, in the extent to which they adopt some or all of the supposed cultural artefacts (such as dress, musical tastes, legal and illicit drug use and adherence to particular forms of participation) associated with lifestyle sports. In fact, many young people who take part in more established sports also adopt some of the behaviours and attitudes associated with lifestyle activities. Indeed, many of the characteristic styles associated with particular lifestyle sports – such as baggy trousers, beanie hats, wrist bands and beads – are also features of

more generalized youth **identities** (which include many who do not participate in sport). All told, claims that participants are immersed in or 'live' the
subcultures that are said to surround activities such as surfing, deliberately seeking a distinctive, alternative lifestyle which provides them with a particular and
exclusive personal and social identity (Wheaton, 2004) – in other words, that
lifestyle sports offer an alternative culture to dominant sporting subcultural as
well as broader cultural practices – tend to be exaggerated. While 'sports' such
as surfing and climbing may offer alternative cultures to those participating in
them, whether or not participants are in fact significantly influenced by these
alternative cultures (let alone engage in them) are empirical matters; that is
to say, they need measuring and as yet the jury is out. In fact, according to
Tomlinson *et al.* (2005), limited market research suggests that around one-in-ten
of the adult population is interested in lifestyle sports and that the majority of
this 10 per cent is drawn from a narrow **age** and socio-demographic grouping:
15–24-year-olds, mainly men, from the higher socio-economic classifications.
Participation, they add, is split between a relatively small core of regular participants (typically less than 1 per cent of the adult population) and a larger group
of occasional participants, some of whom learn and participate predominantly as
a holiday activity.

The argument that the post-modern conception of lifestyle sports tends to
exaggerate differences between supposedly distinct sporting groups is also
applicable to the claim that lifestyle sports offer a counter to the commercially
exploitative world of mainstream sport. Many young people embrace rather
than eschew competition and/or **commercialization**, even in such 'alternative'
activities as skateboarding and BMX. Internationally, Summer and Winter X
Games feature competition alongside exhibition, while in the United Kingdom,
events such as the Urban Games (London), Gold Coast Ocean fest (Devon),
National Adventure Sports (Somerset) and World Skateboard Championships
(London) are gaining popularity year-on-year. In addition, many young people
take part in both conventional sporting forms as well as the newer, more
adventurous activities. Indeed, a feature of sports participation among young
people over the last 40 years has been an increase in the breadth and diversity
of sporting forms undertaken including a preference for more recreational, less
competitive modes of participation – often alongside competitive and conventional sporting forms. All in all, as Roberts (2009: 326) observes, 'most young
people have never aligned themselves with any particular youth cultures' insist-
ing that they are 'just "normal" or "ordinary"'. Young people may be particularly interested in surfing, skating and blading and the clothing and musical
tastes associated with these, for example, but such activities are unlikely to
dominate let alone dictate their entire lifestyles and are unable to provide
substantial and enduring foundations for their self-identities.

The term lifestyle sports may also exaggerate differences between sporting
forms. Any classification of lifestyle sports would, as Tomlinson *et al.* (2005)
observe, recognize that 'alternative' sporting forms have tended to emerge in

several broad ways. While some do appear to be new types of practice with no antecedents (such as skateboarding) others can be seen as variations on conventional sporting practices (e.g. bouldering and sport climbing from free climbing) or extreme versions of relatively established or newer sporting forms (barefoot snow or water-skiing in the case of the former and volcano boarding in the case of the latter).

In contrast to post-modern perspectives, Coalter's (1996, 1999) conception of lifestyle activities (rather than merely sports) is based on a more conventional use of the term lifestyle – implying a larger element of possible choice characteristic of modern-day consumer societies (Roberts, 2009) – and grounded more in empirical observable patterns and trends (extensive survey data, for example). Put simply, this is a conception of lifestyle sports based upon styles of participation rather than styles of life per se. Coalter describes lifestyle activities in terms of the more-or-less common features of the many and varied activities (new and old) that have become increasingly popular among young people in recent decades. These, he suggests are characterized as being non- or, at least, less-competitive (than traditional team sports), more recreational in nature, flexible, individual or small group activities, sometimes with a **health** and fitness orientation: in other words, activities that can be undertaken *how* (more-or-less competitive, for example), *where* (commercial gyms, voluntary or local authority sports centre), *with whom* (singly or with **friends**) and *when* (in bouts of spare **time**) young people want.

The significance of lifestyle sports and activities for youth sport

In the latter sense of the term, the relative predominance of lifestyle activities over more competitive performance-oriented sports was apparent in the participatory profiles of young people in the six European countries featured in Telama et al.'s (2002) study. Among the 15-year-olds, for example, cycling was the most popular activity for young males in Belgium, Estonia and Finland and the second most popular activity behind soccer for those in Germany. At the same time, a quarter of young women in Estonia, a third of those in Belgium and almost half in Finland and Germany cycled (Telama et al., 2002) while another popular lifestyle activity, swimming, featured prominently in the participatory profiles of both young males and females in Estonia, Germany and Belgium. Elsewhere, Dollman et al. (2005) observe that, according to several large cross-sectional surveys of Australian youngsters, the participation rates of children in 'organized sport' at schools and/or community groups has decreased substantially over the past two decades. The implication seems to be that participation in traditional team sports has fallen in direct proportion to increased engagement with less structured, more recreational lifestyle activities. The picture is not, however, quite as straightforward as it seems at first glance. As with their counterparts in the United Kingdom, sport and team games as well as lifestyle activities have become an integral feature of young people's participation both inside and outside school in many European countries (De Knop and De Martelaer, 2001; Scheerder et al., 2005a; Telama et al., 2005). Rather than simply replacing traditional sporting styles, 'new styles of physical activities have been added to the sports scene' (Scheerder et al., 2005a: 337) – as in the case of the increasing popularity of in-line skating in countries such as Slovenia (Kovač, Sloan and Starc, 2008). The most popular activities among 16–19-year-olds in Norway in 2007 neatly encapsulated the shift towards lifestyle activities at the relative expense of traditional sports. The top ten were jogging, fast-walking/weight training, cross-country skiing, downhill skiing and snow-boarding, football, cycling, volleyball, swimming and aerobics (Vaage, 2009). It is worthy of note, however, that even the popularity of the various lifestyle activities waxes and wanes. Between 2004 and 2007 in Norway, there was a drop in the absolute and relative popularity of cycling and downhill skiing alongside a rise in popularity for fast walking, cross-country skiing and weight-training. Outside the top 10 notable climbers were martial arts and athletics while notable fallers were basketball, handball, tennis, bandy and indoor bandy and golf (Vaage, 2009).

Telama, Laakso and Yang's (1994) observation regarding Finland in the mid-1990s – where 'the most popular types of sports (or, rather, physical activities) among adolescents (were) ... cycling, swimming, walking and running' (p. 68) *alongside* other more competitive, performance-oriented team sports such as soccer and basketball – is equally applicable to many countries in the developed and developing world contemporarily. In China, for example, among the most popular of the increased range of available activities has been aerobics, martial arts, dance, badminton, Tai-chi and tennis (Xiong, 2007). In this vein, schools throughout in England have, in recent years, supplemented curricular and extra-curricular **PE** with a host of sports and activities that conventionally lie outside school PE curricula: such as boxing, horse riding, rowing, triathlon, orienteering, golf, bowls and archery as well as some of the newer lifestyle activities (e.g. BMX and cycling more generally, skateboarding and various forms of contemporary dance) and adventure sports such as sailing, skiing, mountaineering and canoeing (Quick et al., 2009).

Increases in participation in games that might be deemed lifestyle or recreational activities – such as tenpin bowling and bowls – alongside those that are more stereotypically sporting in orientation – such as basketball – reflect the complexity of the youth sports participation scene. Even though lifestyle activities become an increasingly prominent feature of the participation profiles of youth and adults, it is evident that a number of sports – golf, badminton and martial arts, for example – are not only popular among secondary-age young-sters (Sport England, 2003a) in their leisure time but also track into youth and through to adulthood for significant numbers of people (UK Sport/Sport England, 2001).

All in all, it seems that sport, as well as lifestyle activities, is integral to many young people's leisure lifestyles. In Brettschneider and Naul's (2004) study of six European countries, recreational or lifestyle sport was the sixth most popular leisure activity among young people while organized sport was ninth. Not only have lifestyle activities 'experienced substantial increases in participation' (Coalter, 2004a: 79) among young people but they are also 'among those with the most regular participants' (p. 80). While the evident shift in participatory terms, towards more individualistic, recreational and lifestyle activities may not signal the end of sport in its more competitive, institutionalized forms, it may, at the very least, signal a 'redrawing of the traditional boundaries and meaning of sport' (Coalter, 1999: 37). Nevertheless, the substantial shift towards lifestyle activities cannot be taken to indicate that sport – and especially competitive games – is in terminal decline among young people. The trends in leisure-time sport among young people reflect a broadening and diversification of participation, to incorporate lifestyle sports and activities, rather than a wholesale rejection of sport per se.

MORAL PANIC

The term 'moral panic' refers to the process by which the general public (often based upon limited and impressionistic evidence) becomes anxious about and/ or takes offence at a particular social phenomenon. Moral panics characteristically involve a public reaction out of proportion to the event(s) to which they are a response. In this manner, perceived as threatening normative values and practices (Jones, 2009) social phenomena such as drug usage and 'binge' drinking become generalized into threats to society at large (Welch, Price and Yankey, 2002) and in need of urgent response (Lawson and Garrod, 2003). Thus, in presenting them as 'folk devils', moral panic often leads to a more generalized panic about particular groups (young people, drinkers and Muslims, for example) as a whole (Jones, 2009). Central to the process of moral panic is the media who, in their choice and depiction of newsworthy stories (and with their own ideological perspectives prominent and commercial interests paramount), tend to present distorted, often sensationalized and stereotypical images of their target groups.

Public and political concern over issues such as childhood and youth **obesity** and the supposedly declining levels of sports **participation** among young people are recent examples of moral panic. In morally evaluating particular behaviours and norms, media and political caricatures of folk devils – such as obese and sedentary youngsters – serve to reinforce adult tendencies to hold generally negative views of young people, characterizing them 'as rebellious, irresponsible and prone to display problematic behaviour' (Minnebo and Eggermont, 2007: 131). In Japan, for example, the media have identified and targeted a group they refer to as 'hikikomori' – young people (mostly male) who spend what is viewed as a disproportionate and unhealthy amount of **time** alone playing computer games or generally being online. In addition to the

116

allegedly negative consequences of such practices for the physical and mental **health** of the youngsters concerned, their reclusive behaviours are often portrayed in terms of removing themselves from or shunning society thereby threatening to undermine national culture.

This tendency is nothing new, however: 'Since the emergence of distinct **youth** (sub)**cultures** during the 1950s, young people's lifestyles have frequently been portrayed as threatening' (Furlong and Cartmel, 2007: 82). Bramham and Cauldwell (2005) point to the work of Stanley Cohen in the 1970s and 1980s demonstrating how media items regularly and repeatedly simplified, trivialized, personalized and dramatized young people's **leisure** such that news stories became 'morality tales where the good are rewarded, the weak are saved and evil is duly exposed and punished' (p. v). From 'teddy boys' through 'mods and rockers' to 'skinheads', football hooligans, 'hoodies' and **drug**-users at different times, in different places and circumstances various groups of young people have been seen as in some way or other abnormal or deviant, representing a challenge to the existing social order.

Negative media coverage defines deviancy in relation to normative contours and, in the process of clarifying and emphasizing the contrast, tends to not only reaffirm interpretation of particular behaviours as deviant but also consolidate the behaviour among the folk devils themselves (Jones, 2009). In this regard, it is always worth remembering that attributes of individuals and groups deemed negative by outsiders may not be viewed thus by members of the group themselves.

The significance of moral panic for youth sport

Over time, a wide variety of young people's leisure activities have been portrayed as undesirable, even threatening. In the nineteenth and early twentieth centuries, for example, it tended to be youngsters playing games such as football and cricket on the streets of Britain (Holt, 1990). Nowadays the tendency for young skateboarders, riders and traceurs to colonize suitable urban spaces (such as town centres for skateboarding, BMX and parkour or free-running) and rural areas (such as woodlands for mountain biking) for their activities – and sometimes in addition or in preference to **facilities and venues** set aside for them – is often reported as an index of growing disregard among young people for property and even their fellow citizens (see **informalization**).

Nowhere is this proclivity to demonize young people as folk devils better illustrated than in debate surrounding young people's presumed lack of sporting involvement alongside leisure lifestyles ostensibly based around fast food, alcohol, tobacco, drugs, unprotected sex, TV, the Internet and video games (Bramham, 2005). Since the early 1990s, media attention has repeatedly focused upon the supposedly growing levels of physical inactivity among young people, the apparent decline in sports participation – especially among young people – and the alleged dearth of (team) sport in state schools. Young people around the world, or so it is claimed, are 'slipping into a life of excess' (Bramham and Cauldwell, 2005: v) in which they are simply immune to the lure of sport and physical **activity**. The 'folk devils' in this case have, at various times, been not only the youngsters themselves but also the 'trendy', politically left-leaning teachers portrayed as abandoning 'traditional' **PE** and school sport. However, Roberts' (1996a) analysis of the first nationwide survey of young people's levels and patterns of involvement in sport and physical activity in school PE lessons and in their leisure time (Mason, 1995) – alongside surveys of the youth service (Department for Education, 1995) and sports facilities (Hunter, 1995) – revealed that contrary to the assumptions underpinning the moral panic expressed in much of the contemporary media and political rhetoric, evidence from the Government's own surveys disarmed fears and forecasts that sport in schools in England was in decline. More specifically, Roberts observed that by the middle of the 1990s:

> young people were playing more sports in and out of school than in the past … the drop-out rate on completion of statutory schooling had fallen dramatically … **social class** and **gender** differences had narrowed (and) … sports had higher youth participation and retention than any other structured forms of leisure.
>
> (Roberts, 1996b: 105)

Roberts (1996a) concluded that, while there continued to be wide variations in the amount young people played, their levels of sport and physical activity participation in 1994 remained 'well above the levels (of) … the 1950s and 1960s' (p. 52); having increased especially rapidly since the 1980s. Despite this, over the two decades since its own research demonstrated the gross inaccuracies in media and political claims regarding youth sport, UK government **policy** has consistently fanned the flames of moral panic surrounding the ostensible decline in young people's participation levels in sport, steadfastly refusing to give up the (false) claim that in many schools PE and sport have declined dramatically. The persistent tendency for media and political pronouncements to encourage moral panic over contemporary youth physical and mental **health** while advocating a misguided cure for a 'fictitious illness' (Roberts, 1996a) was neatly reflected in a debate in a national 'broadsheet' newspaper in the spring of 2005. Headlines such as 'Young people are being driven out of sport' and 'Youngsters put off sport for life by state of sport in schools' (Campbell, 2005) reflected the persistence of the kind of taken-for-granted assumptions among politicians and newspaper columnists that Roberts had shown to be inadequate in the mid-1990s.

All in all, the concept of moral panic reminds us of the truth in Bramham's (2005) observation that each generation voices its concern about contemporary youth. It also helps towards a sense of perspective on the 'frequent expressions' of moral panic and public outrage 'against troublesome and disorderly youth' (Bramham and Cauldwell, 2005: v) that are manifest in media stories and, for that matter, government proclamations and related policy. Media reporting of, as well as government policy towards, the overweight/obesity 'epidemic', physical inactivity and the relationship between these and youth sport neatly illustrates the tendency of such groups to caricature reality for their own commercial and political purposes by focusing on 'the worst of the worst'; that is, the small minority who reside at one extreme end of continua of levels of physical activity, weight or alcohol consumption, for example. As Malcolm (2008: 171) observes, the crucial point about the notion of moral panic is the way in which the intended and unintended consequences of media exaggeration and caricature serve to distract attention from the real causes of a particular social issue by scapegoating particular groups (and often various groups of young people) and presenting them, symbolically, as the bearers of blame for various social phenomena.

MOTIVATION

Motivation refers to the 'causes' of behaviours. It is, in effect, an umbrella term for 'those factors which initiate or energise behaviour' (Moran, 2004: 38) – the thing(s) which 'get people going' in the sense of inciting or incentivizing them to do particular things, such as play sport and exercise. What motivates young people to start, continue with, drop-out and return to sport has long been the subject of research and debate in academic, public and political circles.

The significance of motivation for youth sport

Much of the plentiful research into motives for **participation** in sport focuses (in line with the dominant social-cognitive approach) upon the self-reported reasons (or attributions) provided by participants (Biddle and Mutrie, 2008). With young people (as with adults) motivation can take multiple forms 'including fun and enjoyment, learning and improving skills, being with **friends**, success and winning, and physical fitness and **health**' (Biddle and Mutrie, 2008: 48). Nonetheless, in many studies fun and enjoyment consistently emerge as the major motives for participation in sport. Children of primary (or elementary) school **age** tend to be enthusiastic about physical **activity** and motivated in particular by the enjoyment to be gained from the activities themselves as well as the social dimension (being with friends) of participation. While having fun is also a major motivation for secondary school aged youngsters, being with friends and improving bodily self-image become increasingly important motives as they grow older. Whereas lack of **time** and sporting competence are major barriers to participation in sport among adults, the main 'demotivators' for young people are perceived lack of competence, past experiences of sport (including **physical education**), feelings of embarrassment (often related to physical self-image [see **identities**]) and insufficient support from significant others (such as parents and friends) (Biddle and Mutrie, 2008).

One particularly productive area of research into motivation towards sport addresses so-called achievement goal orientations – the personal meaning individuals attach to the achievement contexts that are believed to sustain motivation. Goal orientations tend, at a fundamental level, to be divided into two categories: task- and ego-orientations. The latter – ego-oriented dispositions – involve the individual being primarily predisposed towards a concern for performance outcomes and comparisons with others. By contrast, task-oriented outlooks focus more upon the mastery of skills; in other words, learning and improving in particular sports. Much extant research concludes that intrinsic reward (or intrinsically-motivated experiences) – wherein the impetus for engaging in sport is derived from the satisfaction and pleasure gained from taking part (Moran, 2004) – and, thus, a task-orientation, is a more powerful motivator of behaviour, especially over the longer-term, than extrinsic reward and an ego-orientation. It seems, then, that a learning environment or climate (e.g. in school PE or sports **clubs**) which emphasizes the mastery of skills and techniques (for the pleasure they bring as much as overall improvements in performance and efficacy in particular sports) tends to be strongly positively correlated with psychological outcomes such as satisfaction and enjoyment. Conversely, environments that focus on demonstrating high levels of **ability** and achieving success in sporting **competition** tend to be particularly demotivating for many young people (Biddle *et al.*, 2008).

Enjoyment is evidently a central dimension of intrinsic motivation. From their study of the impact of goals, beliefs and self-determination in girls' PE in Singapore, Wang and Liu (2007: 159) concluded that 'when (female) students were more self-determined or intrinsically motivated, they enjoyed their PE experience more'. Although it is difficult to pinpoint exactly what constitutes pleasure or enjoyment there is evidence to suggest that 'optimal experiences', if not simply enjoyment, revolve around striking a balance in any activity between the participant's skill-levels and the challenge s/he faces – what Csikszentmihalyi (1990) refers to as 'flow'. All told, it appears that very many adherents to sport participate not so much for extrinsic reasons (such as health promotion) as the sheer pleasure of playing; put another way, reasons to do with the intrinsic pleasures to be gained in performance of the activity itself (and the pursuit of 'flow'-like experiences) rather than any externalities that might accrue. In effect, people learn the satisfactions to be had from doing particular sports and want to repeat them. The upshot is that young people are more likely to engage in and continue with an activity when they enjoy what they are doing. Girls, in particular, are far more likely to participate in sport if their primary motivation is intrinsic; that is to say, the activity is viewed as being enjoyable in its own right with the emphasis on fun and enjoyment. Biddle *et al.* (2005) found that girls in Scotland whose main motivation was intrinsic were less likely to feel self-conscious about taking part than those for whom changing their **body**-image was the main motivation.

Unsurprisingly *competence* – the ability to perform a task to an appropriate and acceptable (to the participant) standard – tends to be strongly correlated with enjoyment. Indeed, some argue that competence is the best predictor of partici-pation in sport (Biddle, 2006). When faced with choices – for example, in their **leisure** – young people's dispositions are framed by their perceptions of what *can* be done and central to this are their perceptions of their own competencies (their beliefs about their ability to perform in ways likely to achieve desired outcomes). Youngsters' beliefs about their competencies are rooted in their prior experiences of sporting success or failure, and they adjust their choices and aspi-rations accordingly. Thus, 'Poor motivation is as much a consequence of negative experience as a cause of it' (Catan, 2004; cited in Jones, 2009: 82). If people (and especially young people) feel that their skill-levels and all-round competence in an activity is good enough or improving they will be a good deal more likely to enjoy that activity and, as a consequence, continue participating.

A number of studies offer support for the idea that promoting perceived competence is a significant factor in encouraging adherence to particular sports (Telama *et al.*, 2005) and that skill levels can be a predictor of levels of involve-ment (Iwasaki and Havitz, 2004). In the case of tennis, for example, Casper (2007) found that the higher the skill level, the more participants in the United States were likely to play tennis throughout the year. Wallhead and Buckworth's (2004) research in the United States noted that 'perceived competence is a powerful psychological correlate of youth physical activity' and concluded that if those involved in teaching sport were able to increase young people's per-ceived competence and subsequent enjoyment of their sporting experiences, these affective outcomes would 'transfer into motivation to adopt a physically active lifestyle out of school' (p. 295). It seems, therefore, that for very many young people motivation is often intimately related to perceptions of compe-tence and, given a choice, they are unlikely to choose leisure activities in which they feel incompetent. Girls, in particular, are more likely to participate if they feel competent enough to do so. Biddle *et al.'s* (2005) study of 10–15-year-old girls in Scotland found that perceived competence was 'particularly influential' in the withdrawal of girls from sport. Interestingly, failure to achieve competence in one field (sport, for example) often, it seems, leads to increased efforts to achieve it in other areas (Jones, 2009) (such as schoolwork or even parenthood); in other words, displacement.

All this begs questions about the optimum conditions for young people to become competent, to gain enjoyment and thus feel motivated towards participation? In PE and sport, an approach to content and teaching styles that focus upon effort towards and improvement in the mastery of skills and activities (rather than focusing upon competition and identifying winners) – while, at the same time, allowing pupils sufficient time to learn these skills – is considered to be more likely to encourage both competence and enjoyment.

In this regard, girls appear more likely to approach school sport with a task-orientation and boys with an ego-orientation (attributable to their **socialization** into masculine norms of achievement) and this may begin to explain why boys are less influenced by different teaching styles than girls (Salvara *et al.*, 2006).

Taken together, participation and perceptions of competence appear mutually reinforcing. A variety of studies have shown that those individuals most active in participatory terms were the ones most likely to perceive themselves as competent (in those activities in which they participated) and to persist at becoming better at the tasks involved in the sports they were undertaking (Telama *et al.*, 2005). This is what psychologists refer to as *self-efficacy* – belief in one's ability to successfully undertake a course of action, such as playing football – and it is particularly significant for youth at a time in their lives when developing positive self-images and identities are of paramount concern. This realization led Biddle *et al.* (2008: 197) to conclude that self-efficacy is 'one of the most consistent predictors of physical activity behaviours and is key to promoting activity in young people'. In this regard, in examining the contribution of secondary PE to lifetime physical activity, Fairclough *et al.* (2002: 71) highlight a 'cycle of perceived incompetence' whereby youngsters convinced that they cannot perform the necessary skills shy away from sporting activities both in and out of school.

Along with enjoyment and competence (as well as self-efficacy), *voluntariness* is a key dimension to sports participation. Studies of childhood per se suggest that where children are given responsibility and, if necessary, guidance they frequently demonstrate levels of competence much higher than that adults anticipate – children learn by experience and competence grows with experience (James and James, 2009). For all young people, the motivation to take part in sport – in the form of the enjoyment they expect to gain from the activity itself and being with friends – tends to be enhanced when an element of self-determination or autonomy, particularly in the form of choice, is available to them (Biddle *et al.*, 2008). Voluntariness and choice are especially important for girls: when girls feel that they are 'forced' to participate, it impacts negatively on their overall participation (Biddle *et al.*, 2005).

Anticipated enjoyment, competence and voluntariness all appear to influence young people's attitudes – a favourable or unfavourable evaluation of something, such as sport (Hagger and Chatzisarantis, 2008) – to sports participation and attitudes are believed to pre-empt intentions which then find expression in behaviours. Attitudes inevitably have emotional and rational dimensions. The affective (or emotional) element is clearly likely to be the more significant aspect of youngsters' attitudes with regard to leisure activities such as sport and music even though there will inevitably be times and activities that they view instrumentally, in relation to developing and sustaining friendships for example. Unsurprisingly, young people's favourable or unfavourable evaluation of sport tends to be acquired and internalized as **habitus** via socialization among **parents and family** in the first instance but increasingly, as they approach youth, among friends and peers.

As useful as the goal orientation approach to the psychology of motivation has been there are a number of problems with presenting the issue of motivation in dichotomous typological terms (intrinsic versus extrinsic), not least of which is the tendency to overlook the interplay between the two (Moran, 2004). Similarly, much is assumed about the need to inculcate the 'right' attitudes towards sports participation (as well as healthy lifestyles) among young people 'even though there is considerable evidence to suggest that such a simple, deterministic relationship is erroneous' (Hagger and Chatzisarantis, 2008: 167). In this regard, theories of behaviour change as a means of describing and explaining the various processes underlying changes in behaviour in relation to sport (Lorentzen, 2007) have become increasingly popular. Such theories refer to progression through a series of stages over time with individuals found at differing stages in relation to 'their level of psychological readiness to change or continue behaviour' (Lorentzen, 2007: 16). These theories tend, however, to place undue emphasis on the significance of deliberate, rational decisions to engage in activity, paying insufficient attention to socialization and the resultant habits and predispositions. In seeking to identify 'causes' – in the form of prior motives for initiating sports participation – there is a risk of overlooking the tendency of young people to make sporting 'choices' in relation to what they have grown accustomed to enjoying during their early lives. In other words, viewing motives as a priori 'causes' ignores the significance of the habits and habitus derived from family and peer group experiences. Similarly, the tendency to conceptualize motivation in terms of reasons (rather than, for example, affect or even custom) risks misconstruing the nature of motivation. Thus, rather than engaging in rational means–end calculations regarding the pros and cons of sports participation, let alone reflecting on what they find motivating or demotivating, youngsters often simply carry on with things they have grown (often quite unreflexively) accustomed to enjoying and deriving pleasures and benefits from, whatever those may be. Rather than being the product of deliberate, reasoned action based on a cost-benefit analysis of taking part in sport, initial participation is often better understood as the product of socialization and the competencies, enjoyment and predispositions towards particular sports that results. On this view, experiences of pleasurable excitement (which, in turn, generates intrinsic motivation) alongside being constrained and/or encouraged to participate in activities on a sufficiently regular basis tends to motivation becoming part and parcel of a young person's predispositions or habitus.

Although motivational theories appear limited in explaining initial involvement in sport, they are helpful in making sense of the way ongoing participation is, in Moran's (2004) terms, 'energised'. The significance of young people's sporting predispositions or habituses notwithstanding, there are evidently many cases where they have become motivated and deliberately chosen to change their behaviours towards sport for any number of reasons including fun and enjoyment, being with friends, challenge and achievement and physical fitness and health.

All in all, research into motivation confirms the intuitive belief that young people are more likely to be motivated to participate in sporting activities if they derive some pleasure from them rather than if they are constrained or forced (e.g. in school PE) to take part.

OBESITY

Weight gain is a function of an imbalance between energy consumption and energy expenditure. Obesity, on the other hand, results from a chronic (long-term) energy imbalance and represents a judgement based on a clinical assessment of the relationship between weight and **health** and, in particular, the (increased) **risk** to health of being 'excessively' overweight. Overweight and obesity are largely the result of insufficient physical **activity** (and **sedentary** lifestyles generally) in conjunction with a poor diet (e.g. high in fat and sugar), both of which have become commonplace in modern, 'obesogenic' societies in which energy-dense and cheap foods, labour-saving devices, motorized transport and sedentary lifestyles are commonplace.

Recent claims that increases in obesity levels have stalled (Gard, 2010), notwithstanding, the prevalence of excess weight among the young has increased rapidly over the past 50 years, particularly in the economically developed countries of the Western world. In the United Kingdom, for example, childhood and youth obesity is said to have reached epidemic proportions (Waine, 2007): 62 per cent of adults and 30 per cent of children are classified as overweight with 24 per cent of adults and 16 per cent of children obese – the highest obesity rate in Europe (ESRC, 2009a). More than one in two obese children are likely to become obese adults (Choi *et al.*, 2005), and it is estimated that by the middle of the twenty-first century 90 per cent of children in the United Kingdom will be obese (Rowlands, 2009). In the United States, Cohen, Perales and Steadman (2005: 154) point to 'the tripling of overweight young people (ages 16–19) over the last 30 years'. Elsewhere, Welk *et al.* (2006) highlight the prevalence of obesity among Australian, Canadian, Chinese and Spanish youth. Exacerbated by apparent increases in 'binge-eating' (a tendency not only to overeat but also to eat large quantities in a short space of time, when not hungry and in private), obesity is anticipated, in the near future, to lead to a reversal in the life expectancy gains witnessed over a century or more in the developed world. In addition, it is forecast to increase the numbers of cancers and to overtake alcohol as the major cause of liver cirrhosis.

Despite the seemingly overwhelming claims regarding the prevalence of obesity and its significance for ill health, a number of authors (see, for example,

124

Evans and Davies, 2006; Gard and Wright, 2005) have pointed in recent years to what they take to be the limitations of 'scientific' claims regarding the relationship between obesity and health, expressing two distinct concerns: first, with the science itself; and, second, with the ideological underpinnings and consequences of the scientific discourse.

In the first instance, critics point to the problems associated with measurement. It has become increasingly apparent that satisfactory measures of overweight and obesity (and the associated definitions thereof) are difficult to establish. The most frequently used measure of overweight/obesity is the Body Mass Index (BMI). BMI is calculated by dividing weight in kilograms by height in metres squared: in adults, a score of less than 18.5 is classified as underweight, 18.5–24.9 as normal, 25–29.9 as overweight and 30 or more as obese. BMI is frequently criticized, however, for being imprecise not merely because it allows for some mesomorphic sportsmen and women to be classified as obese but also because of 'the changes that occur in the ratio of velocity of weight gain to height gain' (Schenker, 2005: 10) during the normal growth phases of children and young people. Crucially, BMI is also viewed as unhelpful, because it measures mass rather than **body** fat content – adipose tissue or fat lying wrapped around the heart and vital organs (and especially the abdomen in men) and streaked through muscles poses the biggest threat to health (Welk *et al.*, 2006). It is this 'internal fat' – rather than subcutaneous fat – that sends out the chemical signals which eventually lead to insulin resistance, diabetes and heart conditions, even in especially slim people who do not exercise. Those jokingly referred to as TOFIs (thin on the outside, fat on the inside) are, it seems, as susceptible to fat infiltration of the liver, for example, as overweight and obese people. This is especially significant in relation to the health of young people, among whom much excess fat surrounds the internal organs rather than simply being subcutaneous. In contrast to BMI, alternative measures in the form of waist:hip ratio and waist circumference are considered to be more strongly correlated with cardiovascular risk and, therefore, more informative measures of obesity (Wu, 2006). Indeed, because it is significantly correlated with percentage body fat, waist circumference is likely to be the most promising surrogate measure of body fatness with children.

Issues related to the difficulties of obtaining accurate measurements notwithstanding, some question the assumption that there is, in fact, a significant health problem associated with being overweight. Rich *et al.* (2005), for example, observe that while there are likely to be health risks for individuals at the extreme ends of the weight continuum the relationships between weight, diet, physical activity and health are far more complex and uncertain than is frequently suggested. Rich *et al.* (2005) point to studies indicating that individuals who are 'overweight' but physically active may, in fact, be healthier than their thinner but relatively inactive counterparts – being active is more important in health terms than being thin and being fit but slightly overweight is not only relatively common among young people but usually perfectly healthy.

Put simply, it is better to be fat and fit than thin and unfit. Granberg *et al.*'s (2008) study of 343 African-American girls (aged 12–14) provides support for the argument that size and weight might not be the straightforward health issue it is widely assumed to be. Despite the evidence for a link between being overweight and depression among girls, the African-American girls were generally more satisfied with their bodies. Indeed, it seems that overweight African-American adolescent girls have generally positive self-images, particularly when compared with overweight females from other racial and ethnic groups (Granberg *et al.*, 2009).

Concern is also expressed by critics about the ways in which scientific knowledge about health (and overweight and obesity in particular) tends to be distorted in translation and subsequent communication to young people. Professionals in the world of sport display a tendency to exaggerate and distort the relationship between health and overweight/obesity when, for example, conveying the impression that youngsters must be thin and fit if they are to be healthy. Such simplistic messages are said to be dangerous not least because by reducing the issue of health to one of weight management they can impact negatively upon youngsters' (and particularly girls') **identities** and subsequent **risk** behaviours (in the form of eating disorders, for example). The issue of weight – and, in particular, 'shared peer norms for thinness' (Dohnt and Tiggerman, 2005: 103) and having a desirable figure – is particularly significant for young women (Cox *et al.*, 2005). Almost twice as many 12–13 and 14–15-year-old females, for example, 'would like to lose weight' compared to similar **age** boys (SHEU, 2007) and, as a result, approximately one quarter of 14–15-year-old females in England are likely to have nothing at all to eat for breakfast on any one morning. It seems, then, that conventional definitions and measurements of overweight and obesity, alongside the crude strategies recommended to combat the 'problem', may result in a number of unhealthy and unnecessary responses by young people encouraged to believe that they must be thin in order to be healthy (Evans and Davies, 2006). As a consequence, the well-meaning actions of those engaged in health promotion with young people, such as teachers and health experts, may only serve to further stigmatize some children and even constrain girls and young women towards eating disorders, such as anorexia nervosa and bulimia (Rich *et al.*, 2005). On top of this, as the *British Cohort Study* (BCS) demonstrates, 'eating problems' (at age 10) are negatively associated with sports **participation** in adolescence (Feinstein *et al.*, 2005).

With objections such as these in mind, critics highlight what they view as a profound consequence of the science of health and weight: the tendency to portray overweight and obesity as an individual matter and something that individuals have a responsibility, even duty, to do something about. This 'ideology of healthism' (Colquhoun, 1991), as it is called, incorporates an assumption of individual responsibility that reduces the complex aetiology of so-called 'lifestyle diseases' to under-exercising. In doing so, it also ignores the various social, economic and cultural 'determinants' of health, such as the pervasive influence of the food industry and the fact that overweight and obesity are well documented as structural conditions 'exacerbated by low socio-economic status' (Royal College of Physicians *et al.*, 2004: 21) in particular. While the reasons for the chronic energy imbalance characteristic of obesity vary between individuals, in general terms they are said to result from a combination of genetic, intrauterine, postnatal, environmental and social factors and, although active involvement in sport and physical activity can make a difference to individuals' health, it simply cannot eradicate or necessarily even lessen the inequalities associated with, for example, **social class** and **gender**: 32 per cent of women in the bottom fifth income distribution are obese compared with 19 per cent of women in the top fifth (ESRC, 2009a).

The *EarlyBird* study – set up in 2000 at Peninsula Medical School, Plymouth, United Kingdom, to collect longitudinal data from a cohort study of Plymouth school children recruited at the age of 5 years and combining annual measures of physical activity, body composition as well as additional measures such as insulin resistance and its metabolic correlates – has found that 'up to 90 percent of excess weight gained by 10 years is gained before school age' (Wilkin, 2007: 3). In addition, the study found no evidence that more opportunity (e.g. additional time spent in **PE**) led to more physical activity or that attendance at sports **clubs** had any impact upon BMI. Nor, indeed, did it find that more physical activity resulted in lower BMI: those who met BMI norms were no less adipose (Wilkin, 2007). These criticisms of the science of overweight and obesity and its implications notwithstanding, there are a number of caveats worthy of mention. First, with regard to measurements such as BMI, critics often overlook the fact that because BMI has been the most commonly used measure over a long period, it does allow for broad trends to be identified. Second, in probabilistic terms, physical activity and fitness is more likely to be associated with recommended weight than with overweight. Third, in terms of life expectancy, it is better to be slightly underweight than overweight. Finally, it is important not to overlook the fact that the best predictor of future weight is current weight: fat children are demonstrably more likely to become fat adults and being overweight in childhood and youth is associated with adverse health consequences including metabolic abnormalities, increased risk of type 2 diabetes and psychological problems.

The significance of overweight and obesity for youth sport

Sport – and sport in schools, in the form of PE, in particular – is viewed by many as both the best setting and the solution to the overweight/obesity 'crisis' among young people. It is viewed as a solution because physical activity produces the same health-related benefits for youngsters as for adults: it reduces body fatness and aids the management of obesity, lowers high blood pressure, increases bone mineral density and enhances psychological well-being

(Winsley and Armstrong, 2005). In addition, it confers health benefits that can be experienced by ordinary participants across all socio-demographic groups and which act in addition to other favourable lifestyle practices such as healthy diets (Roberts and Brodie, 1992). Youth sport is seen as an appropriate setting for health promotion in two main ways. First, sport is expected to provide opportunities for pupils to engage in health-enhancing levels of physical activity. Second, to the extent that playing sport in their early lives increases the likelihood that young people will remain sports active throughout their adult lives, childhood and youth sport is seen as an important vehicle for promoting lifelong adherence to health-related physical activity.

There are, however, two fundamental problems with the health case for youth sport: first, the abundant reservations about just what difference sports participation can actually make to health; and, second, the oft-ignored health 'costs' of sport (see health). In terms of the contribution of sport and physical activity to health, young people seldom meet current recommendations – as problematic as they may be (Rowlands, 2009) – regarding so-called MVPA (moderate to vigorous physical activity). While getting young people to participate in sport is not an issue getting them to participate often enough and at sufficient intensity to improve their health is – most young people simply do not do sport regularly enough to lose weight or improve their health substantially if at all. Indeed, the very nature of much sport is such that levels of physical activity when playing tend to be sporadic and intermittent. In addition, there is the problem of persistence. For benefits to be life long, it is necessary to be a lifelong participant and in order to improve normal day-to-day health (in terms of lowering body fat, lowering cholesterol and improving physiological functioning generally) people need to raise their heart rate by exercising regularly throughout the life-course. The question then becomes 'to what extent can and does youth sport (especially in schools) make **lifelong participation** more likely?'

All in all, promoting youth sport as both the setting and solution to the health/obesity 'crisis' exaggerates the role of the kinds of sports and exercise young people are introduced to at school as well as those they tend to engage with in their **leisure**. It also exaggerates the contribution of sport per se. Lifestyle changes over the last 20–30 years are the major contributory cause of the rapid increase in obesity; in particular, the consumption of processed and larger and larger portions of (often 'fast') food at the expense of fruit and vegetables – carbonated drinks and unhealthy snacks form a substantial proportion of young people's calorie intake. Thus, it seems that any potential weight-related benefits to be gained from increasing levels of physical activity and exercise are most likely to have a profound effect on the reversal of so-called 'metabolic syndrome' if they occur in conjunction with modifications in diets (Anderssen et al., 2007) and both of these are intimately related to issues of social class, gender and **ethnicity** among other structural factors.

Advocating youth sport in relation to health promotion among young people also sends exaggerated messages 'about self-discipline, control and will-power'

(Tinning, 1991: 40). In playing up 'the pseudo-sovereignty' (Frew and McGillivray, 2005: 173) of the individual, the neo-liberal individualistic ideologies that lie at the heart of healthism reduce complex social processes to the individual level and explain them purely in psychological terms while ignoring the aforementioned structural dimensions of social processes such as weight gain. A corollary of the presumption of individualism built into the ideology of healthism is **moral panic** and the moral condemnation of those who fail to adopt active, healthy lifestyles.

Finally, it is worth considering the findings from the *British Cohort Study* (BCS) which throw many of the claims made about sport in relation to health into sharp relief. Among other things, the BCS revealed no statistically significant connection between obesity and leisure activities in general (Feinstein *et al.*, 2005), whether the activities were sporting or otherwise.

PARENTS AND FAMILY

In the twentieth century, the normative model of the modern family was 'based upon a monogamous, lifelong partnership between a breadwinning husband and a nurturing, domesticated wife' (Roberts *et al.*, 2009: 151). Consequently, there remains a tendency to conceptualize the family in ortho-dox, conventional Western terms as 'nuclear' (an adult couple and their birth, adopted or step-children) and 'extended' (the basic nuclear unit extended ver-tically by grandparents or horizontally by the brothers and sisters of parents and their nuclear families). In reality, however, cohabitation is now common-place, separation and divorce rates have risen, and there are more children and young people living in reconstituted families or being reared by single parents. In so far as there is still a norm for monogamy, it is nowadays serial monogamy (Roberts *et al.*, 2009c). Such developments – including increases in so-called lone-parent (one parent plus children) and beanpole (successive single child) families as well as families involving step-parents or 'carers' along-side or even instead of living biological relatives (Saelens and Kerr, 2008) – have made defining the family far more problematic. Nonetheless, and despite changes in the family structure such that increasing numbers of children live with single, lone- or step-parents, approximately two-thirds of families in the United Kingdom, for example, are still headed by a married couple and by far the most common arrangement for young people remains living with their two biological parents: 71 per cent of 13–16-year-olds in the LSYPE (*Longitudinal Study of Young People in England*) lived with both parents compared with 26 per cent living with a single parent (almost invariably the mother only) (DCSF, 2008). Beyond the United Kingdom, in Mediterranean and Eastern Europe, for example, living in the parental home 'never ceased to be the norm' (Roberts, 2009c: 165). The fragility of present-day marital relation-ships notwithstanding, the nuclear family remains the normal residential unit.

It is worth bearing in mind cultural variations on this pattern, however. Despite the steady decline in three-generational families in Western societies, youngsters from ethnic minority backgrounds living in the West 'are still more likely to grow up in a household where three or more generations live together' (James and James, 2009: 57).

Some of the socio-demographic trends outlined above have encouraged the view that in the supposedly post-modern age, parents and family have become less important in terms of **socialization** while people and groups outside the family – **friends and peers**, in particular, but also **role models** more generally – have become correspondingly more significant. This view is reinforced by time-use data from developed industrial countries which reveal that 'teens' relationships and contact with parents, peers, and mass media have tilted in the past 15–20 years heavily in favour of peers and mass media' (Zuzanek, 2005: 410). Nonetheless, and despite the fact that a wider variety of family forms are now evident and friends and peers have become more prominent in the social networks of youth, the enduring centrality and significance of the family in young people's lives should not be overlooked nor underestimated. In the case of white, middle and affluent working-class 17–20-year-olds in one Finnish study, for example, the family remained a sufficiently significant aspect of their lives such that their parents were still providing them with important material resources and socio-psychological support at the **age** of 20 (Lahelma and Gordon, 2008). In general, the young Finns relied upon their parents and respected their opinions and wishes with the consequence that they remained semi-dependent on them well into adult life, only moving gradually towards independence.

All told, parents and families remain highly significant in transmitting between generations not only wealth and psychological support but also skills, social networks, aspirations and values (Jones, 2009).

The significance of parents and family for youth sport

Families in general and parents in particular are especially significant in relation to young people's sporting predispositions and tendencies. Birchwood *et al.'s* (2008: 291) South Caucasus study led them to conclude 'that a distinct and enduring propensity to play sport is acquired during childhood via a culture transmitted by the family'. They observed that family background was still making a difference to sports **participation** (in other words, having effects additional to those generated by life-stage **transitions** to parenthood, employment and so forth) when respondents were in their 20s. Indeed, much of the sport participation among their sample appeared fixed by age 16 (see **lifelong participation**).

Parents can play a key role in the sports participation of their offspring not least because 'participation usually depends on parental expenditures of money, time and energy' (Coakley, 2009: 46). Perhaps the most significant role of parents, however, comes in the form of the socialization of young people into sport. In terms of shaping their children's sporting predispositions and habits, parental influences can be broadly described as passive and/or active. They can be passive in the sense that, while not actively promoted or encouraged, sporting and exercise attitudes and behaviours are modelled by parents and imitated by their children (Fredricks and Eccles, 2005b; Hendry et al., 1993; Roberts, 1999; Scheerder et al., 2005b): 'children infer information about their parents' beliefs, behaviours, and goals, and such information influences their psycho-social development' (Holt, Tamminen, Black, Mandigo and Fox, 2009: 38). Parental influences are said to be active when, for example, they (i) participate with and/or alongside their children (when playing racket games or kick-about football, skiing or sailing, for instance); (ii) provide sporting experiences and transportation to sporting venues and activities; (iii) play a significant role in the sports participation decisions of their offspring and (iv) offer verbal encouragement and positive perceptions of their children's **ability** (Fredricks and Eccles, 2005b; Scheerder et al., 2005b; Saelens and Kerr, 2008). In Canada, for example, while sports participation was highest in 2005 among children whose parents were involved in refereeing, coaching or in sports administration, children's participation rates more than doubled if their parents were involved in sports in any way, even just as spectators of amateur sports (Clark, 2008). Clark (2008) observes that on an average day about 7 per cent of parents of 5–14-year-old Canadians tended to be involved in some form of sports activity with their children, whether it was participating in sports, coaching or attending a professional or amateur sporting event as a spectator. In total, 57 per cent of parents in Canada were involved in some way at some time or other with sports as participants, spectators, coaches, referees, sports administrators, organizers or members of sports organizations. Not only did the parents spend an average of 2.5 hours doing these sports-related activities with their children, they also tended to be participants in many sports-related activities on their own account.

With regard to imitation, Scheerder et al. (2005c: 5) concluded from their studies of Flanders youth that parental sports participation could play a substantial role in youngsters' active involvement in sport in conjunction with **gender** and school PE programmes. They noted that participation tended to be more frequent among Flemish high school boys and girls whose parents were both active sports participants and that these youngsters were more involved in **leisure**-time sports than those whose parents did not participate. Simple passive modelling of sports participation by parents and families, however, does not appear to be as effective as active participation in sport by parents (or family members) alongside their children or the mere provision of logistical and emotional support. Interestingly, sports-specific modelling appeared more influential than modelling of general levels of physical **activity** in Scheerder et al.'s (2005c) study. In the absence of empirical evidence it seems plausible to assume that while co-participation alongside modelling of sports behaviour may be more influential in the socialization of younger children, logistical support in the form of, for example, transportation, sports club membership, equipment and emotional support at sports venues is likely to be more influential for teenagers and youth.

In addition to promoting the value of, as well as facilitating, active participation among their children, parents can play a significant role in youngsters' perceptions of their own sporting abilities and competence (Fredricks and Eccles, 2005b). Children report higher levels of athletic competence and intrinsic **motivation** when they receive frequent positive comments from their parents and perceive positive parental beliefs about their competencies (Holt *et al.*, 2009). From their survey of junior tennis coaches, Gould, Lauer, Rolo, Jannes and Pennisi (2006) reported parents as very important for junior tennis success. Once again, positive parental behaviours included providing logistical, financial and social and emotional support, as well as tennis opportunities and unconditional love. Parents can also enhance perceived enjoyment: children tend to report enhanced sporting enjoyment when they perceive their parents to be positively involved and satisfied with their sport participation (Holt *et al.*, 2009).

It is worth bearing in mind that the significance of parents and family for youth sport takes the form not only of encouragement and facilitation (via modelling and support) but also constraint borne out of such things as parental concern for their children's safety (Saelens and Kerr, 2008). One form of indirect constraint is **sedentary** parental behaviour which appears to be more 'contagious' than sports participation, possibly because the former is 'more easily shared across generations' (Saelens and Kerr, 2008: 278). Parents can also militate against sports participation – and not merely by being inactive themselves. The actions of parents ostensibly keen to support their children's involvement in sport can, for example, have unplanned outcomes: children report heightened anxiety when they perceive their parents are over-involved, unduly critical, hold excessively high expectations, overemphasize winning and exert too much pressure on youngsters to perform (Holt *et al.*, 2009).

Unsurprisingly, perhaps, parents and families vary in their ability (as well as inclinations) to pass on to their children the kinds of social and cultural **capital** that may be useful in sporting terms. Parents are particularly significant mediators of **social class**. Middle-class parents are not only more likely to possess the material resources, or economic capital, to enable their offspring to engage in sport but are also more likely to be in a position to transfer their social and cultural capital by virtue of being already actively involved themselves and inclined to pass their 'love of sport' on to their children (Roberts and Brodie, 1992). They are, in other words, more likely to provide passive support (via modelling) and active support (via involvement and resources) for their youngsters' sporting lives. In short, middle-class parents often go to great lengths to ensure that their offspring enjoy a breadth of abilities and advantages. They tend, in other words, to 'invest heavily in the cultivation of the physical capital of their offspring from a very early age' (Evans, 2004: 101). In doing so, middle-class parents not only 'inculcate "the right" attitudes, values, motivations, predispositions, representations but also the right physical capital in terms of skills, techniques and understanding' (Evans, 2004: 101). In contrast, Macdonald *et al.* (2004) found evidence from their study of lower primary school children in Australia to confirm the commonplace observation that children from single-parent families and families in lower socio-economic groups tend not to receive the amounts and kinds of support for involvement in sport that their middle-class counterparts do.

Class-related parental and family effects notwithstanding, differences in participation cannot be entirely explained in structural terms. The propensity to participate in sport appears related to but partly independent of – and, therefore, irreducible to – family social class (Birchwood *et al.*, 2008). Put another way, family cultures appear able to cut across socio-economic effects. While middle-class parents and families are more likely to be the ones that socialize their youngsters into sport, there are some sports-active working-class parents and families that have the same effects. It seems that crucial sporting dispositions (or **habitus**) are transmitted through families laying down 'a mini-max range' within which other processes (such as adult transitions) and developments (**policy** interventions via **physical education** or the provision of **facilities and venues**, for example) can be effective (Birchwood *et al.*, 2008).

As well as being mediators of social class effects on young people's sports socialization, families also tend to be significant in terms of **gender socialization** and mothers and fathers tend to be **gender** stereotyped in their sporting beliefs and practices (Fredricks and Eccles, 2005b). The historically gendered nature of sports socialization notwithstanding, one consequence of recent family trends – that may have positive ramifications for youth sport – has been changes in the role of fathers in youngsters' leisure-sport. High levels of maternal employment, increased breakdown and reconstitution of families and concomitant rises in remarriage and cohabitation have played a part in the changing conditions of fatherhood (Kay, 2009b) – and changes in men's relationships with the leisure of the young – in recent decades. Nowadays, '"good" fathering means "being with" the children' (Such, 2009: 86). Although women spend two to three times as much time with children as men do, since the 1970s fathers (and middle-class fathers especially) have been spending far more time with their children, such that the amount of contact between fathers and their offspring is somewhere between one and two hours per day in the United Kingdom, Australia, Canada and the United States (Kay, 2009b). Because leisure lies at the heart of family relationships and of fathers' parenting roles in particular, these changes are significant for sport. Indeed, fathers increasingly use leisure as a key means of fulfilling their fathering role and 'place leisure at the heart of their parenting' (Kay, 2009a:1). 'As fathers seek to become increasingly involved in their children's lives, youth sports provide parenting contexts that ... enable fathers to nurture relationships ["bond", in colloquial terms] with sons and daughters and claim that they are sharing childrearing responsibilities with their wives, former wives, or partners' (Coakley, 2009: 49). Nonresident fathers, in particular, attach a great deal of importance to leisure as a means of being good fathers (Kay, 2009a).

Fathers' involvement in their children's leisure and sport tends to be purposive: they seek, for example, to use the opportunities sport provides for them as parents to share experiences with their children, to guide them and to inculcate values (Harrington, 2009). For some, perhaps many, fathers play, games and sport are contexts in which they feel competent and consequently comfortable based on their knowledge of sports and past experiences (Coakley, 2009). In addition, sport and active recreation are forms of leisure that fathers can be involved with their children in a manner consistent with conventional (albeit changing) views of masculinity. According to Coakley, there has been 'a generational shift in popular perceptions of a father's role in the sports participation of his sons and daughters' (p. 40): in the United States, for example, 'fathers are expected to support and guide children as they learn to play sports' (p. 40) and some fathers take this expectation seriously serving as 'teachers, coaches, managers, agents, mentors, and advocates for their child athletes' (p. 40). In Canada, fathers were twice as likely as mothers to be in these roles, at 20 per cent versus 11 per cent (Clark, 2008). Consequently, 'when sons and daughters excel in sports, their success is directly attributed to parents, most often to fathers' (Coakley, 2009: 40). From his study of Canadian youngsters, Clark (2008) concluded that, 'The attitudes of fathers play a key role in the likelihood that their children play sports' and the outlook of fathers who exhibited very positive attitudes towards sports participation was associated with significantly higher sports participation for their children (77 per cent) compared with children whose fathers whose attitudes towards sport were not particularly positive (54 per cent). Clark also found that in contrast with fathers' attitudes, the level of importance mothers placed on their own sports participation made little difference to that of their children. Nevertheless, he adds, 'there is a significant difference when mothers participated in sports in any way: their children's participation rate was much higher (71 per cent) than that of children whose mothers did not'.

As well as class and gender and ethnic dimensions to parental and family support for sports participation among their children, there can also be a broader ethinic and cultural dimension to parental support. Ha et al.'s (2009) study of physical activity among primary and secondary schoolchildren in Australia and Hong Kong highlighted the marked differences in parental support between the two 'with more than twice the number of boys and girls in Australia reporting frequent levels of support from both mother and father compared with their Hong Kong counterparts' (pp. 165–66). Ha et al. (2009) point to the widespread belief that in some cultures, such as Hong Kong, parents' overriding concerns are with things other than sport, such as their children's academic success.

It is interesting to speculate on the significance of socio-demographic trends (and developments in the family in particular) for the 'intergenerational reproduction' (Scheerder *et al.*, 2005c: 22) of sports participation. At a time when children in lone-parent families are more likely to live with their mother than with their father and the vast majority of lone-parents tend, in fact, to be lone mothers (with the likely consequences for gendered socialization into sport which that implies), it will be interesting to see how the rapid changes in family structures, the greater diversity in family' living arrangements and the possibility of young people living under different family arrangements impact upon family' sporting cultures and young people's sporting habituses. In Canada, the highest children's sport participation rates occurred in intact families where both birth parents were present (Clark, 2008). Whereas boys' sporting participation was almost the same for all family types, however, girls in lone-parent families were a good deal less likely to be sports participants than girls from intact families. Lone-parent families, especially those headed by women, were more likely to experience financial difficulties and Clark (2008) surmises that, under the strain of financial problems, lone parents may sacrifice the sports participation of their daughters, reasoning that sports have traditionally not been as important to young girls' **identities** as they have been for boys. It will also be interesting to observe how youngsters' prolonged reliance on parental support and changing economic roles will impact on the sporting habituses of youth. Findings from the realm of paid **work** add to the growing evidence that parental behaviours during childhood have long-reaching consequences for children's behaviours (van Putten *et al.*, 2008). Increasing numbers of families have both parents in employment and some for longer hours than hitherto (van Putten *et al.*, 2008) and this may threaten modelling of, involvement in, and support for sports socialization. As is frequently the case with young people, the United States may be modelling a prototype for the future. According to Saelens and Kerr (2008), as a consequence of changes in family structure, composition and responsibilities in the United States, more parents are relying on after-school programmes to provide sporting opportunities than that they did in the past.

In addition to developments in the family, the expansion of post-school education in countries such as England makes young people more dependent, and for longer, on their parents and families. Generational change has been so great that parents with no history of post-school education are now expected to support children while they study. Consequently, parents have increased power to affect their children's transitions and young people without parental support tend to be severely disadvantaged – in sport as in education, young people's opportunities vary considerably according to whether their parents can and will support them in their endeavours (Jones, 2009).

When it comes to the effects of family members beyond parents not a great deal is known about the impact on young people's sports participation of their siblings. Nonetheless, Sallis *et al.* (2000) review of correlates of physical activity of children and adolescents suggest that adolescents' physical activity (rather than sports participation per se) is correlated with that of their siblings. As far as grandparents are concerned, a recent study suggested that they can also play an important part in young people's lives generally by providing not only caretaking and financial support but also sharing young people's interests and activities (ESRC, 2009b).

Although young people learn a great deal from observing and modelling the behaviour of significant others (people whose views and approval matter to them), including their friends, parents and families continue (albeit to varying degrees) to provide the resources, sites, experiences, role models and encouragement crucial in enabling and nurturing the sporting involvement of their youngsters. Thus, parents in particular as well as families more generally remain central to young people's socialization into sport and the concomitant sports-related social and cultural capital they develop.

PARTICIPATION

Participation in sport (and, for that matter, **leisure**) tends to be measured in terms of one or more of the following:

- *Rates*: the numbers and proportions (usually expressed in percentage terms) of young people taking part in sport.
- *Frequency*: the number of times young people, take part (each week, month or year, for example).
- *Duration*: the length of each 'bout' of participation.
- *Type*: the form of participation – in general terms (such as games and **lifestyle sports and activities**) as well as more specific activities (e.g. football, skateboarding and swimming).

It can also be interesting to know something about the *context* of participation, such as the **facilities and venues** used (private gym, public playing fields or swimming baths, school sports hall or even local neighbourhood and town centre streets), the **time** of day or week (e.g. after-school, weekends and school holidays), who young people are most likely to participate with (such as **friends** and family) as well as the manner (e.g. more-or-less organized or informal) of participation. For those concerned with young people's **health** and fitness it is also useful to know something about the intensity of participation in terms of both energy expenditure and the physiological demands of **activity and exercise** (in other words, whether single or repeated bouts of physical activity are most likely to contribute to health and fitness). Because participation in sport within school **physical education** lessons is usually compulsory, young people's involvement with sport in their **leisure** is taken as a far more useful indicator of the penetration and significance of sport in their lives.

Almost all studies of participation have one weakness – the tendency to rely upon self-reported data. Self-reported data is problematic for several reasons: (i) the difficulty of recall – especially when it involves remembering relatively less structured activities such as lifestyle activities; (ii) the likely impact on recall of social desirability (i.e. the tendency for people to overestimate involvement in activities viewed positively by wider society – such as sports participation – and under-report behaviours that may be viewed negatively – such as smoking or 'binge-drinking') and (iii) the difficulties obtaining the rich, nuanced data necessary to accurately represent the often complex nature of participation.

The significance of participation for youth sport

Notwithstanding the aforementioned limitations and the fact that sports participation data may be 'somewhat conservative', providing 'little evidence about the intensity and quality of the activity' (Coalter, 1999: 25), the use of similar, repeated methods within (if not between) studies over time (alongside studies providing a snapshot of a particular time and place) provides substantial evidence of a clear trend towards increased participation among young people and adults across the developed (and, occasionally, the developing) world since the 1970s. Increases in participation (over various time periods) have, for example, been reported in:

- Australia (Dollman *et al.*, 2005)
- Belgium (Telama *et al.*, 2002)
- Canada (Clark, 2008)
- China (Xiong, 2007)
- England (Roberts, 1996a, 1996b; Sport England, 2003)
- Estonia (Telama *et al.*, 2002)
- Finland (Borodulin *et al.*, 2008; Koska, 2005; Laakso *et al.*, 2008; Telama and Yang, 2000; Telama *et al.*, 2002)
- Flanders (De Knop and De Martelaer, 2001; Scheerder *et al.*, 2002, 2003, 2005a, 2005b; Vanreusel *et al.*, 1997)
- Germany (Brettschneider and Sack, 1996)
- Iceland (Eiðsdóttir *et al.*, 2008)
- Ireland (Fahey *et al.*, 2005)
- Netherlands (Breedveld, 2003; De Knop and De Martelaer, 2001)
- Norway (Breivik, 2007; Vaage, 2009)
- Spain (Puig, 1996)
- United States (Caine, 2010)
- Various European countries (Samdal *et al.*, 2006; van Bottenburg *et al.*, 2005)

Studies of participation among young people in several Scandinavian countries have consistently pointed towards relatively continuous increases in participation in recent decades. In Finland, for example, Laakso *et al.* (2008: 151) have noted that 'Leisure time physical activity [including sport] among young people increased ... from 1977 to 2007', especially among young women. In Norway, levels of physical activity among people aged 15 and over increased from 31 per cent in 1985 to 42 per cent in 2003 (Breivik, 2007). Those categorized as 'active' (defined as one or more times per week) 1–4 times per week increased from 46–56 per cent over the same period while those participating five or more times per week increased from 10.8 per cent in 1985 to 13 per cent in 2003. A pattern of substantial increases in regular participation is evident across all **age** groups in Norway with 50 per cent increases in almost daily activity among 20–24-year-olds and 45-year-olds and over and 100 per cent increases in almost daily activity among 25–34 and 35–44 age groups. All told, over half (c.51 per cent) of the older youth population in Norway – 60 per cent of 16–19-year-olds and 43 per cent of 20–24-year-olds – were taking part three times per week or more in sport and physically active recreation in 2007 (Vaage, 2009). In their study of trends in vigorous physical activity and participation in sports **clubs** (defined as engaging in moderately intensive activity four times or more a week) among cohorts of Icelandic adolescents in 1992, 1997, 2000 and 2006, Eiðsdóttir *et al.* (2008) observed 'an overall increase in vigorous physical activity and participation in sports clubs over the past decade among both genders' (p. 289). Growth in participation has also taken place in developing countries in the Far East. In China, for instance, sports participation increased substantially from the 1980s onwards and dramatically so since the 1990s (in cities in particular) (Xiong, 2007) – albeit from a very low base: in 1996, 15.5 per cent of urban Chinese regularly took part in sport or exercises (at least three times per week) whereas four years later, in 2000, the number had increased to 18.3 per cent. According to the *Investigation and Research on Chinese Mass Sport*, 35 per cent of Chinese people over 16 years old participated in sport at least once a week in 2000 (0.65 per cent higher than 1996) (Xiong, 2007). Studies of participation in sport in the United Kingdom reflect a similar trend towards increased participation among young people (Roberts, 1996a; Sport England, 2003a, 2003b, 2008) and, for that matter, adults (Sport England, 2005; Sports Council for Wales, 2000, 2003; *SportScotland*, 2001, 2002) since the 1980s. Overall, alongside an increase in levels of participation, there has been a marked decline in the drop-out rate during late adolescence and young people are much more likely to continue participating in sport and physical activities after completing their full-time education (Roberts, 1996a; Green *et al.*, 2005). Between 2005–06 and 2007–08, youth and young adult groups in England experienced increases in the percentages taking part in sport and physically active recreation at least three times per week (at moderate intensity) from 33–34 per cent among 16–19-year-olds, roughly 27–29 per cent among 20–24-year-olds and 23–25 per cent among 25–29-year-olds (Sport England, 2008).

Whether the 'good news' story of sports participation among young and old over the last 30–40 years is likely to continue remains to be seen. While sports participation among young people and adults is by no means collapsing, there does appear to have been a slight decline in some countries during the last decade or so. The United Kingdom, for example, experienced stagnation in overall participation in the 1990s followed by a slight downturn in the early noughties (2000 and beyond) – predominantly among youth aged 16–24 (Sport England, 2003a). Similarly, research across several European countries (e.g. Samdal et al., 2006) has also indicated that while sport and physical activity participation among young people has increased rapidly over the past three decades, it has stabilized or, at least, increased less substantially since the 1990s. Zuzanek's (2005) overview of time-use among adolescents in several European countries as well as Canada, the United States and Australia, portrays a somewhat more negative scene. Zuzanek identifies falling levels of participation (or, at best, a levelling-off) in physically active leisure over the last decade or so: adolescent participation in sports and outdoor activities declined in Germany, Australia and the United States, and remained at approximately the same levels as in the 1980s in France, Finland and the Netherlands.

Despite these caveats and the fact that, just as with adults, there remains a significant minority of young people doing relatively little or absolutely nothing in participatory terms, more young people are doing more sport than 40 years or so ago. Participation in children's and youth sports has become increasingly popular and widespread, in Western societies in particular (Caine, 2010). Utilizing club membership figures and survey data (or, where this was not possible due to the lack of data, a geographical example of several member states) over the last twenty years in the 25 EU member states, a study by the Mulier Institute (van Bottenburg et al., 2005) compared and contrasted empirical data on the nature and extent of sports participation and concluded that participation in sport was very extensive within the member states of the European Union. The data drawn from Telama et al.'s European studies was based primarily upon the results of a cross-sectional study which explored, among other things, the leisure-time sport – in what the authors call 'organised competitive sport' and 'recreational sport' – of a sample of 6,479 12- and 15-year-olds (3270 males, 3209 females) from six European countries (Belgium, Estonia, Finland, Germany, Hungary and the Czech Republic) (Telama et al., 2002). Telama et al.'s (2005) research corroborated the findings of earlier studies in various European countries (see, for example, Breedveld, 2003; De Knop and De Martelaer, 2001; De Knop et al., 1996; Scheerder et al., 2003; Scheerder et al., 2005) suggesting that 'physical activities and sports (continue to) belong to the most popular (leisure) activities of young people' (Telama et al., 2002: 140).

Several country-specific studies point to the same conclusion. Elling and Knoppers (2005) study of 1025 young people between 14 and 20 years of age in the Netherlands, for example, found that, in general, nearly two-thirds of the respondents actively participated in sport, with a mean intensity of three times a week. Similarly, the *TellUs3* survey (OFSTED, 2008) of children and young people across England found that 71 per cent did at least 30 minutes of sport more than three times in the past week. Beyond school, 58 per cent had played sport at a sports club in the previous four weeks, 46 per cent had been to a swimming pool and 27 per cent to a gym. Among 14–16-year-olds in the *Longitudinal Study of Young People in England* (LSYPE), approximately 70 per cent males and just over 40 per cent females had taken part in any sport out of school in the last four weeks (DCSF, 2008). In North America, the United States and Canada have witnessed trends towards increased participation as well as a lengthening of the duration of bouts of participation among children and youth and girls, in particular.

Alongside increases in participation rates over time, there has been a broadening (in terms of numbers of sports) and diversification (different sports) in sports participation. From their *Cross-Cultural Studies on Youth Sport in Europe*, Telama *et al.* (2002: 141) concluded that 'there were many more physical activities and sports mentioned both as recreational and competitive sports than those in which young people participated, say, 20 years ago'. While in many Central European countries (such as Belgium) young people's participation in sport has traditionally been 'mainly organized' and taken place in sports clubs, in countries such as Finland young people are said to 'participate more in unorganized physical activity than in organized sport' (Telama *et al.*, 2005: 128). A particular feature of this trend has been a shift towards so-called **lifestyle sports and activities** in young people's leisure lives. Telama *et al.'s* (2002) study, for example, highlighted the popularity of cycling, swimming and jogging among male and female 15-year-olds in Belgium, Estonia, Finland and Germany.

When placed alongside the fact that only a small minority play competitive sports in their adult lives the shift towards lifestyle activities begs the question whether current trends are signalling the terminal decline of sport – and competitive games in particular – among young people? The short answer is 'no'. The trends in leisure-time sport among youth reflect a broadening and diversification of participation rather than a wholesale rejection of sport per se. Indeed, the growing popularity of lifestyle activities notwithstanding, 'the traditional style characterized by participation in a formal organizational context (e.g. sports club, extra-curricular school sports), remains very popular … among young people of school age' (Scheerder *et al.*, 2005b: 337) not only in Flanders but Europe-wide. Laakso *et al.* (2008) noted that while 'the frequency of unorganized spontaneous leisure time physical activity had remained at the same level or increased slightly' (p. 149), some of the biggest increases in youth sports participation had been observed in sports clubs which, by extension, involve organized sports. Kristen, Patriksson and Fridlund (2003: 25) have pointed towards the alleged 'dominance' of sport in the lives of young people in Sweden and described the 'sports movement' as being the country's 'largest and most vigorous popular movement' (p. 24). In Finland, participation in sport increased between the mid-1980s and 2007. Laakso et al. (2008) note an upward trend in Finnish adolescents' leisure time physical activity in organized sport, in particular, including a bigger increase of activity among girls than in boys. Similarly, in Iceland in 2007 more 14–15-year-olds reported participating in sport and physical activity overall and in sports clubs than in 1992 (Eiðsdóttir et al., 2008).

In Europe, at least, it seems that sport and team games remain an integral feature of many young people's participation *alongside* lifestyle activities (De Knop and De Martelaer, 2001; Scheerder et al., 2001; Telama et al., 2002; Telama et al., 2005). Instead of replacing traditional sporting styles, 'new styles of physical activities have been added to the sports scene' (Scheerder et al., 2005b: 337). Telama et al.'s observation that in Finland – 'the most popular types of sports (or, rather, physical activities) among adolescents are ... cycling, swimming, walking and running' (Telama et al., 1994: 68) alongside other more competitive, performance-oriented team sports such as soccer and basketball – can be equally applied across Europe. The most popular activities among Dutch youth, according to Elling and Knoppers (2005), are a mixture of sports (e.g. soccer, hockey, basketball and tennis) alongside lifestyle activities (such as swimming, fitness, martial arts, dance/ballet and horse-riding). In Norway, while participation levels and rates among some games (e.g. football, bandy and ice-hockey) remained relatively stable, decreases in games such as basketball, handball, squash and tennis have occurred alongside increases in others (such as volleyball) and, most notably, in individual, flexible games such as golf, bowling and badminton [after a major downturn between 1985 and 1993] (Breivik, 2007). In Portugal, as in Israel (Ben-Porat, 2009), soccer is consistently the first choice for males followed by swimming and other team sports (Seabra et al., 2007). For females, it varies with age with swimming the most popular between 10–12 years and soccer between 13–16 years. In Wales, the slight increases in the early 2000s in young people's (especially girls') participation in and out of school were 'generated by increases in traditional sports as well as activities which promote general health and fitness' (SCW, 2003: 4).

While competitive sport and games retain a place alongside lifestyle activities in young people's participatory profiles, it is noteworthy that partner sports appear to have lost ground (Scheerder et al., 2005b; Sport England, 2003a). In the United Kingdom, for example, following substantial growth in the 1980s, partner sports such as squash and snooker experienced sharp downturns – among young people in particular – during the 1990s and the early years of the new millennium, respectively.

Alongside increases in participation in lifestyle or recreational pursuits and a broadening of the range of activities in which young people are engaged, another noteworthy feature of their patterns of participation is *diversity*, in the form of an increase in the number of different sports and physical activities young people do frequently out-of-school (Sport England, 2003a). Diversity in the shape of co-occurring increases in participation in games that might be deemed lifestyle or recreational activities (such as tenpin bowling) alongside those that are more stereotypically sporting in orientation (e.g. basketball) reflects the complexity of the youth sports participation scene. Even though lifestyle activities become an increasingly prominent feature of the participation profiles of youth and adults it is evident that a number of sports – such as golf, badminton and martial arts – are not only popular among secondary age youngsters (Sport England, 2003a) in their leisure time but also track into youth and through to adulthood for significant numbers of people (UK Sport/Sport England, 2001).

On the basis of numerous national and international surveys, it seems that sports – as well as lifestyle activities – have become integral to many youngsters' leisure lifestyles. That said, for many young people 'it is clear that individualistic and flexible activities dominate' (Coalter, 2004a: 80) their participatory profiles. Indeed, lifestyle activities have, as Coalter (2004a: 79) observes, not only 'experienced substantial increases in participation' by young people, they 'are among those with the most regular participants' (p. 80), as they turn towards health and fitness-oriented activities during their mid-teenage years. All in all, while the evident shift, in participatory term – towards more individualistic, recreational and lifestyle activities – may not signal the end of sport in its more competitive, institutionalized forms, it may, at least, signal a 'redrawing of the traditional boundaries and meaning of sport' (Coalter, 1999: 37).

Amid the general picture of growth in sports participation over the course of roughly half a century, it is important to add a caveat: growth in participation has been far from global. There are considerable variations in amounts of sporting involvement internationally and regionally. In terms of 'sports and physically active leisure', Zuzanek (2005) observed that in the late 1990s, adolescents from Canada and Finland spent approximately 7 hours per week in out-of-school sporting and outdoor activities, compared to around 5 hours in France and the United States and 3–3.5 hours in the United Kingdom and the Netherlands. The Mulier study (Van Bottenburg et al., 2005) also pointed to clearly identifiable geographical and social patterns with respect to sports participation in the European Union. The highest proportion of the EU population taking part in sport and exercise occurred in the Scandinavian member states, followed by the Western and Central European countries. Finland, in particular, is 'one of the most active nations … probably the most active' (Koska, 2005: 295) in both participatory and energy expenditure terms in sport and physical activity more generally. Far lower levels of sports participation are evident in the Southern European member states. The many exceptions to the patterns of quite widespread participation in sport found among young people in the Western world are predominantly to be found in the less-developed and developing regions of the world. Birchwood *et al.* (2008) observe that in the countries of the South Caucasus, participation in sport is a marginal interest to youths and adults seeking Western lifestyles. Similarly, in the Far East, sport involvement is minimal to non-existent among both male and female Korean adolescents, for example, due to heavy school requirements (Staempfli, 2005: 680). Regional differences are also observable within nations. The 2006 *SportScotland* report identified significant geographical variations in sports participation – such as the low rates of participation (especially for women) in urban west–central Scotland – that did not appear explainable in terms of standard socio-demographic factors. By the same token sports participation rates in urban areas of China tend to be considerably higher, more than double, that in the rural areas (Xiong, 2007).

It is clear from the findings of a variety of studies across Europe in recent decades that participation in sport has assumed a significant place in the leisure and educational experiences of young people in the latter decades of the twentieth century and the early years of the twenty-first century. Although there is a significant minority of youngsters doing relatively little or absolutely nothing, it remains the case that young people in Europe are taking part in more sport and physical **activity** than previous generations. All told, involvement in sport and physical activity among young people is sufficiently commonplace for us to refer to the 'sportization' of young people's lives (Brettschneider, 1992; Telama *et al.*, 2005).

Young people's participation in sport is influenced by a wide variety of factors including such things as **age, gender, social class, ethnicity, parents and family** and geographic location. Youngsters approaching or in their early teens – that is to say, those in the 10–14 years age group – are more likely to be sports active than youth. Although boys are more likely than girls and to participate in sport the gender gap is narrowing to the point where it is justifiable to talk of degrees of convergence. The same is also broadly true for distinctions based on social class. Nonetheless, children whose parents have high incomes, are well educated and are involved in sports activities themselves are the most likely to be sports participants (Clark, 2008).

It remains a moot point whether levels of sports participation are currently near saturation levels and no longer rising or, at least, only modestly so. From their evidence in the South Caucasus, Birchwood *et al.* (2008: 297) observed that there appeared to be 'a level beneath which sport participation would not fall even in the least propitious circumstances'. They concluded that 'it is likely that even when sport is not a priority in schools or in families, and when local facilities are non-existent, some young people will still play, maybe because they are exceptionally talented or just exceptionally motivated for whatever reasons'. On the other hand, it may be that there is a 'natural' constraint on maximal levels of sports participation. Because challenging or competitive physical amusements (such as sport) necessarily involve testing oneself against others directly or indirectly, it might be that the pleasure associated with being good, or at least better than some others, will not by definition be achievable by everyone.

PHYSICAL EDUCATION (PE)

Although it is conventional to view education in school systems as specifically concerned with the development of the cognitive and intellectual abilities of young people, a more comprehensive conceptualization would be 'socialisation which takes place in specialised institutions' (Roberts, 2009: 74). While, in principle, education (in the more restricted intellectual sense associated with academic subjects) is distinguishable from training – 'where people are taught specific skills in order to perform particular tasks' (p. 74) – both education and training are features of the **socialization** process that occurs in educational institutions. In broad terms, *physical* education (PE) involves the socialization of young people into sporting and physical **activity** skills and cultures. In more formal terms, however, PE refers to 'the planned teaching and learning pro-gramme in *curriculum* time' (Quick, 2007: 6); emphasis in the original) that, in the case of England and Wales, 'meets the requirements of the National Curriculum for PE [NCPE]'. This definition of PE distinguishes curricular from **extra-curricular PE** or, as many prefer to view it, school sport. A more empirically adequate definition of PE, however – and one more in keeping with the views of teachers (and, for that matter, the perceptions of pupils regarding the practice of PE) – would be those physical activities and sports organized (and usually overseen) by PE teachers or their representatives during the (sometimes extended – see extra-curricular PE) school day and week.

Among a vast array of claims for the benefits of PE, successive PE curricula in England and Wales have tended to conceptualize the subject in terms of both sides of a long-standing philosophical debate regarding its nature and purposes: in other words, as an educational subject (in the more restricted sense, with a strong theoretical or cognitive element) and/or as the initiation (or socialization) of young people into sport for its own sake. Thus, in claiming that PE 'educates young people *in* and *through* the use and knowledge of the **body** and its movement', the original NCPE for England and Wales (DES, 1991; emphases added) grounded the justification for the subject in both the development of theoretical knowledge and practical skills and the initiation of youngsters into the practices and traditions of sport (as a 'valued cultural practice'). The most recent iteration of the NCPE sustains the supposedly cog-nitive or theoretical dimension to PE by requiring pupils to demonstrate, among other things, 'an understanding of the concepts that underpin success', 'how to select and apply appropriate tactics, strategies and compositional ideas' as well as how to 'take on different roles and responsibilities, including leader-ship, coaching and officiating'. Despite the long-established tendency for the routine of PE to remain wedded to the practice of sport, even PE teachers

144

(rhetorically at least) share the view implicit in the NCPE that PE should not simply be reduced to training in sport but be viewed, at least in part, as an aspect of 'the education of the whole child' and 'an activity undertaken to provide that education' (Mason, 1995: 3).

Be that as it may – and notwithstanding the rapid growth and development of academic qualifications in PE – in reality, the subject continues to be dominated by the teaching of sports and sports skills. Unsurprisingly, this is pretty much how young people experience PE: pupils in secondary schools across the world view the subject as primarily about 'enjoyment' of sport and physical activity and a break from more academic **work** (Dyson, 2006; Laws and Fisher, 1999; O'Sullivan, 2002; Smith and Parr, 2007). In short, what amount to non-educational (in the academic sense of the term) justifications for the subject – revolving around recreational fun and social interaction with their peers – tend to be the major **motivation**s for young people engaging in PE. Indeed, youngsters tend not to recognize the supposed educational purpose and value of the subject (Jones and Cheetham, 2001).

The significance of PE for youth sport

Whatever other socializing functions they may have, schools, as 'the primary and most common institutions of education' (Sivan, 2006: 437), are expected to prepare young people for adult life. With the increase in free **time** over the second half of the twentieth century and growing concern with the alleged **health/obesity** crisis, education for (active) **leisure** has become an increasingly prominent feature of education in general and PE in particular. It begs the question, however, how best to enhance young people's **participation** in sport in a manner likely to bring about their ongoing adherence to active leisure, particularly in the shape of sport?

One of the more obvious ways in which physical educationalists in the United Kingdom have set about responding to this objective has been via a broadening of the PE curriculum (especially for older **age** pupils), incorporating more diverse activities than the staple-diet of sport and team games especially (Roberts, 1996a, 1996b). Although Scheerder et al. (2006) were unable to show, in detail, just what it was about the particular school PE programmes that impacted positively upon the late-adolescents in their Flemish study, Smith, Thurston, Green and Lamb's (2007a, 2007b) research with 15–16-year-olds suggested that it is likely to be something about the relative breadth and informality of PE programmes that might facilitate the development of **sporting** repertoires among young people and which may, in turn, constitute a 'school effect' on youth sport participation. Despite constraints caused by prescribed national curricula, timetable pressures and so forth, schools in England are continuing to broaden their PE curricula to include a breadth of activities including tag-rugby, trampolining, handball, baseball, boxing, fencing, horse riding, triathlon, orienteering, golf, bowls and archery as well as such diverse

145

pastimes as rock-it-ball (a variation on pop-lacrosse), ultimate Frisbee (Frisbee played to American football rules), and even underwater hockey together with some of the newer lifestyle activities such as cheerleading, yoga, circus skills, skateboarding and various forms of cycling (Quick *et al.*, 2009; Sykes, 2008). This broadening of provision notwithstanding, the PE curricula of the vast majority (possibly even all) of secondary schools in countries like England continue to privilege competitive sport generally and team games in particular. The 2008–09 *PE and School Sport Survey* in England confirms the pre-eminence of 'traditional' sports and games in PE and out of hours (extra-curricular) school sport in the vast majority (at least four in five) schools, albeit supplemented by a range of other activities (Quick *et al.*, 2009). By contrast, in Scandinavian countries (which have some of the highest rates of youth sport participation in the world), such as Norway, PE lessons are more likely to revolve around multi-skill games with an emphasis on enjoyment and physical activity than particular sports per se.

A breadth of content in PE curricula is not, however, sufficient on its own to promote youth sport participation more generally. However important enjoyment and perceived competence (see **motivation**) may be for initial involvement in sport, the latter in particular appears crucial for maintaining involvement (Brustad *et al.*, 2008). A number of studies offer support for the idea that promoting perceived competence is a significant factor in encouraging adherence to particular sports (Telama *et al.*, 2005) – unsurprisingly, perhaps, it seems that if young people believe themselves to be good at an activity then they will tend to like it and stick with it. On top of enjoyment and competence, it seems that young people also want a degree of self-determination in their leisure lifestyles, hence the significance of pupil choice in PE. Placed alongside competence and enjoyment, opportunity and choice appear significant variables for participation (Wallhead and Buckworth, 2004). Motivation, it seems, is essentially enhanced when students are given a choice in the content and style of PE lessons. Bramham's (2003) study of 15-year-old boys in inner-city schools in England concluded that they not only valued the opportunities to choose activities in PE but also, in some cases, where levels and forms of choice were unsatisfactory, pupils responded by not taking their kit to lessons. Unsurprisingly, in the light of broader trends towards lifestyle activities, dissatisfaction among some pupils occurred where the choices they were offered 'were structured in such a way to make outdoor games compulsory' (p. 66). In this regard, Bramham also found that the minority of boys with little commitment to PE tended to 'favour indoor, individualized activities such as trampolining, badminton and volleyball' (p. 67).

Although the continued dominance of PE programmes in many countries by sport (and team games in particular) cannot be justified in terms of trends in participation among young people, this should not be taken to suggest that sport-based PE nor, for that matter, multi-activity PE programmes, are devoid of merit in relation to the goals of promoting youth leisure sport and, ultimately,

lifelong participation. Sport and team games continue to hold a place in both the preferences and participatory repertoires of young people. Fisher (2003: 145) points to studies in Denmark, Germany and Switzerland indicating not only 'that pupils like a range of experience' or 'rich curriculum' but that, in the case of countries such as Germany, so-called 'traditional sports' remained popular in PE. In relation to the promotion of participation in sport and physically active recreation among young people there is, therefore, a strong case for retaining multi-activity programmes. It seems that young people want the more 'traditional', sporting activities supplemented by other activities in broader curricula, rather than simply expunged. Hence, Roberts *et al*'s (2001) observation on leisure education is equally applicable to multi-activity PE programmes; that is to say, they will not merely help but are likely to be crucial in so far as they provide every youngster with a broad base of interests and skills, and encourage them to be discriminating, so that they can pick their own mixes from the opportunities that are available, thereby using PE and school sport as a basis for constructing and expressing their individual identities while becoming integrated into their particular social milieu.

There is one other aspect of schooling which may be significant for ongoing sports participation. To the extent that late adolescence can play a role in linking sports participation from youth through to adulthood it is suggested that delaying adulthood – with its associated barriers to participation in the form of working and domestic roles and responsibilities – by remaining in education, may serve to reinforce a commitment to sport. 'All over the world young people are remaining in education for longer than ever before' (Roberts, 2008: 43) and, whatever their role in inculcating or developing sporting habituses or enhancing those already laid down in families, schools and universities do provide opportunities and **facilities**, free time and like-minded peers with which to establish sport as an aspect of young people's self-**identities** – something which may be particularly important for women.

The claims for a 'PE effect' notwithstanding, there is reason to suspect that the impact of PE on youth sport participation may be far less significant that physical educationalists may want to believe and that **parents and family** and, to a lesser extent, **social class** are the major 'determinants' of young people's engagement with sport.

POLICY

Policy is a statement of intent regarding achieving, maintaining, modifying or changing something. In this vein, Penney and Evans (2005: 21) define policy as 'someone's (an individual's, institution's, local or central government's) authoritative decision about how "things" should be'. Policies can range from the simple to the complex and because the term 'implies a desire to move from what is perceived to be an unsatisfactory state of affairs to a more satisfactory one'

(Murphy, 1998: 104), policies tend to begin life as issues. In sport as elsewhere, vested (political) interest in achieving results as swiftly as possible means that policies tend to be oriented more towards the short-to-medium term rather than the longer term.

Traditionally, the path from policy to practice is viewed as a relatively straightforward one: people, with authority to do so, generate and send forth policy for those on the ground – sports officials, development officers, coaches and **PE** teachers, for example – to receive and implement. This ideal-type, hierarchical and linear model of policy implementation distorts, however, a more complex, contingent and dynamic process. The traditional view of policy implementation simply underestimates, among other things, the propensity of policy-makers to introduce policies with multiple goals that may be neither straightforward to implement, nor compatible, nor result in the outcomes anticipated. Neither should the policy process be viewed as democratic and rational. Struggles over values, interests and goals develop as a consequence of the differential power relations of the (interdependent) people and/or groups of people (with their own particular interests, aims and objectives) involved in generating and delivering policy. Recognizing and appreciating the particular ties between people and groups – and the power relationships associated with these – is fundamental to understanding policy formation and implementation. Because no group or individual will have anything remotely approaching total knowledge of any particular area or situation, the outcomes of policies are inevitably 'blind' insofar as they frequently have unintended as well as intended outcomes. Indeed, the consequences of today's policy responses to pressing issues provide the context for the formulation of tomorrow's policies and practices (Murphy, 1998).

When considering policy towards youth sport, it is necessary to bear in mind that in countries such as England not only is there no government department with youth in its title (Roberts, 2003) but the ministry concerned with sport might also hold responsibilities for other areas, such as the arts, culture and media. This is likely to be part of the explanation for the emergence and implementation of differing, sometimes conflicting, policies on youth, youth sport, PE, sports **facilities** and so forth which variously emphasize and target youth delinquency, anti-social behaviour, crime and so-called 'exclusion', competitive sport, as well as the identification of gifted and talented young sports men and women.

Nevertheless, since the mid-1990s, 'there has been a renewed focus on young people in social policy' (Robb, 2007c: 5) generally in the United Kingdom, including a number of more recent initiatives in school and youth sport. The policies and strategies that emanate from these reveal government's tendency to view sport as a social service (Coalter, 2007); in other words, as a vehicle for achieving a range of political objectives from curbing **health** problems (such as childhood **obesity**) to cheaper, alternative vehicles for integrating alienated and disruptive youth. In this regard, sport is almost invariably valued more by policy-makers for its instrumental worth rather than merely any intrinsic benefits that participants or practitioners may see it as possessing (Coalter, 2009).

The significance of policy for youth sport

Governments in very many developed nations of the world have, over the last quarter of a century of more, developed policies towards sport in both elite performance and recreational participatory forms (Nicholson *et al.*, 2009). Growing concern with youth sport, in particular, and the uses to which it might be put has resulted in a plethora of initiatives aimed at young people (Coalter, 1999). Norway is just one among numerous countries that have begun to use sport as a means for the integration of minority youth (Walseth, 2006a, 2006b). According to Green (2009: 123), 'the struggle to cajole, encourage or persuade the public at large to take part (more often) in sport, recreation or physical **activity** programmes has characterised sport policy interventions by governments of different persuasions'. In England, for example, the *Physical Education, School Sport and Club Links strategy* (PESSCL) [Department for Education and Skills/Department for Culture, Media and Sport (DfES/DCMS), 2003] and, more latterly, the *Physical Education and Sport Strategy for Young People* (PESSYP) [Department for Children, Schools and Families (DCSF), 2008] have among their objectives the aim of developing links between sport in school and sport after school, especially at sports **clubs**. Supposedly, building on the PESSCL strategy the PESSYP is supported by an investment of £783 million to improve the quality and quantity of PE and sport undertaken by young people aged 5–19, including the opportunity for young people to participate in three hours of sporting activities each week (to be provided by schools, further education colleges, clubs and community providers) in addition to at least two hours per week of PE and sport in school (Bloyce and Smith, 2009).

A plethora of policies in countries around the world target increases in youth sport even though it is unlikely that a level of **participation** will ever be reached that would be deemed satisfactory (by the various interested parties) and make redundant the apparent need to urge 'more'! Indeed, such policies tend to overlook several things. First, the fact that **age**-related decline in sports participation is almost inevitable – in part because the implicit baseline measure tends to be young people's sports participation while at school and this is artificially high due to the fact that PE is obligatory in many countries. Second, policy interventions via education inevitably boost sport participation to unsustainable levels either 'because they exceed the proportions of young people who are genuinely motivated to play or because there are insufficient facilities to enable them to continue to do so in conditions that the young people would find acceptable' (Birchwood *et al.*, 2008: 297). Third, where unequal propensities to participate are set during childhood (see **socialization**) the impact of policy-led interventions in terms of boosting

149

participation thereafter is likely to be minimal (Birchwood *et al.*, 2008). Finally, and crucially, policies aimed at bringing about equality are not only impossible in stratified societies, they are impossible in relation to sport because of its very nature: in its competitive form, at least, sport is a zero-sum activity (see **competition**).

The tendency for policy-makers to develop and implement superficially plausible but ultimately confused, contradictory and misguided policies is particularly evident in England in relation to youth sport. The gap often found between policy rhetoric and the 'evidence-base' is illustrated in policies aimed at raising participation levels among young people in particular (DCMS/ Strategy Unit, 2002). In the United Kingdom, for example, the available evidence (much of it generated by government itself) suggests quite clearly that the perception of decline in sports participation among young people is misguided – overall levels of participation have risen in recent decades (Roberts, 1996a, 1996b; Sport England, 2003a) and, in the process, dispersed across a wider range of traditional and more recreational **lifestyle activities**.

The fact that policies towards youth sport often appear doomed to failure is probably best explained by the policy-makers tendency to think in terms of what they hope to achieve rather than what might realistically be achieved and, consequently, they tend to set unrealistic goals and targets. This situation is both caused and compounded by policy-makers' frequently inadequate grasp of patterns and trends in sports participation among young people and, for that matter, of **youth lifestyles** as a whole. Indeed, governments frequently overestimate the significance of policy. The potential to change (young) people's individual and collective behaviours directly through policy-making – is often quite limited. Educational campaigns towards alcohol, smoking and **drugs** are examples of generally ineffective policies. In the case of sport as a vehicle for promoting health, it is readily apparent that young people know and understand the benefits of physical **activity and exercise** but tend not to act upon that knowledge – by taking part in (more) sport, physical activity or exercise – unless they are already predisposed to do so or unless (usually later in their lives) they experience a health crisis, by when it is usually too late! All told, a more detached, less ideologically tainted perspective on youth sport might recognize, along with Coalter (2007), the abundant research which suggests that because sport is only one aspect of young people's lives its likely effects on attitudes and behaviours are inevitably limited. It is, to say the least, unlikely that sports programmes will have a substantial, let alone direct, impact on young people's participation in sport as a whole let alone lead to reductions in anti-social and risky behaviours among young people.

The various caveats notwithstanding, short-term policy interventions aimed at increasing sports participation among young people are not always and inevitably doomed to failure. The message from research such as that of Birchwood *et al.* (2008) is that interventions may well be effective – albeit within a 'mini-max' range laid down during early sports socialization in the family.

With this in mind, the obvious policy implication of much of the extant research (into patterns and trends in sports participation) is to maximize participation among children and then minimize drop-out during the next life-stage – youth – rather than try to reclaim those who lapse as they grow older. In other words, 'the best way to boost levels of adult participation will be to push the childhood start-point as high as possible, then try to prevent drop-out during the vulnerable years which ... follow exits from full-time education' (Birchwood *et al.*, 2008: 286).

RISK

Since the late 1980s, so-called 'risky behaviours' among youth have become major social and public **health** issues (Peretti-Watel *et al.*, 2004). Alcohol, tobacco, illicit **drugs**, sex, gambling and adventure sports are just some of the risk-taking behaviours young people engage in (ESRC, 2009c).

The notion of the *Risk Society* was introduced by Ulrich Beck's (1992) influential book of the same name in which he argued that people's increased knowledge of the world and, in particular, the dangers inherent in modern societies (resulting from the very things – science and **technology** – which had promised to free humankind from famine, pestilence, flood and the like [Roberts, 2009]) have resulted in a heightened awareness of risk. Because, the argument goes, 'the world is perceived as a dangerous place in which people are constantly confronted with risk' (Furlong and Cartmel, 2007: 3) they inevitably 'live in a climate of heightened risk awareness' (Jackson and Scott, 2006: 226). The point is neatly illustrated by the growth over the last decade or so of bureaucratic requirements for teachers, coaches and sports centre operatives to undertake risk assessments for the various activities they provide.

The concept of risk is, however, contentious – not least because there is tendency to use the term too simplistically while failing to recognize that risk can take a variety of forms (Soule, 2008). There are, for example, those risks associated with simply being young and growing up among friends, those inherent in life-stage transitions (moving from education to **work**, for example), and those associated with actively seeking fun or pleasure (particularly in the form of sport). It is worth saying a little more about each of these.

In mere play – and especially when utilizing play in establishing their **independence** – youngsters can become exposed to risk 'through curiosity and/or experimentation' (Carter *et al.*, 2003: 225). In such cases, risk can occur in quite mundane situations. In addition, young people as a whole are an 'at-risk' group in terms, for example, of contracting sexual disease, being physically or psychologically abused, or merely sustaining injury. Anxieties about the welfare of children (and child **abuse**, in particular) are associated with the modern idea of childhood innocence which emerged in the nineteenth century and the tendency for the lives of young people in modern Western societies to be bounded by surveillance (Jackson and Scott, 2006) is one consequence of the everyday world of childhood no longer appearing so safe and predictable. All forms of risk behaviour associated with being young are likely to be reinforced by the presence of **friends and peers** – peer pressure is particularly strongly associated with risk-taking (Carter *et al.*, 2003) through the modelling of behaviours within peer groups and the influences young people exert on one another. This is particularly so where young people seek to achieve status within their friendship and/or peer groups and lose sight of the risks of physical danger or social disapprobation in the process. In such situations, young people's ability to assess risk can be compromised by either ignorance of the possible or likely consequences of their behaviours or by an overriding **motivation** for persisting, such as peer approval. Particularly salient among the risks associated with peer influences among young people are those related to alcohol consumption as well as illicit drug and tobacco use: 'high levels of consumption of alcohol and binge drinking', for example, not only distinguish the behaviour of contemporary teenage girls from their mothers' generation (Abbott-Chapman *et al.*, 2008: 131) but also place such young women at risk of assault and exploitation.

Young people's lives are also said to have become more risky in relation to their life-stage **transitions** as a direct consequence of **youth's new condition**. More protracted and more varied transitions for many youngsters (from school to work, for instance, and being single to becoming a parent) have meant that young people can often 'struggle to establish adult **identities** and maintain coherent biographies' (Furlong and Cartmel, 2007: 138). This makes their lives feel more risky and their futures more uncertain while the greater diversity of opportunities and risks results in young people feeling more responsible for their current and future circumstances (Miles, 2000). In libertarian societies, people are constrained to think of themselves as individuals with the consequence that their ability to shape their circumstances tends to be exaggerated. The upshot is that risk becomes individualized in the sense that youth are expected to focus upon their individual experiences and, as a consequence, come to view problems and solutions as lying in their own hands – a failure to succeed is often portrayed and understood as a deficiency of skill or effort (the sine qua non of meritocracies) rather than structural processes largely beyond individuals' immediate experiences and comprehension, such as economic changes. In reality, far from being evenly experienced, risks associated with transitions are disproportionately felt by disadvantaged groups (Furlong and Cartmel, 2007).

In addition to the aforementioned instances of risk, where **leisure** is concerned risk-taking behaviour may also refer to seeking adventure in order to generate fun and excitement, whether in the form of illegal drugs or adventure sports. In other words, young people (like adults) often choose to engage in activities that in one way or another can be considered risky. At one end of a continuum such activities may involve generating the kinds of excitement or thrill-associated risk when, for example, flirting with authority and breaking the law. At the other end, it may lie in the pleasures associated with risks inherent in such sports as martial arts and outdoor pursuits. Paradoxically, although they may go to a great deal of trouble in their daily lives to reduce or eliminate risks (e.g. when working with machinery or driving a car), many people actively seek out risk in their leisure activities in the form of sport and the so-called 'adrenalin (or adventure) sports' (such as bungee-jumping and climbing) in particular.

With these examples in mind, it is necessary to recognize that what constitutes risk depends upon perspective; that is to say, the same behaviour is very often viewed in quite contrasting terms by young people themselves. Similarly, it is interesting to reflect upon the manner in which some behaviours come to be considered too risky and are, as a consequence, prohibited (e.g. illegal drugs) while others are viewed as only requiring careful control rather than prohibition (legal drugs such as alcohol, for instance). It is also worth considering how involvement in some (more-or-less risky) activities (such as team games) can lead to involvement in yet other risky behaviours (such as consuming alcohol). In this regard, Peretti-Watel *et al.* (2004) observe that sporting **activity** and various risky behaviours may not only be both impelled by similar motives and values but also sporting activity itself may provide opportunities to engage in risky behaviours – excess drinking and 'recreational' drugs, for instance, are often used in sport as integrative drugs.

It is also important to note the structural dimensions to risk. It seems that vulnerable youngsters (such as young offenders) – who are far more likely to come from disadvantaged groups such as the lower working classes – are more prone to engage in risky behaviours and to fail to learn from any adverse consequences. In the case of gambling, for example, small successes are likely to lead to such youngsters gambling more whereas it tends to have the opposite effect on 'normal' gamblers (ESRC, 2009c). By contrast, young people from middle-class backgrounds often have the economic and cultural **capital** security which allows them to ignore risk. As well as being cross-cut by **social class**, risk is gendered: 'among young men it may be associated with unemployment or marginal employment; among young women, risk may be associated with teenage pregnancy' (Jones, 2009: 101–2).

The notion of 'risk' is often associated with post-modern theories and the alleged dissolving of the certainties associated with the modern world. Within such theories the concept of 'edgework' (Lyng, 1990) refers to the quest for self-actualization that is said by some to be the motivation for **participation** in adventurous leisure activities (Rojek, 2006). It is important, however, to distinguish between 'real life' and mimetic excitement (Elias and Dunning, 1986). In everyday life, tense excitement (and, therefore, risk) can be generated through, for example, experiences of unemployment, physical violence, natural disasters and political force. These are risks that people try to avoid: they tend to be uncontrolled, uncertain in their outcomes and potentially, physically and psychologically damaging. Although, when it comes to sport, participants may expect to experience similar emotions (such as fear of painful physical contact in martial arts or rugby) and overlapping experiences (physical violence and psychologically damaging results), for the most part these remain under the control of the sportsman or woman to a far greater degree and, more importantly, are consciously undertaken; they are, in other words, chosen rather than imposed. Such controlled de-controlling of the emotions is, therefore, far more likely to result in enjoyable experiences (Elias and Dunning, 1986). In modern societies, people are constrained to exhibit relatively high levels of self-restraint, consequently there are few opportunities for people to exhibit strongly and deeply felt emotions, let alone spontaneity. Consequently, modern sports (some more so than others) offer an arena in which people can experience pleasurable excitement by generating potentially exciting challenges and concomitant tensions, of the kinds associated with sports such as football, climbing, boxing, free-running and mountain-biking.

The significance of risk for youth sport

All of the forms of risk outlined in the foregoing section are to be found in sport and particularly in youth sport – whether they be risks of exploitation and **abuse** associated with being young in sport, risks to do with alcohol and drugs and peer influence, or those to be found in the **individualization** of life transitions vis-à-vis healthy, active lifestyles. Last, but by no means least, there is the culture of risk associated with sport itself (Malcolm, 2008) where sporting activities necessarily involve risk-taking – whether in conventional sports such as rugby and martial arts or physical recreations such as climbing and canoeing. Indeed, risk can be said to be normalized in physically vigorous sports involving **competition** and physical contact in terms of the inevitability of pain and injury and the widespread acceptance that commitment to such sports (and, for that matter, team-mates) necessitates risk-taking (Waddington, 2000).

Taking part in sport at a young **age** inevitably involves particular risk of injury. Youngsters may be especially vulnerable to growth-related injuries during the adolescent growth spurt (e.g. growth plate damage). They are also susceptible to injury due to immature or underdeveloped coordination, skills and perception (Caine, 2010). Young females, in particular, may be at increased risk of non-contact anterior cruciate ligament injuries due to such factors as anatomy, hormones and menstrual cycle, neuromuscular characteristics, muscle strength and flexibility. The frequent and intensive training and competition of young athletes create conditions under which all of these potential risk factors are more likely to surface (Caine, 2010). Varying cultures of risk are, then, deeply embedded in some sporting cultures (Malcolm, 2008) and particularly those that are strongly masculinized.

On the basis of the various commentaries on risk in contemporary society it would be easy, therefore, to overlook the fact that risk can be experienced as a positive thing – in the sense of being a motivating factor (in adventure sport, for example) – as well as viewed as something threatening which needs, at worst, to be avoided or at least protected against and, at best, controlled. Indeed, voluntary risk-taking is often a prominent characteristic of young males' sporting cultures, not least because of the seductive qualities of risk sports where the frisson of the activity may be associated with degrees of fear (e.g. regarding injury) but also the enhancement of self-esteem and identity. It is in this area of courting risk that much contemporary research on **lifestyle sports** devotes time to the ideas of 'high risk' or 'extreme' sports (Soule, 2008) as these grow in popularity. In the United States, children and adolescents are increasingly visiting wilderness recreational destinations and participating in a growing number of adventurous and 'extreme' sports such as skate boarding, BMX, mountain biking and rock climbing (Caine, 2010). 'Extreme' is, however, a relative concept. It is largely taken to involve those sports which court relatively more 'objective' danger (involving risks that cannot be controlled such as rock-fall, extraordinary waves, unpredictable fast-moving water, changing weather and avalanches) – rock-climbing, canoeing and skiing, for instance – rather than team games. In these activities, an elevated consciousness of, and aversion to, risk is likely to have a detrimental effect on the sporting experience. Thus, when commodifying risky adventure sports and activities (turning them, in other words, into 'packages' to be bought by consumers), commercial providers tend to sanitize and detune the risk element in order to provide experiences that are more likely to be experienced as thrilling rather than frightening. They are, in effect, providing an illusion of risk rather than real risk (not least because of the potential litigious consequences the latter may bring). To the extent that such activities limit the possibilities of the participant overcoming a (risky) challenge with their own skills they are not likely to generate profound or deep-seated feelings of satisfaction of the kind associated with feelings of 'flow' (see motivation). This is precisely why the more skilful sports participants become the more adventurous (risky) in order to seek out the challenge needed to sustain a feeling of 'flow' (Csikzentmihalyi, 1990).

It seems that for some young people sport is one vehicle through which they can simultaneously seek pleasure while satisfying a desire to court risk and to flirt with loss of control. For parents, youngsters' involvement in sport highlights the general tension they face between protecting their children from harm while endeavouring to foster (or, at least, not inhibit) their autonomy (Jackson and Scott, 2006). **Parents'** growing anxiety regarding the risks confronting their children has behavioural consequences for all aspects of their lives and play and sport in particular. Nowadays, children below the age of 10 are less likely than their parents' generation to travel to school or sporting venues or play on their own entirely without supervision. Nevertheless, although young people's sporting and leisure experiences are increasingly subject to formal and informal forms of risk assessment, many continue to seek out and engage with unpredictable and risky sporting and recreational experiences.

It is important not to underplay the cultural specificities and differences, not to say complexities in attitudes towards risk in sport. In the case of outdoor pursuits (such as climbing and mountaineering), for example, many people in countries such as the United States and the United Kingdom may be seen as located towards the risk-averse end of a continuum – in both cultural and legal terms – with Scandinavian societies such as Norway and Eastern European countries such as Poland and the Czech Republic positioned towards the risk-embracing pole. However, when it comes to contact-based team sports like rugby, American football, ice hockey and martial arts, all countries appear to have groups of young people for whom the risk involved is deemed acceptable and often identity-enhancing.

When it comes to structural differences in risk, girls are widely believed to have a stronger inclination to avoid risks than boys. Findings from Koska's (2005: 131) study of over 900 Finnish students in school years 11 and 12 and over 1,100 of their parents suggest, however, that **gender** differences in risk taking and perceptions of risk in relation to sport and **health** have narrowed significantly over recent decades. Similarly, Abbott-Chapman et al.'s (2008) study of intergenerational risk-taking in Australia found evidence of increased risk-taking among female adolescents (compared with their mother's genera-tion) alongside a reduction in the gap between levels of teenage male and female risk taking. In terms of **ethnicity**, the The Activities and Experiences of 16 year olds in England in 2007 (DCSF, 2008) revealed very large differences among ethnic groups in the 14–16-year-olds who most commonly reported 'risky behaviours', with the White and Mixed groups most likely to have reported these as such. In relation to social class, the over-representation of working-class youngsters in fighting sports is well-established while middle-class youngsters are disproportionately represented in adventure and risk sports, not least because these can require economic as well as cultural and social capital.

All in all, risk is a significant phenomenon in leisure generally and sport in particular, whether it is experienced as a positive and motivating factor (as in some aspects of adventure sports tourism), or seen as a potential threat to be controlled and protected against (as in the case not only of those same adventure sports such as climbing but also in relation to general issues such as abuse in sport). The control of risk may be seen as a positive aspect of ensuring that children are protected from harm, and that leisure and sporting **facilities** and services are safe and fit for purpose. Conversely, an elevated risk consciousness may in fact narrow leisure opportunities and diminish leisure experiences.

Finally, it is worthy of note that young people's risk-taking is often presented as problematic not only for themselves but also for others (and especially adults) in terms of anti-social, 'out-of-control' behaviours such as skateboard-ing, biking and skating in town centres as well as the culture of youth drinking that sometimes accompany these activities. The upshot can sometimes be the criminalization of such commonplace sporting behaviours and the spread of **moral panic**.

ROLE MODELS

The term 'role model' refers to those whose attitudes and behaviours (young) people are believed to not only admire but also seek to imitate, whether consciously or subconsciously. At various times in young people's lives, parents, teachers, peers, 'pop' musicians and sporting stars, among others, might be perceived or projected as (more or less suitable) role models.

The significance of role models for youth sport

Role models, especially in the form of highly visible elite sportsmen and women, are often portrayed as significant in shaping young people's inclinations towards sport. The impact of role models on young people's **participation** is often misunderstood, however, and frequently overstated. Competitors at the Olympic Games are one oft-cited example of role models believed to inspire young people (e.g. by modelling enthusiasm for sport as well as the rewards involvement can bring), thereby increasing levels of participation in and commitment to sport. Stamatakis and Chaudhury's (2008) study of temporal trends in adults' sports participation patterns in England between 1997 and 2006 suggested a different outcome, nevertheless. Their findings provided support for the conclusion of an earlier study on the London (2012) Olympics legacy (see Coalter, 2004b) regarding comparisons between participation immediately before (2003–04) and one year immediately after (2006) the successful London Olympic bid – and also, they might have added, two years after the Athens Olympic Games (2004) in which Britain achieved notable successes in cycling and rowing. Stamatakis and Chaudhury (2008: 607) observed that, far from indicating an increase, 'participation in major Olympic sports (swimming, cycling, running and team and racquet sports) among young men, the population group that is most likely to adopt role models from the world of sports, showed signs of decrease'. In the same vein, Houlihan *et al.* (2009: 5) cite the University of Toronto Centre for Sport Policy Studies' exploration of the 'inspiration myth' 'in the face of evidence which suggests that there is little or no significant correlation between Olympic success and changes in levels of mass participation in sport'.

It seems that the young people most likely to view top-level sportsmen and women as role models to be imitated are those who perceive themselves as being on a similar trajectory in the same particular sports as the role models themselves. Even then, young and aspiring elite sportspeople tend to be discerning in their choice of characteristics they seek to emulate. Young elite rugby league players, for example, 'admire the technical competence, physical characteristics and temperament' (Fleming *et al.*, 2005: 64) of elite players rather than other aspects of their general lifestyles and behaviours. Beyond aspirant young sportsmen and women, young people generally are unlikely to model the sporting behaviours of the 'stars'. Vescio *et al.* (2005) demonstrate how young people have difficulty identifying with sporting stars that may appear, at the very least, several steps removed from them. Consequently, elite sports men and women are unlikely to be viewed as meaningful role models by young people. This is because the significance of role models lies in their relationship with, and proximity to, young people rather than their sporting and cultural status per se. Youngsters are far more likely to be influenced by those closer (in relational, cultural and geographic terms) and who are, or at least were, similar to them at one point in their lives. Consequently, the 'aspirational model' of 'efficacy expectancy' – focussing attention on those young people who may realistically aspire and/or expect to be like – appears a much better bet than the elite model in terms of modelling desirable behaviours (Coalter *et al.*, 2006a). Hence, the potential impact on sports participation of **friends and peer** groups and, for that matter, **parents and family** members as well as the limited significance for many young people of their **PE** teachers and sporting heroes and heroines. Indeed, there is substantial evidence that families as well as friends act as particularly significant role models in relation to sports **socialization**. Parents and family not only provide the earliest opportunities and experiences as well as financial and emotional support (Street, 2002) they, along with older siblings, provide early models of sporting practices. Beyond childhood, it seems to be during the secondary school years (i.e. 11–15 years) that the involvement in sport of not only parents and siblings but also best friends becomes particularly influential for young people (Brustad *et al.*, 2008). All things considered, it seems that the most effective sporting role models for young people lie far closer to home than is commonly assumed in the rhetoric surrounding sporting 'stars'.

SEDENTARINESS

Coined relatively recently to refer to what appeared to be a growing trend in the developed world during the second half of the twentieth century, the terms sedentary and sedentariness refer, in essence, to physical *in*activity. *The Health Survey for England* (Craig *et al.*, 2009) defines children as sedentary in more specific terms if they either do no physical **activity** at all or less than 30 minutes a day of moderate intensity activity. In terms of the pervasiveness of sedentariness, there is substantial accumulated evidence from around the world (and developed countries in particular) that 'significant numbers of children lead relatively sedentary lives and rarely experience sustained periods of moderate or vigorous physical activity during the weekdays or weekends' (Winsley and Armstrong, 2005: 72) sufficient to enhance their **health** status.

Low and diminishing levels of physical activity – in terms of energy expenditure – are especially marked in females and older children and the activity levels of both these groups deteriorate while the portion of **leisure** time in which they are sedentary grows as they move through the secondary school years (Marshall *et al.*, 2002).

As Biddle *et al.* (2008: 208) point out, however, defining sedentariness merely as an absence of physical activity 'fails to identify what young people are doing while they are sedentary, thus precluding an understanding of *why* they are sedentary' (emphasis in the original). In short, sedentary lifestyles are said to be characterized by an excess of sitting – watching TV, playing computer games or surfing the Internet, for example – alongside a general dearth of physical activity, particularly in the form of sport. Watching TV is now the industrialized world's main pastime, accounting for more **time** than any single activity except **work** and sleep (Sigman, 2007). A recent study of British children's activities and leisure time in 2007 discovered that more than six in ten (63 per cent) youngsters aged 11–15 reported watching TV for between one and three hours a day with 20 per cent watching for four or more hours and only 1 per cent watching none at all (Philo *et al.*, 2009). In Brettschneider and Naul's (2004) European study, the main leisure activities of 12–15-year-olds were watching TV and listening to music and most of the countries featured in Zuzanek's (2005) review of recent surveys witnessed 'increases in adolescent television and video watching' (p. 394) over the past two decades. UK adolescents were the most avid watchers (16 hours per week: approximately 40 per cent of their free time) while Norwegian and Dutch youth watched TV and video the least (both relatively and absolutely) – 10–12 hours per week, approximately 25–27 per cent of their total free time.

It is hardly surprising to find TV viewing feature so prominently in the leisure lives of young people given that more than 40 per cent of American households, for example, have three or more TV sets (McElroy, 2008) and many youngsters not only have TVs in their bedroom but also face no restrictions from their **parents** with regard to how much TV they are allowed to watch. Sigman (2007: 12) points to research indicating that many 11–15-year-olds in Britain spend 55 per cent of their waking lives watching TV; in other words, 53 hours a week or seven and a half hours a day. The average six-year-old will have already watched TV 'for more than one full year of their lives' and by the **age** of 75, 'the average Britain will have spent more than 12 years of 24-hour days watching television' (p. 12).

Despite growth in TV viewing over the last 20 or so years and the prominence of TV in the leisure lives of young and old alike, the amount of time teenagers spend watching TV and videos hovers in many developed countries around 14–15 hours per week (Zuzanek, 2005). Indeed, television viewing appears to have 'stagnated' (Wray, 2006) in recent years as other sedentary activities, and Internet usage in particular, have boomed. Computer use generally has risen substantially since the late 1990s, particularly among younger teenagers attracted by computer and video games which 'now account for a relatively large proportion of young people's time and income' (Furlong and Cartmel, 2007: 77). By contrast, older teenagers spend growing amounts of time using computers to surf the Internet and participate in online chat groups (Zuzanek, 2005) as well, in the evenings, as watch TV. The *Mediascope Europe* study (cited in Wray, 2006) revealed 45 per cent of Internet users online every day of the week sending emails, visiting websites, chatting online and downloading music. Daily usage of the Internet is particularly high among those 16–24-year-olds who have Internet access (Wray, 2006).

TV viewing and use of the Internet have not only been significant aspects of the substantial economic and cultural changes that have occurred over the last half century or more but they are also strongly associated with the rapid growth of so-called 'obesogenic environments' in which sedentary lifestyles have become normalized. Such changes also include a rise in the number of less physically active occupations, the growth of labour-saving devices, increased use of cars and computers, increases in 'low intensity leisure activities' (Dollman *et al.*, 2005: 892), unfriendly walking and cycling environments (Samdal *et al.*, 2006) and changing patterns of family eating, including a notable increase in snacking.

In recent decades, TV-watching and playing or working with computers and other sedentary behaviours have been presented as significant reasons for what are perceived as growing levels of physical inactivity alongside overweight/ **obesity** among young people (Telama *et al.*, 2005). Sedentary behaviours are believed to play a dual role in promoting obesity not only because they involve low energy expenditure but also because they tend to be associated with the intake of high-energy snacks (Brodersen *et al.*, 2007): 'children and adolescents consume snacks and drinks while watching TV … (and) the TV-related consumption of foods is higher among heavy viewers than among lighter viewers' (Brettschneider and Naul, 2004: 138).

The significance of sedentariness for youth sport

Sedentary behaviours and lifestyles have become normalized among children, young people and adults across the developed world. Central to discussions about sedentariness and youth sport is the widespread belief that, in becoming core aspects of (young) people's lives, some things (such as TV and computers) have displaced other activities, such as sport. This is known as the displacement hypothesis. In essence, it explains sedentariness in terms of a hydraulic metaphor: the more young people are doing one thing (e.g. watching TV) the less they are inevitably able to do of another (such as sport). In practice, however, the relationship between activity and inactivity in young people's lives is one of degree or emphasis rather than either/or. Put another way, while almost all young people in developed countries spend time on certain core activities such as watching TV, socializing with **friends**, shopping, playing (computer) games and so on (Furlong and Cartmel, 2007) this does not prevent many from playing sport as well. Data from Canadian children aged 12–14, for example, indicated that only 24 per cent were inactive even though very many watched high levels of TV. The remaining 76 per cent ranged across 'a spectrum of activity levels' (McDermott, 2007: 305). Similarly, Marshall, Biddle, Sallis, McKenzie and Conway's (2002) study of teenagers in the United States and the United Kingdom indicated that sedentary behaviours often coexist with physical activity and some of the most active children in sporting terms are also among the most sedentary overall. This phenomenon is neatly illustrated by Peiro-Velert *et al.'s* (2008) study of 12–16-year-olds in a Mediterranean region of Spain in which approximately two-thirds of the group were categorized as active on a daily basis (with high mean daily energy expenditure) while, at the same time, spending more than two-thirds of their free time in sedentary behaviours, such as screen media use, homework and reading. In practise, rather than simply displacing physical activities such as sport, it seems that some sedentary behaviours (such as watching TV) are more likely to replace other sedentary behaviours (such as reading) (Gard and Wright, 2005; Marshall *et al.*, 2002). What gives way in young people's busy leisure lives tends, in other words, to be TV, social life, resting/sleeping and housework – things that easily expand or contract in the time available – rather than sport per se. Altogether, it seems that involvement in physical activity and sedentary behaviour are often, in reality, two sides of the same coin. This phenomenon is, perhaps, best exemplified by boys who, in virtually all countries surveyed in Zuzanek's (2005) review of adolescent time use, 'spent more time than girls watching television, engaging in sports and outdoor activities, playing computer and video games, and using computers' while 'Girls spent more time than boys reading and doing hobbies' (p. 391). Sleap *et al.'s* (2007) study of affluent (and, for the most part, privately educated) 9–15-year-olds in England found the picture that emerged 'was one of a balance between sedentary pursuits such as television and homework and physical activities such as sport and active play' (p. 459): 'Pupils spent an average of 121 minutes per day participating in physical activities of at least moderate intensity' which, they observed, was considerably more than the public health recommendations. Sleap *et al.* (2007) added the caveat, however, that almost a quarter of the youngsters in their study engaged in less than the 60 minutes of moderate activity recommended. Nonetheless, even allowing for a social desirability bias (in the form of overestimations of levels of activity in the responses), many youngsters in the study were sufficiently active to maintain 'good health'.

The widespread co-existence among young people of sedentary activities and involvement in active sports and recreation notwithstanding, Sigman (2007) points to research in Mexico, New Zealand and China which suggests a strong relationship between the amount of TV viewing and increases in the prevalence of obesity. He highlights a variety of studies that pinpoint TV as a factor in a number of health issues such as sleeping difficulties, attention deficit hyperactivity disorder, and raised blood cholesterol levels. Sigman (2007: 16) concludes that, 'Watching television, irrespective of the content, is increasingly associated with unfavourable biological and cognitive changes.' In fact, the growth of sedentary leisure activities may have consequences not only for physical but also psychological health. Roberts (2005: 5) notes that 'the growth of leisure time and spending has inflated types of leisure activity that are far less likely to leave people feeling fulfilled and satisfied with their lives.' Pattie *et al.* (2004) study of *Citizenship in Britain* appears to substantiate Putnam's (2000) well-rehearsed claim that social capital – and, correspondingly, active citizenship – declines in direct proportion to TV watching: the general effect of watching TV being a corresponding diminution in active involvement with others and with things in general.

All in all, it seems that not only are young people's lifestyles multifaceted so too is sedentariness – which cannot be accurately represented by a single measure such as TV viewing (Marshall *et al.*, 2002; Telama *et al.*, 2005). **Time** left over after school, homework, part-time work and other, often domestic duties (such as eating meals, cleaning bedrooms and visiting relatives) is used by young people for a wide range of activities, some of which can be labelled sedentary others of which are active uses of leisure. Thus, 'High levels of physical activity and sedentary behaviour are able to coexist within the lifestyle of a young person' (Marshall and Welk, 2008: 12). Through young people in the developed world, we appear to be witnessing the normalization of two trends that may appear paradoxical, even irreconcilable, but are, indeed, two sides of the same coin; that is, youngsters with busy leisure lives who – while strongly involved in sport – are, nevertheless, more sedentary overall and more likely to be overweight (even morbidly obese) than ever before.

SOCIAL CLASS

Social class is 'the main form of stratification (socially structured inequality) in modern societies' (Roberts, 2009: 35). Even though the class structure of societies such as Britain has changed in shape over the last half century or so – the middle classes have expanded and become more diverse while the working class has shrunk (Roberts, 2008) – social class remains a key determinant of life chances. Indeed, not only do young people's destinations remain 'linked as firmly as ever to their social class family origins, and to the places they are born and grow up', 'inequalities in origins and destinations are growing wider than ever' (Roberts, 2008: 203).

Despite its social significance, class is a strongly contested term almost impossible to define precisely. Nevertheless, all conceptualizations of class have an economic base (Roberts, 2009), grouping together 'people with similar ways of making their livings'; in other words, 'in similar occupations' (Roberts, 2001: 21).

In broad terms, beyond those people not in **work** (the unemployed, the retired, the infirmed and single parents, for example) there are three main social class groupings: 'the subordinate (manual, wage-paid) classes, the intermediate (salaried or self-employed) classes and the "advantaged classes" (capital and property owners, and employers)' (Payne, 2006: 17). Because the concept of class revolves around how they make their living – in other words, their market situation in terms of labour market experiences, education and life-chances, as well as occupation – the term socio-economic status (SES) is often used as a synonym for social class (Gabe *et al.*, 2004; Roberts, 2001). SES obviates the fact that social class is not reducible merely to occupation and income but has social and cultural as well as economic dimensions: 'class is not just what we do but who we are' (Roberts, 2007: 719) – it governs our social relationships (social **capital**) and pervades our thoughts and behaviours (cultural capital).

Despite the continued significance of social class for all aspects of people's lives it is noteworthy that, while aware of the class, **gender** and other such differences between them, 'young people do not usually perceive these as divisions' (Roberts, 2008: 11): 'They are less conscious of and responsive to constraints and opportunities that are shared with members of any social category than the scope that they as individuals possess to forge their own futures' (p. 11).

The significance of social class for youth sport

While **age** and gender differences in youth sport are reasonably well-documented, the impact of social class on youth sports **participation** is less frequently studied. There is, nevertheless, ample evidence that social class has particularly significant ramifications for young people's **leisure**-time sports participation.

Overall, although many young people are leisure and sporting omnivores – in the sense that they are inclined to dabble in and experiment with a range of activities – the middle classes simply do more. Based on a 30-year study of young people in Flanders, Scheerder *et al.* (2005b) concluded that leisure-sport participation among adolescents continued, by degrees, to be stratified on the basis of social class. A variety of studies have shown how pupils from predominantly working-class schools (Smith, 2006) or vocational or technical schools (Scheerder *et al.*, 2005b) are less likely to participate in organized leisure-**time** and extra-curricular sporting activities than those in middle-class and more academically oriented schools.

The persistence of a class effect on sports participation notwithstanding, in recent years social class divisions in sports participation rates and forms have become less clear cut among young people (and, for that matter, adults) (Scheerder *et al.*, 2005b; Roberts, 1999). Using 'free school meals' as a proxy measure for social class, a Sports Council for Wales (SCW, 2001) study of young people of secondary school age (11–16 years) found that young people's involvement in leisure-time sport and physical **activity** was only marginally lower for those who received free school meals and thus, by extension, were deemed to be working-class. Although pupils living in the top quintile (20 per cent) of deprived areas in England (Sport England, 2003b) were less likely to have taken part in **extra-curricular** PE and sport, the gap in participation between those young people who did (37 per cent) and those who did not (44 per cent) live in the top 20 deprived areas was not as large as might have been expected. More recently, however, the *PE and School Sport Survey 2008/09* in England found a strong link between levels of participation in PE and school sport and eligibility for free school meals (FSM) and indices of multiple deprivations (IMD). Schools with lower levels of participation tended to have relatively high proportions of youngsters eligible for FSM and/or were located in deprived areas with high IMD (Quick *et al.*, 2009). Nevertheless, overall, it seems that although all occupational sectors have experienced increases in sports participation, the greatest increases have been among the lower-middle- and working-class groupings (Coalter, 1999). Indeed, across Europe there is growing 'empirical evidence that social class has weakened as a predictor of participation in youth sports' (Scheerder *et al.*, 2005b: 338), suggesting 'a gradually diminishing relationship between youth sports participation and social class background' (Scheerder *et al.*, 2005a: 6). While these changes represent a blurring rather than an eradication of class (and, for that matter, gender and **ethnic** difference) in relation to the amounts and kinds of sports young people participate in (as well as the variety of sports undertaken within all social groups), 'it is no longer true that all or nearly all participants are young, male and middle-class' (Roberts, 1996a: 54). This is partly explained by the fact that once youth and adults are *in* sport, the effects of social class upon committed participants is minimal and largely restricted to kinds and amounts of involvement (Roberts and Brodie, 1992) – working class sports participants, for example, are more frequent participants in hall and pitch sports (Coalter, 1999). Thus, while young people (especially young males) on middle-class life trajectories continue to have higher levels of sports participation than working-class youngsters, the main social class differences are no longer in whether young people play any sport, but how much, how many and how often as well as the general styles of participation – including who individuals choose to play with, the **clubs** they belong to and the **facilities and venues** they use. Blurring is also partially explained by the fact that there are 'phases during the youth life-stage when there is considerable overlap between the leisure activities, tastes, scenes and places of young people from different social class backgrounds and heading towards different social class destinations' (Roberts *et al.*, 2009: 274).

Against the backdrop of a weakening of the correlation between social class and youth sports participation, it is interesting to note the findings from a recent study of 214 7- and 8-year-old (early secondary school) boys and girls in Plymouth, England. Voss *et al.* (2007: 1) observed that it is often assumed that 'children from low-income families suffer most where there is a lack of structured **physical education** in school' and, as a consequence, 'provision of additional facilities for sport and other forms of active recreation tend to target areas of socio-economic deprivation' (Voss *et al.*, 2007: 1). Their study revealed, however, that while children from low-income families had less access to sports facilities they were no less physically active. Indeed, while 'children from low-income families attended significantly fewer sessions of out-of-school activities than those of wealthier families ... total physical activity ... over seven continuous days, showed no relationship between parental income and the mean activity level of the children' (p. 1). Voss *et al.* (2007) concluded that, even though they made less use of facilities for structured out-of-school activity, what these disadvantaged youngsters lacked in opportunity they appeared to make up for in the form of unstructured exercise. As a result, they queried whether improving provision for sport would actually lead to the expected rise in activity levels among such youngsters. Similarly, on the basis of findings from the *British Cohort Study*, Feinstein *et al.* (2005: 17) comment that sport 'is quite distinctive in largely attracting young people independently of their socio-economic background' and those engaged in sporting activities tend to be 'fairly representative of the general population of adolescents' (p. 19) and 'less likely to be influenced by social origin' than many other leisure pursuits.

Evidence for the blurring of social class differences notwithstanding, how might the evident persistence of differential rates and forms of participation in sport among young people be explained in relation to social class? Well, at least in part, youth sport can be understood in terms of the economic capital at young middle-class people's disposal, often via their parents: in other words, the ability and tendency of middle-class parents to utilize economic resources to enable their sons and daughters to maintain varied and costly leisure and sporting lifestyles (Evans, 2004). In short, economic inequalities 'lead inexorably to inequalities in leisure' (Roberts, 2001: 171) and the middle classes, young and old, are better able to afford to do the sports and active recreations (such as attend private **health** and fitness gyms and join 'exclusive' sports clubs) that cost money. Leisure and sports participation cannot, nevertheless, simply be reduced to questions of control over economic resources. Class-based patterns of youth sport participation often reflect more than mere differences in disposable income. Middle-class parents not only possess the material resources, or economic capital, to enable their offspring to engage in sport, but they are also in a strong position to pass on social and cultural sporting capital by virtue of being already actively involved themselves and inclined to pass their 'love of sport' on (Roberts and Brodie, 1992). Indeed, middle-class parents often go to great lengths to ensure that their offspring enjoy a breadth of abilities and advantages – the middle classes 'invest heavily in the cultivation of the physical capital of their offspring from a very early age' (Evans, 2004: 101). In doing so, **parents and family** not only 'inculcat(e) "the right" attitudes, values, **motivations**, predispositions, [and] representations but also the right physical capital in terms of skills, techniques and understanding' (Evans, 2004: 101) (see **sociali-zation**). All in all, social class differences in young people's uses of leisure and patterns of sports participation arise from 'different family origins that provide different levels of financial, social and cultural support' (Roberts, 2008: 204).

Probably through the medium of social and cultural (as well as economic) capital, the social networks young people inhabit tend to amplify their leisure and sporting advantages or disadvantages. Young people are likely to form friendship groups and spend their leisure time with others from the same class than across class lines and, in the process, develop relatively similar outlooks and tastes. In this regard, Coalter (2007: 50) cites Bourdieu's (1984) view that sport acts 'as a vehicle for expressing and reaffirming class difference – class-restricted sports, or similar sports participated in at different locations with different social conventions (private tennis club/golf club versus municipal courts/ courses)'.

The class-related picture of sports participation among youth is not, however, straightforward. There are evidently some upper social class families with 'pro-letarian' non-sporting cultures and some aspirational or sunken middle-class/ lower SES families where children are both academically and sport motivated (Birchwood *et al.*, 2008). Nevertheless, class cultures do tend to be self-fulfilling in the sense that because lower-income parents are less likely to be involved in sport in the first place, they are correspondingly less likely to possess either the kinds of dispositions that would **(role) model** sports participation for their children nor the economic, social and cultural capital that might facilitate their sporting involvement.

Nor are the sporting capital benefits of being middle class simply related to the 'here and now' of participation. As implied by the notions of social and cultural capital, the benefits tend to be enduring, particularly in terms of ongoing participation in sport and physical activity throughout the life-course. Middle-class social and cultural capital gives middle-class youth greater 'staying power'; in effect, they are more likely to develop the kind of wide **sporting repertoires** (Roberts and Brodie, 1992) that appear to 'lock' people into sport and physical activity throughout the course of their adult lives. As well as possessing broader experiences of sport middle-class youngsters tend also to be better at sport (judged by the origins of elite sports players) – they have, in other words, greater physical capital (in the forms of fitness, physique and skills). All told, different economic and cultural resources have a strong tendency to result in different leisure and sporting opportunities and experiences.

One seemingly important aspect of cultural capital and, as a consequence, middle-class sporting advantage is education. Scheerder *et al.* (2006: 427) found that 'sports participation is more frequent among people with higher education levels than among people with lower socioeducational levels' and the differen-tial participation rates in early adulthood between those with degrees and those without is maintained through all age groups. In short, participation in higher education appears to predict sports participation – going to university increases the likelihood of sports participation. There is a view, however, that higher education might not have quite the profound effect on sports participation commonly assumed. On the basis of their research in the South Caucasus, Birchwood *et al.* (2008) point to the higher sport participation rates of, for example, university students and graduates prior to their actually entering university and hypothesize that a distinct and enduring propensity to play sport is acquired during childhood via a culture transmitted by the family. More specifically, Birchwood *et al.* (2008) found that after age 16, participation declined at exactly the same pace – there was exactly the same age effect – in each of the SES bands. Beyond age 16, SES neither widened nor narrowed the distance between the groups' participation rates. Thus, Birchwood *et al.* (2008) observe that while family socio-economic status or social class and, for that matter, education is important, it is not the whole answer. Although young people staying-on in education are more likely to experience more extensive formal and informal opportunities to play sport – and differences in the class conditions in which young people grow up tend to lead to differing cohort experiences – this is not as likely as their primary socialization to impact upon their predispositions towards sport and physical activity. Birchwood *et al.* (2008) conclude that cultural differences precede higher education and are pre-eminent in their effects. Thus, social class inequalities in levels of sport participation, like gender differences, may to all intents and purposes be fixed by age 16.

Overall, social class persists as a form of inequality and active sports involvement continues to be correlated with social class (Scheerder *et al.*, 2005a, 2005b) – in both leisure and sporting terms, children of the working classes continue to do less. Class as a form of collective habitus (Bourdieu, 1984) is mediated by parents and families and **friends and peers** and the particular forms of social and cultural capital passed on by families is likely to point youngsters towards or away from particular leisure activities, such as sport. Nevertheless, as with leisure, involvement in sport is more adequately described as class-*related* rather than class-*based* in the sense that there has been a democratization of sporting involvement and the differences between the classes has become blurred. This is not the same, however, as equality. The middle classes not only continue to do a wider variety of sport, they also do more of most sporting activities.

SOCIALIZATION AND HABITUS

The term socialization refers to the processes through which people are taught (directly or indirectly, explicitly or implicitly, intentionally or unintentionally) and internalize the values, beliefs, expectations, knowledge, skills, habits and practices prevalent in their groups and societies. It amounts, in other words, to people learning the culture or ways of life of the networks into which they are born and live. Among other things, socialization becomes manifest in what young people take for granted or think of as 'natural' (Maynard, 1989). Values – defined as beliefs that certain goals or behaviours are more or less preferable to their alternatives (Lee *et al.*, 2008) – tend to be a particularly significant aspect of socialization.

The concept of socialization is often criticized in two broad ways. First, socialization is said to be far too static a concept, implying a once and for all occurrence rather than a process; in other words, something that is never total or complete but, rather, ongoing and developmental. Second, socialization is criticized for being too deterministic, failing to account for the ways in which (young) people mediate, interpret, adapt and sometimes reject what they learn from their families, peers and schools, for example. Whereas a term like education implies deliberate guidance, the term socialization is often taken to imply conditioned responses to various social influences. It is a gross oversimplification, however, to imagine that the social environment conditions or shapes young people any more than young people are entirely free to shape themselves. Socialization is neither a 'homogenizing' nor 'all-embracing' process (Malcolm, 2008: 232). The relationship between young people and socializing agencies such as the family and school is best conceptualized as reciprocal and interactive and one that is, to some extent, contingent upon the former's interpretations of the influences of the latter. This is why social scientists talk of 'negotiation' between young people and others in their social networks in an attempt to convey the significance of their interpretations of the explicit and implicit 'messages' they receive from the networks they are a part of. Much research into socialization is, as a consequence, ecological in the sense that it explores socialization processes within the complex networks of relationships that young people inhabit (e.g. family, friends and school) often at one and the same time. The fact that they do not simply conform to all the norms they are imbued with during socialization is evident in the numerous examples of young people negotiating and compromising on, even rejecting, particular behaviours (e.g. sport and drinking alcohol) as well as embracing them. This is especially apparent when teenagers begin, more overtly, to construct their own **identities** from the material of early socialization.

Negotiation notwithstanding, socialization is inevitable. As young people live, they cannot help but learn something, '*somewhere* with *somebody*' (Tolonen, 2005: 344; emphases in the original) and the people and groups that (intentionally or unintentionally, directly or directly) pass on particular values, practices and so forth are said to be agents of socialization. Agents of socialization are characteristically subdivided into two categories: primary and secondary. Primary socialization refers to the initial and potentially most influential form of socialization, usually experienced within the family – particularly from **parents** but also siblings. Secondary socialization, in contrast, refers to those areas of life, beyond the family – such as the school and peer groups – where young people also inevitably experience socialization processes. Other potentially significant secondary agents of socialization (in terms of **time** and/or influence) include sports **clubs**, part-time workplaces and, in particular, the mass media and TV and the Internet. Socialization amounts to a more or less deliberate and conscious process depending upon the socializing agent(s) and media. Schools, for example, engage consciously (via the formal curriculum) as well as informally (via the so-called 'hidden' or 'informal' curriculum) in the process of (secondary) socialization. The socializing effects of friendship groups, by contrast, tend to be informal via imitation and constraint.

A term commonly associated with socialization is 'significant others'; in other words, people who have a significant influence on the thoughts and practices of young people. In the case of youth sport, this might be expected to be PE teachers and sports club coaches and officials. In practice, particularly significant others for young people are their **friends and peers** and, through the teenage years especially, these become more significant as agents of socialization than their parents. This is particularly so with regard to young people's tastes and practices in general and in relation to sport in particular (De Knop *et al.*, 1996). In fact, while 'peer group influence' is often regarded in a negative light (see **moral panic**) by adults 'it can also provide the arena in which children and young people offer help and support to each other that are lacking in their relationships with adults' (James and James, 2009: 97). Indeed, processes of **informalization** and the growing influence of friends and peers means that socialization of young people as they grow older is, if it ever was, far from straightforward or unidirectional. Secondary socialization from peers can and often does challenge primary socialization in the family and secondary socialization in school (Jones, 2009).

Despite the fact that socialization is a lifelong process in which peers become increasingly prominent, the significance of early life experiences (and those within the family, in particular) should not be underestimated. While socialization does not end with adulthood, later stages of the socialization process inevitably build in some way or other upon the foundations laid early on (Roberts, 2009). The significance of early life socialization lies, therefore, in the impact it has on people's predispositions or **habitus**. Habitus can be defined as 'the durable and generalized disposition that suffuses a person's action throughout an entire domain of life or, in the extreme instance, throughout all of life – in which case the term comes to mean the whole manner, turn, cast, or mould of the personality' (Camic, 1986; cited in Van Krieken, 1998: 47). On this view, 'the real forces which govern us' (p. 47) are our habits or habitus and it is because we tend not to be aware of the ways in which our seemingly free choices are influenced by our deep-seated predispositions (or second nature) that 'the choices involved seem to be made naturally' (Tolonen, 2005: 356). Young people's habituses, for instance, are expressed when they make sporting and **leisure** lifestyle choices (albeit often within the parameters of their **social class, gender, ethnic** and other sociocultural conditions). There is, nonetheless, a view that in late- or post-modernity – as their lives have become increasingly individualized – young people can self-socialize by reflexively and consciously choosing groups (such as surfers or climbers) that will shape them in ways they wish to be shaped.

Whatever reservations there may be regarding the concept of socialization, it remains alive and well in the social sciences and nowhere more so than in the world of sport, particularly in debates about how best to influence young people's (pre)dispositions towards sport. Indeed, the family and the school are regularly blamed by politicians and the media for their alleged failure to socialize youngsters into sport.

The significance of socialization and habitus for youth sport

Because childhood and youth are especially impressionable phases of life, when their personalities are still developing, young people's biographies and their early attachments (or otherwise) to sport appear to have a profound impact on their later life involvement therein. Specific habits (e.g. playing football) and more general predispositions (towards being physically active) tend to be deeply embedded or internalized during childhood and youth. Socialization is a gradual and pervasive process and because habitus is slow to develop, it tends to be slow to change. Consequently, socialization into sport while young can be very significant for **lifelong participation**. According to Birchwood *et al.* (2008: 284), the crucial dispositions among young people towards or away from sport 'are transmitted through families via something akin to ... "habitus", which lays down a mini-max range within which **policy** interventions (via school programmes or providing **facilities**, for example) can be effective'. Parents provide the earliest opportunities and experiences, financial and emotional support (Stroot, 2002) and, along with older siblings, early **role models** of sporting practices: 'If the parents are not actively involved, nor intentionally provide sporting experiences for the child, the chance that the child will be exposed to the sporting world at an early **age** is limited' (Stroot, 2002: 131). Sporting socialization usually amounts to more than simply exposing young people to different activities and opportunities. Rather, it tends to involve the transmission and teaching of values and norms that are adopted by youngsters (Dixon, Warner and Bruenig, 2008) and in both cases, parents and family are crucial. Even recreational engagement in play before more formal engagement with sport can be fundamental in youngsters valuing sport, expecting to play sport and imitating the sporting practices modelled by their parents and families.

While habitus continues to develop throughout a person's life, their values, attitudes and patterns of behaviour tend, inevitably, to be strongly influenced by their earlier experiences; particularly because their predispositions develop within and are therefore shaped by the networks – such as family and friendship and peer groups – they are a part of. Friends, as well as families, can be significant players in sports socialization and the development of a sporting habitus.

Indeed, peer groups and habitus are likely to be mutually reinforcing as young people seek out for friendship those other young people who are most like them in the sense of sharing similar interests. In this regard, young people's engagement with sport spills over into other domains of their lives, such as their friendship networks. As a result, young people's habituses are inevitably connected to their emerging social networks, and these (friendship groups, for instance) are likely to affect the degree of exercise in which people engage (Fisher, 2002). In this regard, O'Donovan (2003: 1) notes how the 'social involvement' goals of young people 'influence their **participation** in physical education', not least because their 'first agenda is to socialize and have fun'.

Early and deep-seated attachments to sport tends to lead to young people developing particular orientations to sport and active recreation per se. Combining the data for recent participation and participation as a child, a Sport England (2007) study revealed that those encouraged to take part in sports as children had significantly higher recent participation rates than those who were not encouraged (76 and 54 per cent, respectively). Evidently, young people do not arrive at **PE** lessons in primary, let alone secondary school, as tabulae rasae. Rather, they arrive with particular dispositions towards sport and sport becomes a more or less central aspect of their self-identities and, thus, predispositions. Nonetheless, according to Feinstein *et al.* (2007: 307), 'there can be "turning points" where the predicted route changes direction in response to new sources of influence' – relocating and making new friends, for example. In this regard, leisure activity and the settings in which it occurs can reinforce or even reverse past developmental trends. While this is palpably true, it is important to bear in mind that their early lives have a tendency to delimit the horizon of possibilities for young people. Thus, their early experiences are likely to have profound implications for leisure tendencies in later life and their subsequent patterns of participation in sport especially. Indeed, by the age of 16, very many young people have already begun to adopt some of the adult leisure practices that will become features of their adult leisure lifestyles (Roberts, 1999); thereafter, their 'leisure lifestyles tend to become focused around a smaller number of retained pastimes' (Roberts and Brodie, 1992: 39). In this regard, childhood and youth serve as a kind of anticipatory socialization during which lifelong participation in sport may be rehearsed. This is why it is also important to bear in mind that sport is only one of a number of leisure-time activities competing for young people's time (Coalter, 1999) and they are only likely to stick with sport if their experiences are more satisfying and better value for time and money than the other leisure alternatives (Roberts and Brodie, 1992).

Young people's sporting decisions are seldom (arguably never wholly) made in isolation. Indeed, at the very least, they are made against the backdrop of their habituses. To see their decisions otherwise constitutes a form of naïve individualism which denies the influence of primary and secondary socialization in framing young people's perceptions of what they can and cannot do and what they want and do not want to do – in other words, their predispositions or habituses. Young people are dependent upon their parents and thus susceptible through socialization to their 'traditional' practices vis-à-vis sport and leisure. In this manner socialization infiltrates youngsters' subconscious. It is an open question when, if at all, young people become sufficiently detached and reflexive to 'free' themselves from the deep-seated influence of socialization and habitus.

SPORTING REPERTOIRES

What are variously termed 'sporting repertoires' (Roberts and Brodie, 1992), skill or **activity** 'portfolios' (SCW, 2000) or 'sports literacy' (DCMS/Strategy Unit, 2002) broadly refer to the number and differing types of sports and physically active recreations that young people engage in.

The significance of sporting repertoires for youth sport

In relation to sport, the significance of childhood and youth lie in their impact on general leisure and sporting tendencies in later life. This is because adults become more rather than less conservative in their leisure tendencies: people use the relative freedom of leisure as they grow older to stick to the routines they have become accustomed to (via **socialization**) in their younger lives (Roberts, 2006). This seems to be particularly true with regard to **participation** in sport. From their study of men and women who had become 'committed' to sport as adults, Roberts and Brodie (1992) found that virtually all of those who played regularly between the ages of 16 and 30 had become 'locked-in' to sport and were frequently 'established on continuous sports careers' which were 'unlikely to be disrupted for many more years' (p. 37). The chief characteristic of those who became 'locked-in' was that they had been active in several (and usually three or more) sporting activities throughout their previous sporting careers. In other words, as young people, they had possessed what Roberts and Brodie's (1992) referred to as 'wide sporting repertoires'. The point about wide sporting repertoires is that whatever reasons people have for dropping out of particular sports at various points in their lives, where they have been regularly involved with several sports early on in life their sports careers tend to be less vulnerable over time (Roberts and Brodie, 1992). In effect, it is not so much the sheer amount as the number of different sports that young people play that appears crucial in determining whether they remain sports active into and through adulthood.

What appears to matter in terms of facilitating wide sporting repertoires among young people is not so much which activities those charged with increasing the levels of sports participation among the young might anticipate young people doing as adults, or even what the young people are currently doing; whether youngsters experience precisely the same activities at school or in their leisure as those they are likely to engage in as adults does not appear crucial. What seems to matter more is whether or not they develop a repertoire or portfolio of sports (Roberts and Brodie, 1992). If they do, then some activities are likely to endure while others will be replaced, supplemented or even dropped as young people's lives unfold and the forms of activity in which they find pleasurable excitement change in the course of their development.

While necessary, breadth of sporting content does not, however, appear sufficient on its own. Nor, for that matter, is a pedagogical approach that prioritizes either enjoyment of the task at hand or the development of a basic level of competence (see **motivation**) enough. As significant as these things are, young people also benefit from a degree of self-determination or choice in moulding their own sporting repertoires (Wallhead and Buckworth, 2004). In short, motivation is enhanced when students are given a choice in the content and style of, for example, sporting opportunities and PE lessons. Roberts (1996a) argues that increases in participation in recent decades are a consequence of the fact that the mode of delivery of school sport has, to a greater extent than hitherto, coincided with the **age** group's preferred leisure styles and the process of **individualization** more generally. Hence, the importance – in the promotion of involvement in sport – of preparing young people for 'choice biographies' (du Bois-Reymond, 1995; cited in Roberts, 1996b); that is to say, of enabling young people to do the things they choose with the people they choose, when, where and how they choose.

Although childhood and youth are the life-stages where the foundations for long-term uses of leisure are laid and wide sporting repertoires developed, during their teenage years young people 'typically dabble and experiment with a wide range of leisure interests, many of which are soon dropped' (Roberts and Brodie, 1992: 39). Thus, while young people are the age group most receptive to 'doing new things' their leisure interests are characterized by changeability; they are 'the section of the population with highest levels and most diverse patterns of cultural consumption' (Roberts, 1997: 3). Consequently, instability is an attendant feature of young people's leisure lifestyles (Iacovou and Berthoud, 2001; Roberts, 1999; Schizzerotto and Lucchini, 2002); hence, the significance of wide sporting repertoires. Using two national surveys in the United States, Sabo and Veliz (2008: 125) show how 'Participation in sports fluctuates a good deal across childhood and adolescence'. While some young people are locked into sport more or less permanently and others drop out never to return, the pattern of involvement among very many is more complex and fluid (Sabo and Veliz, 2008). Of the 2,000-plus school-age youngsters in the two *Women's Sports Federation* studies, 'Nearly half of all current sport team players stopped or dropped out at some point' (Sabo and Veliz, 2008: 125) and the drop-out rate increased among both boys and girls as the youngsters grew older.

173

All told, the significance of a wide-sporting repertoires lies in the fact that they appear to increase the likelihood that youngsters will remain sports active during the periods in their lives when they are dabbling in and experimenting with a variety of leisure activities and subsequently when they experience the impact of **age and life-stage transitions** and events.

TECHNOLOGY/IES

Technology (and information and communication technology, especially) is an increasingly significant aspect of youth lifestyles and, in particular, youth **leisure** and sport. For the present purposes, the term technology can be taken to refer to the 'machines, equipment and implements which, allied to appropriate techniques, are used to produce goods, services and experiences' (Roberts, 2009: 290) as well as to control and develop aspects of the physical and social environments. Specific technologies are often linked with specific (sometimes overlapping) areas of activity or industry; hence, the commonplace references to industrial technology, medical technology, electronic technology (which incorporates information and communication technologies) and even sports technology. The tools and techniques of sports technology include machines (such as mountain bikes and skateboards as well as cars and computers), materials and facilities (e.g. all-weather sports surfaces, artificial surfing reefs, dry-ski slopes and indoor climbing walls) and equipment (such as wetsuits, climbing hardware, carbon bicycles and rackets, titanium golf clubs and padded cricket gloves and rugby jerseys). Sports technology also incorporates the kinds of computer packages increasingly to be found in elite-level sport as a means of analysing and enhancing the sports performance of individuals and teams.

One particularly significant aspect of technological development in leisure generally and sport in particular is that of electronic technology and, within that, information and communication technologies, as well as virtual technologies including the increasingly commonplace computer-simulated virtual leisure and sports worlds. Information technology refers to 'any non-human means of storing, processing and transmitting information' (Roberts, 2009: 134). Nowadays, the term is taken to specifically mean 'electronic, digitised information and communication technologies associated with the computer and the Internet' (p. 134).

Today's young people 'are the first to grow up in a digitally connected world – where geographical boundaries provide no limitations and information can be accessed on a 24/7 basis' (Blacke, 2009: 12). They have, in other words, grown up with computers, the Internet, the World Wide Web, mobile phones, bipods, Google, blogging, Facebook, YouTube, Twitter and many more communication technologies as standard or taken-for-granted aspects of their life-worlds (Naughton, 2006). With information technologies commonplace (in the developed world at least), much of young people's entertainment is nowadays obtained via electronic media (Zuzanek, 2005). Computers are used not only to play computer games but also to access the Internet. The SHEU (2007) archive of 68,495 youngsters between the ages of 10 and 15 from across the United Kingdom revealed up to 16 per cent of males spending more than three hours on computer games after school 'yesterday' and 79 per cent of 14–15-year-old males browsing the Internet. Internet usage continues to boom across Europe and the developed world with many young people sending emails, visiting websites, chatting online and downloading music or just 'surfing the net' on a daily basis. Daily usage of the Internet is particularly high among the 16–24-year **age** group among those who have Internet access (Wray, 2006). Another, earlier, technological advance that has impacted significantly on leisure and over half a century or more and has contributed to privatism in the form of an increase in home and family-centred leisure – television – appears to be suffering from **competition** with the Internet (see **sedentariness**).

New technologies are providing young people with new and alternative ways to communicate with their **friends** and develop their hobbies online. Weekly use of computers rose with age in Philo *et al.*'s (2009) study of children's activities and leisure **time** in England and Wales in 2007 and 90 per cent of the 11–15-year-olds reported owning a mobile phone. While time spent playing computer/video games and surfing the Internet has grown substantially during the last decade alone, social networking has experienced the most dramatic growth – especially among 16–24-year-olds – with the help of developing technologies. Four in five young people now have access to the Internet at home and use it for several hours a night to socialize with friends accessing a variety of social networking tools. Online social networking makes it easier for young people to talk to their peers, access information, gain advice and so forth and social network sites have driven a massive growth in young people's online social networking since the emergence of MySpace in 2003. So-called 'online youth' can join global communities (Roberts, 2008) in 'cyberspace' and almost a quarter of Internet users across Europe visit social networking sites at least once a month. Rather than isolating them, information technology appears to be helping young people foster wider networks and they tend to be more sophisticated and discriminating when doing so than they are typically given credit for (James and James, 2009). In fact, although young people in particular are said to be driving the social networking phenomena, the reality may be quite different: only one in 10 UK Twitter users are aged 17 or younger and that on teenagers only account for 14 per cent of MySpace users and 9 per cent of Facebook (Naughton, 2009). What teenagers are using the Internet for is as a source of entertainment and although nearly all 8–17-year-olds in the *Norton Online Living Report – Survey, 2008* reported using the Internet, this was mainly for playing games and downloading (Roberts, 2008).

One of the **risks** of instant connectivity is said to be the erosion of personal time and time engaged with other leisure activities, especially physically active recreation such as sport. In their study of young people's time use over the past 30 years, Feinstein *et al.* (2008) expected to find that the introduction of new technologies had changed how adolescents spent their time, and the research did, indeed, reveal that the use of nearly all traditional forms of media declined in line with mounting computer use – with one exception: time spent by 11–19-year-olds reading books had increased since the early nineties – and the general uptake of new media technologies. Several other studies indicate how media pursuits have, inevitably, displaced some elements of young people's sleep, homework and physically active leisure (Zuzanek, 2005). Nonetheless, despite the **moral panic** about youngsters' assumed subservience to information technology it seems that many of them are aware and conscious of the risks said to be associated with being 'online'. Online social networking, for example, has become not so much a distinct activity as part of their day-to-day communication and interaction with peers (Blacke, 2009). Indeed, there is evidence that not only is online social networking is not only less popular than is often claimed (see the following section), rather than displacing sport electronic media have found a place alongside active leisure in young people's lives (Marshall *et al.*, 2002).

The seemingly inevitable fashion dimension to technology is particularly pronounced among young people, where their endeavours to stand out in socially acceptable ways among their **friends and peers** often involves not only play with but also display of the latest technology – especially information and communication technology and the entertainment media. In this regard, there is a commonplace assumption that the media industries have a hold over young people's imaginations, transcending national and local boundaries and cultures and strongly influencing the tastes and behaviours of global youth as well as the **identities** young people seek through media representations of 'cool' youth. Here too, however, young people are somewhat more 'tech savvy' and discriminating than is often assumed – they are by no means 'cultural dupes'.

Despite the increasing prevalence of information and communication technologies, youth engagement with and experiences of them are not, however, homogenous. While middle-class teenagers use the Internet daily – approximately a fifth have access in their bedrooms – and nearly all children and young people in the West use the Internet at some time (usually at school), one in five children make little or no use of the Internet (Womack, 2008). Neither are all young people actively using social networking sites – those from disadvantaged backgrounds have less access and are more infrequent users. Of the 10 European countries surveyed in the *Mediascope Europe* survey (cited in Wray, 2006), Denmark was in the vanguard of Internet users with Germany in the rear. In more global terms, electronic technology generally is far more prevalent among young people in Europe and the developed world than in areas of the world such as Africa, India and the 'third world' countries. Despite such differences, overall, the 'digital divide' 'between the rich West and most of the rest of the world' (Roberts, 2008: 121) is narrowing. In a similar vein, while there remains a **gender** dimension to electronic media usage – computer and video games are disproportionately the preserve of boys while social networking in contrast has a preponderance of girls – there has been a narrowing of the 'digital gap' between the genders over the last decade (Zuzanek, 2005).

The significance of technology for youth sport

The question often posed nowadays with regard to technological developments is what will the effects of the rapid growth of information technology (and, more specifically, the Internet) be on all areas of young people's lives and active uses of leisure in particular? More specifically, will it lead to young people becoming more sedentary? Might it stop them doing sport or even going out or seeing friends? As contemporary as such issues may appear, questions such as these have actually been around – in relation, for example, to staples of young people's leisure such as comics, TV and radio – for over half a century. However, rather than necessarily detracting from **participation** in sport and active recreation, it seems that the products of the electronic technologies amount to an added dimension of **youth cultures** rather than substitutes for active leisure, including sport. The *Taking Part Survey* (Sport England, 2007) of people in England, including youth aged 16–24-year-olds, revealed that three-fifths (64 per cent) of the 72 per cent who had either taken part in an active sport in person or accessed a sport website had engaged in sport in person only, with one-third (33 per cent) having engaged in person and accessed online services and only the remaining 3 per cent having used Web sites only.

Although information technology does not appear to have impacted detrimentally on sports participation per se, the sports young people play (and, for that matter, access to them) do, indeed, tend to be influenced by technological developments. In some cases technological developments have been a precondition for participation among some groups (e.g. the tampon in the case of young women) and in particular activities (such as indoor climbing and skiing, mountain biking and surf canoeing). BMX biking, skateboarding, windsurfing and even games such as KwikCricket and short tennis are dependent upon technological developments not only for (user-friendly) equipment but also suitable and appealing **facilities and venues** and surfaces. In this regard, the role of technological development in providing the preconditions for particular forms and levels of participation is also noteworthy. Technology has affected sport and its venues in a variety of ways. It has, for example, played a substantial part in (and, in some cases, been a precondition for) the emergence of new activities (e.g. skateboarding, kitesurfing and Nintendo's Wii *Fit*), the development of different versions of familiar activities (such as snowboarding, surf-canoeing and indoor climbing), access to activities requiring improvements

177

in clothing technology and affordability (water sports) and advances in some well-established sports (with golf clubs and tennis and squash rackets, for example). Some of these technological developments have facilitated increased levels of participation among young people in the form, for example, of climbing walls in school gymnasia and public sports halls, skateboard parks, mountain bike trails, and mechanized **health** and fitness **clubs**.

Time will tell whether and which modern technologies have had or are having a more-or-less significant impact upon sport generally and youth sport in particular. Relatively recent technological developments such as the Internet may well have as transformative an effect on leisure lives as did the radio, TV and the motor car from the 1930s onwards. Whether the application of modern technologies to sport will prove to be as transformative as the invention of the ball or the bicycle remains to be seen. Debates continue over whether technology has, in some way or other, fundamentally altered the character of particular sports and, as a consequence, whether this has been beneficial for or to the detriment of participants' enjoyment; whether, in other words, the pleasures associated with adventure sports (such as climbing), for example, have been sanitized and neutralized (by the development of indoor venues with 'bolted' protection and the provision of soft landing areas). In this regard, concern is often expressed about whether young people are becoming mere observers of endless leisure and sporting spectacles (Roberts, 2009) leading to them losing touch with reality while living in increasingly virtual (and isolated) worlds and a state of hyper-reality. However, even though they are spending more and more time online virtual reality seems more likely to add another dimension to the 'conventional real world activities, relationships and interests' (Roberts, 2009: 311) of young people rather than to revolutionize them. Similar caution needs to be exercised when blaming technology (and TV and computers, in particular) for the health/**obesity** epidemic (McElroy, 2008). It is simply not clear whether young people substitute TV and computer usage for physical **activity**, other sedentary activities or both. Biddle, Gorely, Marshall, Murdey and Cameron (2004) have shown that watching TV and playing video games are not strongly correlated with physical inactivity. Either way, the application of technology to sport is part of a wider process of scientific rationalization – in other words, the spread of calculating rationally how best to improve sports performance and/or the appeal of sports – that is likely to gather pace rather than diminish.

TIME

Time, as Roberts (2009) observes, is one of the major ways in which we organize our lives: 'Most things have proper times or best times, and need enough time' (p. 293). Beyond school **physical education**, much of young people's sports **participation** takes place during their **leisure**: that is to say, in the spare time left over after (school and part-time paid) **work** and so-called 'obligatory activities' (such as personal care and domestic chores). In this regard, time is conceived of as a resource which young people are relatively 'free' to use as they please.

Despite predictions in the 1960s and early 1970s that life would become more leisurely for young and old alike, time is a resource that more and more young people claim to be short of (Tremblay and Thoemmes, 2008) both absolutely and in relation to previous generations. Young people in industrialized societies are increasingly likely to report experiencing the so-called 'time crunch' (Roberts, 2009) as a result of growing time pressures (Zuzanek, 2005). Perceptions of increased time pressures notwithstanding, the trends in young people's 'free' or 'available' time are quite complex. Zuzanek's (2005) review of various studies of adolescents' time use and experience sampling in countries in Europe, North America and Australia revealed a number of interesting features. As with participation in sport, the amounts of free time adolescents reported tended to decline with **age**, particularly in the United Kingdom. The biggest source of time-pressure (and, consequently, 'stress') among teenagers in many countries was school – pupils from most of the countries reviewed by Zuzanek (2005) were spending approximately eight hours each day on school-related activities including approximately one hour of homework each day. Unsurprisingly, older adolescents spent more time on homework than their younger counterparts. An additional source of time pressure took the form of part-time paid work and there have been substantial increases in the amounts of time young people give over to this.

Paradoxically, however, despite widespread perceptions among young people that their stock of time is increasingly pressurized (by the demands of homework and the 'need' for paid work, in particular), in virtually all of the countries in Zuzanek's (2005) review, adolescents gained rather than lost free time during the 1990s. In addition, there were quite considerable differences in the amounts of free time available to young people in different countries. Students from the Scandinavian countries of Norway and Finland had the most free time – approximately 49 hours per week (or six hours on weekdays and longer on weekends) – while those from the Central European countries of Belgium, France, Holland as well as the United Kingdom had less – at 37–42 hours per week (Zuzanek, 2005).

The significance of time for youth sport

Time is, of course, a necessary resource for sport. Some sports (such as games of basketball, cricket and football) require set times for matches (and practices) and can consume several hours, while other games (such as squash) and physical recreations (e.g. aerobics) take up less time. Among adults, organized sport (especially in the form of team and club sport) is under pressure because of the difficulties people face in coordinating their schedules in order that they are all available at the same time once or twice a week (Roberts, 2009). In a similar vein, the shift away from highly organized activities in their leisure time by young people appears related to their preference for more convenient as well as more recreational and informal activities. Activities such as 'shooting hoops', kickabout soccer, skating of various kinds and biking of one sort or another have added appeal because they can be undertaken in small pockets of time at convenient locations (e.g. close to home in the street or a local venue), often alongside other pastimes such as socializing with a handful of the same and/or opposite sex **friends**, and can be picked up and dropped at the whim of the individual or group without time constraints being a hindrance.

Consistent with their perceptions of mounting time pressures, a lack of time is often cited as a barrier to general sports participation among young people. Time pressures are, however, unlikely to be a major reason for instances of non-participation in sport. After all, many young people who play sport face similar time constraints to those who do not participate as much. They cope by cutting back on such things as watching TV and sleeping and/or by multi-tasking. The amount of time spent by adolescents on 'personal needs', for example, declined in most countries over the two decades from the mid-1980s (Zuzanek, 2005) and most of this decline could be explained in terms of a reduction in time spent eating at home and, to a lesser extent, shortened sleep. The additional time pressures often reported by girls emanate in particular from their tendency to allocate more time to personal needs than boys (Zuzanek, 2005), especially in relation to personal care, dressing and grooming. In terms of multi-tasking, the average (undergraduate) student in a class of 130 polled at Kansas State University 'sleeps seven hours each night, spends one and a half hours watching TV, three and a half hours a day online, two and a half listening to music, two hours on the mobile phone, three hours in class, two hours eating, two hours working and three hours studying' (Attwood, 2008: 7) – a total of 26.5 hours! Studies such as this suggest that students – and, by extension, young people – are, indeed, adept at 'multi-tasking'.

Although young people evidently do experience time pressures brought about by part-time work, housework and increasing levels of school homework as they get older, time may be better viewed as a proxy justification for competing leisure interests in the sense that they may simply prefer to do other activities than playing sport. Where young people are already predisposed to participate in particular activities they tend to find the time to take part in one way or another. This is especially true of middle-class youth who are cultural and sporting omnivores. They, in particular, find the time to do most of most things by watching less TV, sleeping less and cutting back on their socializing. On top of this, time pressures exacerbate young people's tendency to engage with leisure activities (such as **lifestyle sports**) that are flexible and easy to fit into their busy lives.

In terms of youth sports participation it seems that 'what matters is not the amount of residual free time available to adolescents, but rather how and with whom young people spend their leisure time' (Staempfli, 2005: 679). In this regard, the significance of time for youth sport lies not merely in the availability of spare time but also how that time is organized (e.g. in the kinds of rigid patterns dictated by **club and organization**-based sport) and by whom (such as adults) and the ways in which some youngsters perceive such features of sport as undesirable, insofar as they restrict their freedom to choose not only what they do and when they do it but also who they do it with and the manner in which they participate (see **informalization** and lifestyle sports).

According to Feinstein *et al.* (2008), the largest changes in young people's time use over the past 30 years – most apparent in large increases in time spent travelling to leisure activities (most likely shopping and other consumer activities) and for domestic reasons – are the result of a growth in affluence and economic access to resources over this period. Increases in access to and use of personal transport/motor cars, and participation in leisure activities away from the home indicate a greater facility for expenditure in these areas as well, perhaps, as greater monitoring of children's activities by **parents**. Overall, over the last quarter of a century or more, young people have changed how they spend their time and this has been most apparent in their use of, and access to, transport and resources away from the home alongside their uptake of new media technologies. While young people continue to spend their discretionary time in ways that may not be deemed by various social commentators as either fruitful or productive, there is, according to Feinstein *et al.* (2008), little or no evidence that trends in young people's uses of time over the past 30 years have increased in a way likely to be deleterious to their physical and mental **health** or, one might add, their involvement in sport.

TRANSITIONS

Transitions are types of change – 'from a start point to a known destination' (Roberts, 2009: 299) – and the life-course of the individual (in other words, their social biography) is structured by these socially constructed transitions as much as by biological **age**. As far as youth are concerned, these transitions amount to moving toward adulthood via a number of economically and socially significant status transitions from full-time education to starting **work**, leaving home and becoming a householder, entering into a 'serious' relationship or relationships and starting a family (Roberts, 2009). Transitions to adulthood are the central dynamic in youth (Jones, 2009) and are often 'associated with social experimentation, the emergence from the family, and the development of the social self and of social **identity**' (James and James, 2009: 150) resulting in greater degrees of **independence** (including separation from parents and financial self-sufficiency) and the establishment of sexual identities and relationships.

Historically, 'the transition from childhood to adulthood, and thus the period described as youth was relatively short, with clearly defined and culturally pre-scribed rites of passage to mark the transition' (James and James, 2009: 150). Half a century ago, 'a person's early life could be conceptualized as consisting of well-defined phases' (Iacovou and Berthoud, 2001: 1) leading from childhood through youth – a period, characterized by the aforementioned transitions – to adulthood. For young people nowadays, however, things have changed and their experiences of growing up in the contemporary world 'are quite different from those encountered by earlier generations' (Furlong and Cartmel, 2007: 138). In recent decades, the life-course has become de-standardized in the sense that the ages at which young people experience the various transitions have ceased to be as predictable as they were through most of the twentieth century. Consequently, normative models of transition 'as linear, one-way, and relatively brief' (Jones, 2009: 85) no longer fit the lived experiences of young people and adults, 'Age has become less reliable as a marker of adult independence' (Jones, 2009: 95). In short, transitions to adulthood have, for many young people, become 'more diverse, complex and unequal than in previous generations' (Robb, 2007: 5).

To compound matters, adulthood itself has become less stable in terms of employment, marriage and parenthood (Jones, 2009). Developments in the global economy (specifically, the loss of the traditional youth labour market) have resulted in protracted labour market transitions as well as a trend towards lengthened participation in education with the result that very many young people remain economically and socially dependent on their **parents and families** for longer (Furlong and Cartmel, 2007). At the same time, however, the age at which the physical growth and development associated with puberty commences has become progressively lower. Altogether, 'youth as a social life space and a stage in the life course has grown' (James and James, 2009: 150) and the protracted transitions to adulthood 'have implications for the lifestyles which young people adopt and for the ways in which they spend their free **time**' (Furlong and Cartmel, 2007: 71). The upshot of these developments has been the normalization in Northern Europe and North America of an inter-mediate stage – between leaving the parental home and compulsory schooling and establishing independent family and economic lives (Roberts, 2003) – encompassing a greater variety in types of employment and family/housing circumstances to which youth transitions lead. For very many young people, not only has the life-stage of youth been prolonged but also their biographies have been individualized (see **individualization**) as the age at which and the order in which they make life-stage transitions (if they make them at all) has grown increasingly varied. Young people can become adult in one area of their lives but not others. Thus, 'While some young people are on extended transitions to adulthood, others are not' (Jones, 2009: 97) and, although most young people still associate independence chiefly with earning an income from work, nowadays they may do so while still living at home. In practice, school-to-work transitions frequently consist of not just one single event but of a sequence of transitions that varies significantly across individuals and countries (Brzinsky-Fay, 2007): leaving home can, for example, involve several leavings (Jones, 2009) with youngsters returning home after completion of full-time education, between jobs, and between accommodation and/or relationships. In sum, youth has become a period within which the paths towards adult roles 'are no longer linear, but synchronical and reversible' (Lahelma and Gordon, 2008: 211).

Despite the prevalence of **youth's new condition**, there are **social class** and **gender** dimensions to transitions. Middle-class transitions (and especially those of males) tend to be more protracted than those of working-class youngsters because of their economic, social and cultural **capital**. They are, for example, more inclined to stay in education longer and delay parenthood, and have the economic and social resources to do so.

The significance of transitions for youth sport

Transitions are potentially significant for sports **participation** because, during transitions, people's **leisure** (and sporting) lives can, and often do, unfreeze and reform: 'In Britain, which is probably a typical Western country in this respect, family transitions (such as marrying and becoming a parent) are junctures where lifestyles tend to unfreeze, some leisure activities are dropped or done less frequently, and are replaced by other pastimes (generally home-based)' (Roberts et al., 2009a: 275). Transitions such as those from education-to-employment and family and housing transitions 'are pivotal youth life-stage transitions in that young people's experiences during and progress through these transitions have implications for all other aspects of their lives' (Roberts, 2008: 197). Transitions from education to work are typically associated with higher levels of discretionary income which, in turn, can open up a range of leisure and sporting opportunities and **facilities and venues**. On the other hand, leaving full-time education will often mean leaving behind the kinds of subsidized, convenient and readily available sports facilities, as well as groups of like-minded peers, that may well sustain engagement with sport among marginal players and embellish that of committed players.

Lengthened transitions associated, for example, with spending longer in education and/or remaining single and childless has tended to result in a larger youth singles scene running alongside, if not quite blending, with twenty- and thirty-somethings in pubs, **clubs** and leisure venues generally. Some transitions, by contrast, may reduce levels of flexibility in young adults' leisure lives. Becoming a parent (and especially a single parent), for instance, tends to have a dramatic impact upon the leisure and sporting lives of those (and especially women) cast in such a role during youth or young adulthood.

In relation to class and gender dimensions to transitions, the middle classes and males are less likely than the working classes and females to reduce their sports **activity** following life-stage transitions to parenthood (Roberts *et al.*, 2009). Indeed, 'it is during young people's education to work and family/ housing transitions that social class and gender differences widen and harden, usually with long-term consequences' (Roberts, 2008: 13) and these tend to be reproduced in other areas of young people's lives, such as leisure and sport. Among working-class youth, as they grow older, street-based leisure gives way to **commercialized**, alcohol-based, young adult leisure: 'The move from the street to pubs and clubs tended to coincide with the cessation of public [state] schooling, physical maturation … the getting of income … and the establishment of new friendship groups via workplaces, training schemes or college course and separation from those made at school' (MacDonald and Shildrick, 2007: 344).

The sporting routes that young people follow are especially heavily constrained/influenced by education-to-work and family transitions. Coleman *et al.* (2008: 633) noted 'the detrimental impact of life transitions such as moving from college to full-time employment' among all groups of 15–19-year-old girls in their study including those who 'always' participated. At the same time, 'the tighter the life cycle squeeze' in youth – the more rapidly young people move from school to work, for example – 'the smaller will be the stocks of leisure capital which individuals preserve or build up and then carry into later life-stages' (Roberts, 2005: 7). Because it is working-class youth who remain most likely to make conventional transitions during their late teenage years, it is they who are most susceptible to doing so with limited stocks of sporting capital.

Transitions offer a useful illustration of why it is impossible to explain what is occurring elsewhere in young people's lives, such as sports **participation**, without understanding what is happening in the sub-structure of their lives and, in particular, the school-to-work and family transitions associated with youth (Roberts, 2003).

TYPOLOGIES

Typologies are the means by which phenomena (e.g. **leisure** and sporting activities) are organized into differing types. They are a way of identifying groups thought to share some common characteristics which, at the same time, distinguish them from other types. Sport, for example, can be subdivided into elite and leisure (or recreational) forms while particular sporting activities are often categorized as games, gymnastic activities, outdoor and adventurous activities and so forth. In a **PE** context, games tend to be further subdivided into invasion, partner and racket games.

Typologies are, therefore, forms of classification systems or schemes and can be developed or derived conceptually and/or empirically. Empirically based typologies arrange evidence into groups or clusters on the basis of observable features. They do so as a basis for further investigation, in the expectation that the empirical features used in the construction of the various types (e.g. sporty or sedentary youth) will have significant implications for understanding the behaviours of those belonging to them. In the social sciences (and, for that matter, in the fields of leisure and sport), it is quite common to construct conceptual typologies that bring together the more prominent or common characteristics of various social phenomena (such as sports **participation** and youth leisure styles) into so-called 'ideal types'. The notion of an ideal type is associated with the work of Max Weber and his desire to typologize or classify views and/or behaviours in order to help researchers move beyond mere description towards interpretation and analysis. Constructing an ideal type involves selecting what are taken to be the most important features of a group, situation or process then relating these to each other, logically (Roberts, 2009). In the process of interpreting patterns of sporting or leisure behaviour, for example, it can be useful to group together (into an ideal type) characteristics that are rarely all found together, empirically, in one person – such as physical inactivity, negative attitudes towards sport, unsatisfactory experiences of PE, overweight, and relatively high TV and computer usage – but constitute features commonly found among people whose overall lifestyles bear certain resemblances. Inevitably, ideal types do not and cannot express all the (descriptive or statistically generated) characteristics of, for example, more-or-less **sedentary** youth. Nor are ideal types intended as ideal versions of social phenomena in the sense of being ideologically or morally desirable. Rather, an ideal type is constructed, conceptually, as a heuristic device through which the emphasis given to certain relatively common elements of phenomena enable researchers to compare and contrast, measure, and interpret their findings from empirical study with the features of some or many similar types. In this regard, ideal or 'pure' types are intended simply as 'shorthand ways of making sense of complex aspects of the social world' (Maynard, 1989: 35) rather than as exact replications of them. As Weber (1949: 90) himself observed: 'An ideal type is formed by the one-sided accentuation of one or more points of view and by the synthesis of a great many diffuse, discrete, more or less present and occasionally absent concrete individual phenomena, which are arranged according to those one-sidedly emphasized viewpoints into a unified analytical construct.'

The significance of typologies for youth sport

In their study of school-**age** young people's participation in PE, **extra-curricular** and leisure sport, Sport England (2003a) generated an empirically based typology of young people's relationship to sport consisting of the following four types: *sporty types, untapped potential, unadventurous* and *reluctant participants*. The latter category of 'reluctant participants' was further subdivided into 'tolerators' and 'couch potatoes'. The *sporty types* (who made up 25 per cent of the youngsters aged 6–16 years in the study) enjoyed sport, had high participation levels and tended to be disproportionately male. Those with *untapped potential* (37 per cent) liked sport, without being as enthusiastic as the 'sporty types', but had relatively lower levels of participation. Younger females were particularly well represented in this group. The *unadventurous* (14 per cent) did not mind sport and had lower levels of participation – 11–14-year-old females were disproportionately over-represented in this latter typification as were particular ethnic groups. The *reluctant participants* (24 per cent) actively disliked sport, had lower participation levels and tended to be disproportionately female 13–16-year-olds. Within the *reluctant participators*, the so-called *tolerators* (15 per cent) – who were demographically representative – disliked sport but had above average levels of participation. By contrast, the *couch potatoes* (9 per cent) – preponderantly secondary school girls – disliked sport intensely and had low participation levels. Viewed graphically, these typologies express the normal distribution found in sports participation generally; that is, along a bell-shaped curve with small minorities at either end doing a lot or a little (often nothing) and, in the middle, the majority doing something on a reasonably frequent basis. Typifying young people in this way was seen by Sport England as a necessary step in targeting **policy** initiatives tailored to meet the needs of each of the categories, such as those with 'untapped potential'.

In Canada, typologies have been used to throw light on the significance of **parents and families** for young people's sports participation. Clark's (2008) review of Canadian survey data on young people's sports participation enabled him to typologize parents into two categories: those with 'no **time** for sports' and those 'keen about sports'. Clark observed that while money and access to sports **facilities** were positively correlated with sports participation, parental apathy appeared to be the biggest 'stumbling block' to participation. When asked about their reasons for not participating in sport, half of the parents who Clark subsequently categorized as 'having no time for sport' gave that as their reason while one quarter said they had no interest in sport. Few, Clark (2008) pointed out, cited a lack of sports facilities or money. He concluded, unsurprisingly perhaps, that the children of parents with no interest in sport had the lower rates of sports participation. On the other hand, parents who Clark referred to as 'I'm keen about sports' (and who participated regularly) were likely to play an important role in their children's attitudes to sport. Categorization of parents in this way led to supplementary questions regarding how strongly they felt about five reasons for their own participation. These parents 'were most likely to view their own participation in sports as very important for recreation and relaxation (71 per cent), as a way of maintaining physical **health** and fitness (67 per cent), and as a family activity (60 per cent). They were less likely to rate achievement and skill development (41 per cent) and developing new friendships (27 per cent) as very important reasons'. On the basis of these typologies, Clark was able to throw light on the ways in which parents might play a significant part in the sporting participation and **socialization** of their children.

WORK

There are three main activities in young people's lives: sleeping, work and **leisure**. For many young people, youth is a period in which paid work of one kind or another becomes an increasingly prominent feature of their lives alongside school work (attending school during the day and completing homework in the evening). Indeed, increasing numbers of young people are experiencing employment (through part-time work) and earning money (over and above pocket money) before they leave school. In England, for example, the percentage of young people with a regular part-time job in 2007 rose from up to 29 per cent among 12–13-year-olds to up to 40 per cent among 14–15-year-olds. Paper and milk rounds were the prime forms of part-time employment for young males while babysitting was commonplace among young females. In addition, paid housework was an important source of income for younger school-age children of both sexes (SHEU, 2007).

Despite the fact that more and more young people are undertaking part-time employment, they do not experience work pressures uniformly (Zuzanek, 2005). Whereas high school students in France, Finland, Germany and Belgium did little paid work (just over one hour per week on average), those in Canada, the United States and Holland carried the heaviest paid work loads, between 5 and 7 hours per week. Up to 24 per cent of the 14–15-year-old workers, in England, worked for more than 8 hours during the week with the average hours of weekly work being around 3.5 for 12–13-year-olds and up to 5.4 among 14–15-year-olds (SHEU, 2007). In their 2007 study of young people aged 11–15 years in England and Wales, Philo et al. (2009) found that around one-third (30 per cent) had worked for money, with older youngsters almost twice as likely as younger ones to report performing paid work. The majority had worked up to five hours in the preceding week.

The income derived from paid work usually supplements 'pocket money' which remains young people's main source of income. Eighty-one per cent of 11–15-year-olds in Philo et al.'s (2009) study received pocket money in the previous week with around one-quarter (26 per cent) receiving less than £5 and one-third (33 per cent) receiving over £12.50. Similarly, approximately one-third of 14–15-year-olds in the SHEU (2007) survey reported receiving more than £10 in pocket money 'last time'. Not all youngsters receive pocket money, however, and even for those who do it may not be a regular nor scheduled occurrence. Although pocket money tends to double in value during the secondary school age years – approximately one-third (29 per cent) of the 14–15-year-olds received more than £10 per week – this does not appear to diminish young people's perceptions of paid work as desirable and, in some

187

cases, necessary if they are to lead the leisure lifestyles they aspire to. While the average earnings of 14–15-year-olds in the SHEU (2007) survey was around £16.50, when pocket money and part-time paid employment were put together almost one in five (18 per cent) earned more than £30 in the previous week.

The significance of work for youth sport

Alongside the media, leisure time activities and consumption, earning money by working part-time is an increasingly prominent feature of **youth lifestyles** (Telama *et al.*, 2005). Nevertheless, the place of paid work in young people's lives is somewhat paradoxical. On the one hand, part-time work tends not only to be limited to menial tasks (e.g. filling supermarket shelves) but also detracts from other areas of young people's lives such as physically active leisure and sleep (Zuzanek, 2005). On the other hand, while paid work adds to young people's perceptions of pressure and stress, it is also viewed as liberating and enabling – income from work gives young people greater control over their leisure lives and, in particular, their consumption habits. Because money is an increasingly significant aspect of young people's leisure (especially around age 16 years and as they approach youth), part-time paid work is typically undertaken to facilitate leisure-time consumption. Although visits to a 'leisure/sports centre' were third (30 per cent) and fourth (28 per cent) in the top four items purchased by 10–11-year-old males and females, respectively, in the SHEU (2007) survey, it disappeared from the top four purchases of 12–13-year-old males and females and older youngsters. Dominating the top items among 14–15-year-old males were sweets, soft drinks, fast food and clothes/footwear and for 14–15-year-olds females sweets, clothes/footwear, soft drinks and cosmetics/toiletries. In this regard, earning and/or acquiring money opens up a broader array of commercialized leisure opportunities to young people than they have been accustomed to during childhood, including those activities typically associated with adult leisure, such as shopping, drinking and 'clubbing'. Thus, part-time incomes and pocket-money are used by youth to fund leisure lives akin to those of adults in terms of expenditure on music, clothing, information **technology**, alcohol and other forms of commercialized leisure.

Overall, by supplementing their other sources of income (predominantly pocket money), paid work provides young people with greater levels of discretionary income thereby allowing them to (i) gain greater (financial) independence from their families and (ii) lead more adult-like and increasingly consumerist lifestyles in the form, for example, of purchasing fashionable clothing and music and 'clubbing'. Income acquired through part-time work opens up a range of opportunities including the opportunity to explore (by imitation) young adult behaviours including those that are risky to **health**, such as consuming alcohol and experimenting with **drugs** – among young people and youth, higher levels of income tend to be associated with a range of health-**risk** behaviours such as smoking, drinking alcohol and consuming fast food (SHEU, 2007). It also enables those inclined to do so to consume more and a wider variety of sporting opportunities, including relatively expensive ones, such as indoor skiing, golf and health and fitness gyms, as well as the relatively inexpensive commercial activities such as tenpin bowling and ice-skating.

YOUTH CULTURES AND LIFESTYLES

All societies generate socially acquired (or learned) forms of beliefs and behaviours – in other words, cultures – and these are 'often distinctive to particular social or ethnic groups' (Jones, 2009: 19). Broadly speaking, therefore, 'culture' refers to more or less shared ways of life and these represent a potentially profound source of **identity** for their members. The concept of youth cultures implies that in some areas of their lives youth adopt similar beliefs, attitudes and behaviours. Youth cultures are, nonetheless, inevitably defined in relation to the broader societal cultures in which they are located. Because they tend to involve a combination of more general societal attitudes and practices alongside those particular to their group, youth cultures are often referred to as 'subcultures' (groups within a group) – containing some shared elements of the host or parent culture alongside some distinctive features. When young people's beliefs and practices are deemed not only distinct but also deviant, even hostile and rebellious, to the dominant or host culture, they are often viewed not only as subcultures but as counter-cultures. In this regard, there is a tendency among the media, politicians and the general public – and even those working with young people in sport – 'to emphasise the unconventional, deviant and nonconformist aspects of sub-cultural groups' (Kehily, 2007a: 23) and, by exaggerating the threat such groups supposedly pose to social order, generate a **moral panic**.

The increasing segregation of young people (e.g. via schools) from the adult world over a century or so has contributed significantly to the development of relatively inward-looking youth subcultures – especially among working-class youngsters. It was, however, the material prosperity of the developed world in the second half of the twentieth century that created the conditions for the emergence of recognizable youth cultures. Although they predate the Second World War, it was during the second half of the twentieth century that youth cultures became sufficiently distinctive (and, in the popular consciousness, problematic) to be identified as such (Miles, 2000; Roberts, 2006). From the 1950s onwards the 'adolescent' peer group became a significant reference point for young people whose self-identities were at least partially formed in the context of peer groups as sites of secondary **socialization**. These subcultures were expressed in dress style, music and language such that by the end of the

1950s, youth cultures or styles had become quite distinctive and increasingly visible (Jones, 2009; Roberts, 2006).

Youth cultures or subcultures amount to the styles that youth peer groups construct from the 'music, dress, places and activities' that they 'cultivate or adopt in their **leisure** time' (Roberts, 2009: 325) and 'much ink has been spilt' (Bramham, 2005: 199) on this topic over half a century or more. In the 1960s, youth cultures were developed and dominated by young, newly affluent skilled working-class men (Roberts, 1999). Nowadays, however, the term has broadened to incorporate youth from all **social class, gender** and **ethnic** groupings and, since the 1970s, young people as a whole have become a substantial new consumer market in the developed world, acquiring in the process seemingly unbounded options from which to choose their own particular and preferred lifestyles (Miles, 2000). Indeed, rising affluence and the process of **individualization** have increasingly been expressed in the splintering and fragmentation of young people's leisure lifestyles and tastes (Miles, 2000; Roberts, 1999). This, in turn, is said by some to have resulted in the death of recognizable subcultures, in the sense that (i) youth cultures 'no longer map neatly onto any other social divisions' (Roberts, 2009: 326) such as social class and (ii) group coherence and consistency is no longer as clear cut as it was – groups are no longer as distinct in terms of values, styles and tastes as, for example, in the 1970s when the term originated (Muggleton, 2005). Nor do contemporary youth subcultures appear to be characterized by a shared identity and commitment to the group among its members. The upshot is that it is better, or so it is claimed, to talk of 'neo-tribes' [or 'clubcultures' as Redhead (1997) has termed them]. On this view, subcultures (neo-tribes/club cultures) are, in reality, 'loose groups of young people whose stylised tastes and lifestyles come together during moments of shared interest' (Kehily, 2007a: 27) rather than enduring groups with a core of shared or common (often class- and gender-based) characteristics; hence, the growing preference for the term 'lifestyle' rather than subculture to describe the patterns of (leisure) consumption of particular groups.

The term lifestyle refers, specifically, to the choices (young) people make in relation to such things as hairstyle, clothes, music and leisure activities in general, and preferred use of **time** and places to visit; in other words, the things young people buy and do and the particular tastes or styles these are taken to represent. Despite the preference in some quarters for terms such as neo-tribe and lifestyle – over subculture – as a means of expressing the shifting and ephemeral nature of collective associations as young people switch from one group to another (Jones, 2009), the fact that such 'bundles of tastes, purchases and activities which cluster together' and constitute youth lifestyles 'confer identities, and allow those concerned to be identified as a particular kind of person' (Roberts, 2009: 149) has, nevertheless, resulted in the persistence of youth *cultures* as the preferred explanatory concept. Indeed, amid any discussion of individualized, consumption-oriented leisure lifestyles among youth, it is important to remember that young people are not and never have been a homogenous group (Roberts, 1999; Telama *et al.*, 2005) and that opportunities to 'construct' lifestyles remain unequally distributed among all social groups (Roberts, 1999). There is, indeed, a tendency in discussion on youth lifestyles and consumption to overlook or downplay social divisions and inequalities while, at the same time, exaggerating 'young people's opportunities freely to pick and choose between the many "lifestyles", "scenes", "neo-tribes" and "clubculture" identities on offer in the contemporary "supermarket of style" ' (MacDonald and Shildrick, 2007: 339). As plausible as the post-modernist claim – that 'the identities that lifestyles confer are displacing and reducing the significance of longer-standing social markers such as social class and gender' (Roberts, 2009: 149) – appears in theory, in practice, 'There is a tendency for the same people to be active in, and to purchase a very wide range of leisure goods and services' (p. 149). This is not to deny, however, that young people can be committed to the relatively identifiable groups (Muggleton, 2005) which continue to provide them with a basis for aspects of their identities, in the form of a sense of belonging and style. All in all, youth cultures in general as well as particular subcultures need to be viewed processually – as fluid and developing entities characterized by continuity as well as change – rather than as fixed and stable groups.

The significance of youth cultures for youth sport

The relationship between youth cultures and sports **participation** patterns is complex not least because of the evident splintering and fragmentation of young people's leisure lifestyles and tastes (Miles, 2000; Roberts, 1999). Increasing demands on young people's **time** is, as Coalter (1999: 29) says of adults' lives, 'paralleled by a shift to more **individualized** activity and a decline in the frequency of some of the most popular activities' such as team games. Nevertheless, it seems that participation in sport and physical **activity** can be, and often is, incorporated into a variety of (youth) lifestyles (Smith, 2006; Telama *et al.*, 2005). In their study of lifestyle and physical activity among 12- and 15-year-olds, Telama *et al.* (2005) found that high levels of physical activity were related to more than one lifestyle group and even among the most active group of young people – the 'sports participants' – sport was not their only interest. They were also active in, among other things, computer games and although, 'Those who were interested in computer games and TV watching were the most inactive' (Telama *et al.*, 2005: 115), many who played computer games were also physically active. **Participation** in sport, it seems, can be and often is incorporated into a variety of lifestyles (Smith, 2006; Telama *et al.*, 2005).

For their part, post-modern theorists of youth sport would argue that too much emphasis has been placed on social structures, such as social class and gender, in relation to youth leisure lifestyles and not enough attention paid

191

to the independence from such structures of aspects of people's lives such as leisure and sport and the significance of consumption in patterns of sports participation (Malcolm, 2008). More attention should be given, they argue, to the ways in which people (and young people in particular) use activities such as sport to develop lifestyles and to enhance their chosen identities in a deliberate, purposeful and self-conscious manner. The emergence and development of different youth sports participation styles over the last three decades or more (Scheerder *et al.*, 2005b) are said to epitomize the trend towards youth independence and consumption in sporting terms. Scheerder *et al.* (2005b: 325) explain the recent growth of **club**-based sports in Flanders as 'characteristic of contemporary zap culture rather than a long-lasting club membership'; in other words, a style of participation more consistent with the widespread growth in popularity of **lifestyle sports**. In contrast, other, more mainstream sociologists of youth and leisure are prone to observe that whatever impressions might be formed regarding the individualized and ephemeral character of much of young people's leisure, in point of fact young people's leisure lifestyles are **age– and life-stage** related (Roberts, 2009). Post-modern and post-structural analyses tend, in other words, to focus too much on 'choice' and not enough on the ways in which, in the words of the famous sociological dictum, people choose but seldom, if ever, in conditions of their own choosing. Put another way, previously clear-cut social divisions have become blurred not simply because they have tended to be portrayed in falsely dichotomous terms, nor due to the fact that young people now live in a post-modern world of endless consumer choices, but rather because more and more youngsters are located in a variety of groups which overlap and thereby camouflage the underlying, if sometimes diluted, consequences of age, class, gender and ethnicity.

Even if they do not constitute a post-modern condition it seems that leisure-time activities have, nevertheless, taken on increasing importance in young people's lifestyles and identities. Days spent in the surf, evenings preoccupied with playing football or basketball, weekends taken up by mountain biking or climbing, weeks spent skiing or months of leisure time given over to perfecting skateboard manoeuvres do, indeed, express the significance of such activities to young people (and, for that matter, adults) at various times in their lives. They are highly unlikely, however, to offer people similar identities to those grounded in gender, social class and ethnicity or, for that matter, occupation.

All told, the concept of subculture can throw light on young people's (sporting) lifestyles and the manner in which distance between such subcultural groups and 'mainstream' cultures (and, for that matter, sporting cultures) appear to emerge and grow. Youth cultures, or subcultures, are most prominent in leisure because of the relative freedom that leisure provides, for example, to establish distinct modes of dress, musical tastes and drink, tobacco and drug habits. Such subcultures are often perceived by the participants or members as involving a search for pleasurable excitement and '**risk**'.

192

YOUTH'S NEW CONDITION

'Youth's new condition' refers to a significant change in the condition of youth in recent decades involving a destabilization of youth as a relatively clearly defined life-stage and associated set of experiences.

In recent decades, the wider economic and social forces 'that have been destabilizing employment, **gender**, and **age** roles' (Hendry *et al.*, 2002: 1) have substantially altered the life-stage of youth. Across Europe, the **transition** between youth and adulthood has become 'a long-drawn-out and unpredictable process' (Iacovou and Berthoud, 2001: 1) as the typical ages at which young people cross thresholds into **work**, parenthood, their own accommodation and the like have risen. Indeed, incomplete transitions to some adult roles are increasingly common in the Western world.

This 'new condition of youth' (Bynner, 2001; Roberts, 2006a) has a number of defining features. First, the life-stage has, in several respects, been prolonged (Hendry *et al.*, 2002; Roberts, 2006a). More young people are spending longer periods in full-time education in order to acquire the advanced educational qualifications and different skills deemed necessary, a consequence of which is delayed transitions into the labour market (Furlong and Cartmel, 1997; Roberts, 2006a). Because more young people are remaining in education longer, their dependence upon their families has also been prolonged (Roberts, 2006a). For increasing numbers of youngsters, however, families are less stable and there is a growing tendency for young people to live alone when they are not living in the parental home (Iacovou and Berthoud, 2001). Second, young people's biographies have become more individualized inasmuch as they have more varied experiences in education (and especially in post-compulsory education), in the workplace, in **leisure** and in the social networks to be found in all these places (Wallace and Kovatcheva, 1998; Iacovou and Berthoud, 2001; Wyn *et al.*, 2002; Roberts, 2006a). More young people are, for example, attending non-local secondary schools and universities (Roberts, 2008) – and moving about more in the process – where they study more individualized combinations of modules and degrees and acquire particular sets of experiences in part-time work. When, eventually, they enter the workforce youth tend to be underemployed: they are, in other words, 'working less than continuously, often for less than full-time hours when they are in work, and for less than full adult salaries' (Roberts, 2008: 199). In addition, 'their typical jobs are well beneath the levels for which they are qualified' (p. 199). One consequence of this has been the difficulty young people experience in establishing self-**identities** around working roles. The upshot is that 'there are no longer "normal" biographies; that is, typical sequences in the transition from youth to adulthood, in contemporary societies' (Schizzerotto and Lucchini, 2002: 7). Third, as a result of the frequent dearth of 'clear pathways to be followed' (Tolonen, 2005: 344), young people's futures have become a good deal more uncertain (Roberts, 2006a). Fourth, and as a corollary of their uncertain futures and the apprehension caused by the economic and social situations in which they find themselves, all the steps that young people might take have a more pronounced sense of uncertainty and **risk** attached to them than hitherto (Roberts, 2006a). To compound matters, the relatively individualized character of their experiences and situations leads young people to feel more responsible for their current and future circumstances.

Overall, half a century ago, young people lived with 'more clearly patterned and predictable life experiences' (Payne, 2006: 11), including greater certainty regarding their prospective work and **leisure** lives. Nowadays, however, as the older 'solid' social formations have decomposed (Roberts, 2008), youth, as a life-stage, has become more individualized (Hendry *et al.*, 2002). One by-product of this has been that the leisure (and leisure-sport) 'tastes and styles' of youth have also fragmented (Hendry *et al.*, 2002: 1).

The significance of youth's new condition for youth sport

As a consequence of the 'changes in the social context' and the 'meaning of childhood and youth' (Wyn *et al.*, 2002: 23) there have been substantial developments in recent decades in young people's day-to-day and week-to-week leisure styles (Roberts, 1996b, 2006a). The upshot has been a trend, over several decades, towards every young person 'having a particular combination of leisure interests and activities, and a unique leisure career' with individuals developing 'personal stocks of leisure skills and interests' (Roberts, 1999: 43) and constructing 'their own leisure biographies' (Zeijl *et al.*, 2001: 380). This process has, in turn, led to corresponding changes in the ways in which young people participate in sport (Roberts, 1996a, 1996b).

One such trend has been the increased appeal of informal, casual, recreational activities. In this respect, patterns of **participation** in leisure-sport in recent years are largely explained by the compatibility of **lifestyle activities** with the broader trends in young people's lives. In particular, the process of **individualization** associated with youth's new condition appears to have played a substantial part in the increased popularity among young people of more individual, more informal leisure and sporting activities over the course of the last 40 years.

The extension of youth as a life-stage has also resulted in young people spending longer periods in education. This has been one of the ways in which an indirect consequence of delayed transitions to adulthood has been an extension of the period of potential **socialization** into sport. Delayed transitions result, for example, in extended dependence on **parents** for various resources while prolonging the potential socializing influence of parents (Jones, 2009) in relation to leisure behaviours. At the same time, longer periods in education mean longer spells in close proximity on a daily basis to **friends and peers** as well as subsidized and plentiful sports **facilities** and, therefore, a range of sporting and leisure opportunities.

Life for many young people in the second half of the twentieth century increasingly involved far more leisure and sporting provision and choice and less socially generated prescription as larger numbers of people – in the developed world at least – became financially better off enabling them to take advantage of newly emerging (windsurfing, mountain-biking and other such adventure sports, for example) and rapidly developing (for instance, golf) as well as increasingly accessible and democratized (such as skiing) sports. This has encouraged some to believe that (young) people's **identities** have become increasingly tied up with what they consume in their leisure **time**, as they are increasingly able to choose what they do. Patterns remain, nonetheless, and the emergence of a new condition for youth has not eradicated predictability in young people's working and leisure lives. Young people from families with low incomes cannot easily choose to ski or to join a golf club. Similarly, while more girls than ever are playing football, it remains a fraction of the numbers of young men doing so. At the same time, disabled youngsters still find it extremely difficult (and often impossible) to access some sporting practices and venues (mountain and water sports being obvious examples). On the other hand, predictability was never so clear cut as sporting patterns of the twentieth century were taken to imply. Even though the contours of youngsters' educational and sporting lives were strongly structured by social class, gender, ethnicity and other social dynamics there remained, by degrees, relatively unique dimensions to their leisure lives. Some working-class young males, for instance, climbed rock faces (there was, for example, a strong and growing tradition of young working-class male climbers pushing back the boundaries of climbing in North Wales and Scotland from the 1950s) and not all middle-class grammar school boys played rugby in preference to soccer. Nevertheless, leisure and sport were far more clearly structured by, among other social dynamics, class and gender than they are contemporarily and the blurring of class and gender patterns of sports participation is a feature of youth's new condition and contemporary youth lifestyles.

REFERENCES

Abbott, P. (2006) 'Gender', in G. Payne (ed) *Social Divisions* (pp. 65–101). Basingstoke: Palgrave MacMillan (first edition, 2000).

Abbott-Chapman, J., Denholm, C., and Wyld, C. (2008) 'Gender differences in adolescent risk taking: Are they diminishing? An Australian Intergenerational Study', *Youth & Society*, 40(1): 131–154.

Alley, T.R. and Hicks, C.M. (2005) 'Peer attitudes towards adolescent participants in male- and female-oriented sports', *Adolescence*, 40: 273–280.

Anderssen, S.A., Carroll, S., Urdal, P., and Holme, I. (2007) 'Combined diet and exercise intervention reverses the metabolic syndrome in middle-aged males: results from the Oslo Diet and Exercise Study', *Scandinavian Journal of Medicine & Science in Sports*, 17(6): 687–695.

Annerstedt, C. (2008) 'Physical education in Scandinavia with a focus on Sweden: A comparative perspective', *Physical Education & Sport Pedagogy*, 13(4): 303–318.

Arai, S. and Pedlar, A. (2003) 'Moving beyond individualism in leisure theory: a critical analysis of concepts of community and social engagement', *Leisure Studies*, 22(3): 185–202.

Armstrong, N. (1991) 'Children's physical activity patterns: The implications for physical education', in N. Armstrong and A. Sparkes (eds) *Issues in Physical Education* (pp. 9–10). Champaign, IL: Human Kinetics.

Armstrong, N. and Welsman, J.R. (2006) 'The physical activity patterns of European youth with reference to methods of assessment', *Sports Medicine*, 36(12): 1067–1086.

Association of Public Health Observatories (APHO) (2009) *Indications of Public Health in the English Regions. 10: Drug Use*. York: Association of Public Health Observatories.

Attwood, R. (2008) 'Student truths generate online hit', *Times Higher Education*, 7–13 August, 2008, No. 1, 857, p. 7.

Bailey, R., Morley, D., and Dismore, H. (2009) 'Talent development in physical education: A national survey of policy and practice in England', *Physical Education and Sport Pedagogy*, 14(1): 59–72.

Balding, J. (2001) *Young People in 2001*. Exeter: Schools Health Education Unit.

Barnes, C., Mercer, G., and Shakespeare, T. (1999) *Exploring Disability. A Sociological Introduction*. Cambridge: Polity Press.

Beck, U. (1992) *Risk Society. Towards a New Modernity*. London: Sage.

Ben-Porat, A. (2009) 'Six decades of sport, from a game to commodity: Football as a parable', *Sport in Society*, 12(8): 999–1012.

Benn, T. (2005) 'Race and physical education, sport and dance', in K. Green and K. Hardman (eds) *Physical Education: Essential Issues* (pp. 197–219). London: Sage Publications.

Biddle, S. (2006) 'Researching the psycho-social outcomes of youth sport'. Paper presented at *Researching Youth Sport: Diverse Pespectives*. Institute of Youth Sport/Institute of Sport Policy Conference, Loughborough University, 20 September, 2006.

Biddle, S., Coalter, F., O'Donovan, T., MacBeth, J., Nevill, M., and Whitehead, S. (2005) *Increasing Demand for Sport and Physical Activity by Girls. Research Report No. 100*. Edinburgh: SportScotland.

Biddle, S.J.H., Gorely, T., Marshall, S.J., Murdey, I., and Cameron, N. (2004) 'Physical activity and sedentary behaviours in youth: Issues and controversies', *Journal of the Royal Society for the Promotion of Health*, 124: 29–33.

Biddle, S.J.H., Gorely, T., and Stensel, D. (2004) 'Health-enhancing physical activity and sedentary behaviour in children and adolescents', *Journal of Sports Sciences*, 22: 679–701.

Biddle, S.J.H., Treasure, D., and Wang, C.K.J. (2008) 'Motivational characteristics', in Alan L. Smith and Stuart J.H. Biddle (eds) *Youth Physical Activity and Sedentary Behavior* (pp. 193–213). Champaign, IL: Human Kinetics.

Biddle, S.J.H. and Mutrie, N. (2008) *Psychology of Physical Activity. Determinants, Well-Being and Interventions*. Abingdon: Routledge (first edition, 2001).

Birchwood, D., Roberts, K., and Pollock, G. (2008) 'Explaining differences in sport participation rates among young adults: Evidence from the South Caucasus', *European Physical Education Review*, 14(3): 283–300.

Blackshaw, T. and Long, J. (2005) 'What's the big idea? A critical exploration of the concept of social capital and its incorporation into leisure policy discourse', *Leisure Studies*, 24(3): 239–258.

Blacke, F. (2009) 'Growing up with the Internet', *Society Now*, 5: 12.

Blauwet, C. (2007) 'Promoting the health and human rights of individuals with a disability through the paralympic movement', in C. Higgs and Y. Vanlandewijck (eds) *Sport for Persons with a Disability* (pp. 21–35). Berlin, International Council on Sport Science and Physical Education.

Bloyce, D. and Smith, A. (2009) *Sport Development and Policy in Society*. London: Routledge.

Boreham, C. and Riddoch, C. (2001) 'The physical activity, fitness and health of children', *Journal of Sports Sciences*, 19: 915–929.

Borodulin, K., Laatikainen, T., Juolevi, A., and Jousilahti, P. (2008) 'Thirty-year trends of physical activity in relation to age, calendar time and birth cohort in Finnish adults', *The European Journal of Public Health*, 18: 339–344.

Bourdieu, P. (1984) *Distinction: A Social Critique of the Judgement of Taste* (R. Nice, Trans.). Cambridge, MA: Harvard University Press.

Brackenridge, C.H. (2001) *Spoilsports: Understanding and Preventing Sexual Exploitation in Sport*. London: Routledge.

Brackenridge, C. (2006) 'Youth sport refocused—a review essay on Paulo David's human rights in youth sport: a critical review of children's rights in competitive sports', *European Physical Education Review*, 12(1): 119–125.

Brackenridge, C. (2008) 'Child sexual abuse', in D. Malcolm (ed) *The Sage Dictionary of Sports* Studies (pp. 41–42). London: Sage Publications.

Braddock, J.H., Sokol-Katz, J., Greene, A., and Basinger-Fleishman, L. (2005) 'Uneven playing fields: State variations in boys' and girls' access to and participation in high school interscholastic sports', *Sociological Spectrum*, 25(2): 231–250.

Bramham, P. (2003) 'Boys, masculinity and PE', *Sport, Education and Society*, 8(1): 57–71.

Bramham, P. (2005) 'Habits of a lifetime? Youth, generation and lifestyles', in Bramham, P. and Caudwell, J. (eds) *Sport, Active Leisure and Youth Cultures*. Brighton: LSA Publications, No. 86: 195–206.

Bramham, P. and Caudwell, J. (2005) 'Editors' introduction: sport, active leisure and youth cultures', in Bramham, P. and Caudwell, J. (eds) *Sport, Active Leisure and Youth Cultures*. Brighton: LSA Publications, No. 86: v–xiii.

197

Breedveld, K. (2003) 'Sport and social capital. Good hopes and high fears'. Paper presented at *2nd World Congress of Sociology of Sport Conference*. Cologne, Germany, 18–21 June.

Breivik, G. (2007) *Norsk Monitor 1985–2007*. Paper presented at Norgeidrettshogskole, Oslo, July, 2007.

Brettschneider, W.-D. (1992) 'Adolescents, leisure, sport and lifestyle', in T. Williams, L. Almond, and A. Sparkes (eds) *Sport and Physical Activity: Moving Towards Excellence. The Proceedings of the AISEP World Convention* (pp. 536–550). Spon: London.

Brettschneider, W-D. and Naul, R. (2004) *Study of Young People's Lifestyles and Sedentariness and the Role of Sport in the Context of Education as a Means of Restoring the Balance*. Brussels: European Commission.

Brettschneider, W.-D. and Sack, H.-G. (1996) 'Germany', in P. De Knop, L.-M. Engstrom, B. Skirstad, and M.R. Weiss (eds) *Worldwide Trends in Youth Sport*. Champaign: Illinois.

Brodersen, N.H., Steptoe, A., Boniface, D.R., and Wardle, J. (2007) 'Trends in physical activity and sedentary behaviour in adolescence: ethnic and socioeconomic differences', *British Journal of Sports Medicine*, 41(3):140–144.

Brustad, R.J., Vilhjmalsson, R., and Fonseca, A.M. (2008) 'Organized sport and physical activity promotion', in Alan L. Smith and Stuart J.H. Biddle (eds) *Youth Physical Activity and Sedentary Behavior* (pp. 351–375). Champaign, IL: Human Kinetics.

Brzinsky-Fay, C. (2007) 'Lost in transition? Labour market entry sequences of school leavers in Europe', *European Sociological Review*, 23(4): 409–422.

Burgess, E. (2007) 'Participation in sport', in C. Higgs and Y. Vanlandewijck (eds) *Sport for Persons with a Disability* (pp. 35–44). Berlin: ICCSPE.

Butterly, R. (2008) 'Fitness for sport and health', in D. Kirk, C. Cooke, A. Flintoff, and J. McKenna (eds) *Key Concepts in Sport and Exercise Sciences* (pp. 62–66). London: Sage Publications.

Bynner, J. (2001) 'British youth transitions in comparative perspective', *Journal of Youth Studies,* 4(1): 5–23.

Caine, D.J. (2010) 'Are kids having a rough time of it in sports?', *British Journal of Sports Medicine*, 44: 1–3.

Campbell, D. (2005) 'Youngsters put off for life by state of sport in schools', *The Observer Sport*, 24th April, 2005, p. 8.

Carless, D. (2008) 'Physical activity and mental health', in D. Kirk, C. Cooke, A. Flintoff, and J. McKenna (eds) *Key Concepts in Sport and Exercise Sciences* (pp. 103–105). London: Sage Publications.

Carter, D.S.G., Bennetts, C., and Carter, S.M. (2003) ' "We're not sheep": Illuminating the nature of the adolescent peer group in effecting lifestyle choice', *British Journal of Sociology of Education*, 24(2): 225–241.

Casper, J. (2007) 'Sport commitment, participation frequency and purchase intention based on age, gender, income and skill level with US tennis participants', *European Sport Management Quarterly*, 7(3): 269–282.

Central Council for Physical Recreation, (CCPR) (2001) *Charter for Physical Education and School Sport*. London: CCPR.

Centre for Sport Policy Studies, University of Toronto (2008) *Opportunity Knocks! Increasing Participation in Canada as a Result of Success at the Vancouver Olympics*. Position paper. Toronto, ON: University of Toronto.

Charilaou, M. Karekla, M., Constantinou, M., and Price, S. (2009) 'Relationship between physical activity and type of smoking behavior among adolescents and young adults in Cyprus', *Nicotine & Tobacco Research*, 11(8): 969–976. http://ntr. oxfordjournals.org/cgi/content/abstract/11/8/96. Downloaded 7 January, 2010.

Choi, B.C., Hunter, D.J., Tsou, W., and Sainsbury, P. (2005) 'Diseases of comfort: primary cause of death in the 22nd century', *Journal of Epidemiology & Community Health*, 59(12): 1030–1034.

Clarke, G. (2006) 'Sexuality and physical education', in D. Kirk, D. Macdonald, and M. O'Sullivan (eds) *The Handbook of Physical Education* (pp. 723–739). London: Sage.

Clark, W. (2008) 'Kid's sports', *Canadian Social Trends*. Statistics Canada, Catalogue No. 11–008.

Coakley, J. (2004) *Sport in Society. Issues and Controversies* (eighth edition). New York: McGraw-Hill (first edition, 1978).

Coakley, J. (2009) 'The good father. Parental expectations and youth sports', in Tess Kay (ed) *Fathering Through Sport and Leisure* (pp. 40–50). London: Routledge.

Coakley, J. and White, A. (1999) 'Making decisions. How young people become involved and stay involved in sports', in J. Coakley and P. Donnelly (eds) *Inside Sports* (pp. 77–85). London: Routledge.

Coalter, F. (1996) *Trends in Sports Participation. Position Paper Prepared for the Sports Council*. Institute for Leisure and Amenity Management Annual Conference. Birmingham.

Coalter, F. (1999) 'Sport and recreation in the United Kingdom: Flow with the flow or buck the trends?' *Managing Leisure*, 4(1): 24–39.

Coalter, F. (2004a) 'Future sports or future challenges to sport?' in Sport England (ed) *Driving Up Participation: The Challenge for Sport* (pp. 79–86). London: Sport England.

Coalter, F. (2004b) 'Stuck in the blocks? A sustainable sporting legacy', in A. Vigor, M. Mean, and C. Tims (eds) *After the Goldrush. A Sustainable Olympics for London*. London: Institute for Public Policy Research and DEMOS.

Coalter, F. (2005) 'Sport, social inclusion and crime reduction', in G.E. Faulkner and A.H. Taylor (eds) *Exercise, Health and Mental Health. Emerging Relationships* (pp. 190–209). Abingdon: Routledge.

Coalter, F. (2007) *A Wider Social Role for Sport. Who's Keeping the Score?* Abingdon: Routledge.

Coalter, F. (2009) *Monitoring and Evaluation: Families of Programmes or Families of Mechanisms?*, Guest lecture, University of Chester, 20 November, 2009.

Cockburn, C. and Clarke, G. (2002) ' "Everybody's looking at you!" Girls negotiating the "femininity deficit" they incur in physical education', *Women's Studies International Forum*, 25(6): 651–665.

Cohen, L., Perales, D.P., and Steadman, C. (2005) 'The O word: Why the focus on obesity is harmful to community health', *Californian Journal of Health Promotion*, 3(3): 154–161.

Coleman, L., Cox, L., and Roker, D. (2008) 'Girls and young women's participation in physical activity: Psychological and social influences', *Health Education Research*, 23(4): 633–647.

Colquhoun, D. (1991) 'Health-based physical education. The ideology of healthism and victim-blaming', *Physical Education Review*, 14(1): 5–13.

Collins, M. (2003) 'Social exclusion from sport and leisure', in Barrie Houlihan (ed) *Sport and Society. A Student Introduction* (pp. 67–88). London: Sage Publications.

Collins, M. (2008) 'Social exclusion from sport and leisure', in Ben Oakley and Martin Rhys (eds) *The Sport and Fitness Sector. An Introduction* (pp. 85–91). Abingdon: Routledge.

Collins, M.F. and Buller, J.R. (2003) 'Social exclusion from high-performance sport. Are all talented young sports people being given an equal opportunity of reaching the Olympic podium?', *Journal of Sport & Social Issues*, 27(4): 420–442.

Cook, D.T. (2006) 'Leisure and consumption', in Chris Rojek, Susan M. Shaw, and Anthony J. Veal (eds) *A Handbook of Leisure Studies* (pp. 304–316). Basingstoke: Palgrave Macmillan.

Cote, J.E. (2002) 'The role of identity capital in the transition to adulthood: The individualisation thesis examined', *Journal of Youth Studies*, 5(2): 117–134.

Cox, L., Coleman, L., and Roker, D. (2005) *Understanding Participation in Sport: What determines Sports Participation Among 15–19 Year Old Women?* London: Sport England/Trust for the Study of Adolescence.

Craig, R., Mindall, J., and Hirani, V. (2009) *Health Survey for England – 2008: Physical Activity and Fitness.* London: ONS.

Csikszentmihalyi, M. (1990) *Flow: The Psychology of Optimal Experience.* New York: Harper and Row.

Curtner-Smith, M.D., Sofo, S., Choiunard, J., and Wallace, S.J. (2007) 'Health-promoting physical activity and extra-curricular sport', *European Physical Education Review*, 13(2): 131–144.

Dagkas, S. and Benn, T. (2006) 'Young Muslim women's experiences of Islam and physical education in Greece and Britain: A comparative study', *Sport, Education and Society*, 11(1): 21–38.

Daley, A. (2002) 'Extra-curricular physical activities and physical self-perceptions in British 14–15-year-old male and female adolescents', *European Physical Education Review*, 8(1): 37–49.

David, P. (2005) *Human Rights in Youth Sport: A Critical Review of Children's Rights.* London: Routledge.

De Knop, P., and De Martelaer, K. (2001) 'Quantitative and qualitative evaluation of youth sport in Flanders and the Netherlands', *Sport, Education and Society*, 6(1): 35–51.

De Knop, P., Skirstad, B., Engstrom, L.-M., Theebom, M., and Wittock, H. (1996), 'Sport in a Changing Society', in P. De Knop, L.-M. Engstrom, B. Skirstad, and M.R. Weiss (eds) (1996) *Worldwide Trends in Youth Sport* (pp. 8–14). Champaign: Human Kinetics.

De Martelaer, K. and Theebom, M. (2006) 'Physical education and youth sport', in D. Kirk, D. Macdonald, and M. O'Sullivan (eds) *The Handbook of Physical Education* (pp. 652–664). London: Sage.

Department for Children, Schools and Families (DCSF) (2008) *Youth Cohort Study & Longitudinal Study of Young People in England: The Activities and Experiences of 16 year olds: England 2007.* London: Office for National Statistics.

Department for Culture, Media and Sport (DCMS)/Strategy Unit (2002) *Game Plan: A Strategy for Delivering Government's Sport and Physical Activity Objectives.* London: DCMS/Strategy Unit.

Department for Education (1995) Young People's Participation in the Youth Service. Statistical Bulletin 1/96. London: DfE.

Department for Education and Science (DES) (1991) *Physical Education for Ages 5 to 16.* London: DES.

Department for Education and Skills (DfES)/Department for Culture, Media and Sport (DCMS) (2003) *Learning Through PE and Sport. A Guide to the Physical Education, School Sport and Club Links Strategy.* London, DfES.

Dixon, M.A., Warner, S.M., and Bruenig, J.E. (2008) 'More than just letting them play: Parental influence on Women's lifetime sport involvement', *Sociology of Sport Journal*, 25: 538–559.

Dohnt, H.K. and Tiggemann, M. (2006) 'Body image concerns in young girls: the role of peers and media prior to adolescence', *Journal of Youth and Adolescence*, 35(2): 135–145.

Dollman, J., Norton, K., Norton, L., and Cleland, V. (2005) 'Evidence for secular trends in children's physical activity behaviour', *British Journal of Sports Medicine*, 39(12): 892–897.

du Bois-Reymond, M. (2005). Book Review: Berry Mayall, 'Towards a Sociology of Childhood. Thinking from Children's Lives'. Buckingham: Open University Press. *Young*, 13(4): 381–382.

Dunning, E. (1986) 'Sport as a male preserve: Notes on the social sources of masculine identity and its transformations', *Theory, Culture and Society*, 3: 79–80.

Dunning, E. (1999) *Sport Matters. Sociological Studies of Sport, Violence and Civilization*. London: Routledge.

Dunning, E. and Waddington, I. (2003) 'Sport as a drug and drugs in sport: Some explanatory comments', *International Review for the Sociology of Sport*, 38(3): 351–368.

Dunning, E. and Sheard, K. (2005) *Barbarians, Gentlemen and Players. A Sociological Study of the Development of Rugby Football* (second edition). London: Routledge.

Dyson, B. (2006) 'Students' perspectives of physical education', in D. Kirk, D. Macdonald, and M. O'Sullivan (eds) *The Handbook of Physical Education* (pp. 326–346). London: Sage.

Economic & Social Research Council (ESRC) (2009a) 'The UK by numbers: Health and well-being', *Society Now*, Spring Issue 3: 18–19.

Economic & Social Research Council (ESRC) (2009b) 'Grandparents are an influence for good', *Society Now*, Spring 2009 Issue 3: 8.

Economic & Social Research Council (ESRC) (2009c) 'The attraction of risk', *Society Now*, Autumn Issue, 5: 8.

Eiðsdóttir, S.Þ., Kristjánsson, Á.L., Sigfúsdóttir, I.D., and Allegrante, J.P. (2008) 'Trends in physical activity and participation in sports clubs among Icelandic adolescents', *The European Journal of Public Health*, 18: 289–293.

Elias, N. (1994) *The Civilizing Process*. Oxford: Blackwell (1939).

Elias, N. (1997) 'The civilizing of parents', in J. Goudsblom and S. Mennell (eds) *The Norbert Elias Reader*. (pp. 189–211). Oxford: Blackwell.

Elias, N. (1998) 'The civilizing of parents', in J. Goudsblom and S. Mennell (eds) *The Norbert Elias Reader* (pp. 189–212). Oxford: Blackwell.

Elias, N. (2001) *The Society of Individuals*. London: Basil Blackwell.

Elias, N., and Dunning, E. (1986) *Quest for Excitement: Sport and Leisure in the Civilizing Process*. Oxford: Blackwell.

Elling, A., and Knoppers, A. (2005) 'Sport, gender and ethnicity: Practices of symbolic inclusion/exclusion', *Journal of Youth and Adolescence*, 34(3): 257–268.

El-Sayed, M.S., Ali, N., and El-Sayed Ali, Z. (2005) 'Interaction between alcohol and exercise: physiological and haematological implications', *Sport Medicine*, 35(3): 257–269.

Engstrom, L.-M. (2008) 'Who is physically active? Cultural capital and sports participation from adolescence to middle age – a 38-year follow-up study', *Physical Education and Sport Pedagogy*, 13(4): 319–343.

European Commission (2003) *Time Use at Different Stages of Life: Results from 13 European Countries*. Luxembourg: Office for Official Publications of the European Community.

European Monitoring Centre for Drugs and Drug Addiction (EMCDDA) (2009) *Annual Report 2008: The State of the Drugs Problem in Europe.* Luxemburg: Office for Official Publications of the European Communities.

Evans, J. (2004) 'Making a difference: Education and "ability" in physical education', *European Physical Education Review,* 10(1): 95–108.

Evans, J. and Davies, B. (2006) 'The sociology of physical education', in D. Kirk, D. Macdonald, and M. O'Sullivan (eds) *The Handbook of Physical Education* (pp. 109–122). London: Sage.

Evans, J., Rich, E., Allwood, R., and Davies, B. (2007) 'Being "able" in a performative culture: Physical education's contribution to a healthy interest in sport?', in Ian Wellard (ed) *Rethinking Gender and Youth Sport* (pp. 51–67). London: Routledge.

Fahey, T., Delaney, L., and Gannon, B. (2005) *School Children and Sport in Ireland.* Dublin: Irish Sports Council.

Fairclough, S., Stratton, G., and Baldwin, G. (2002) 'The contribution of secondary physical education to lifetime physical activity', *European Physical Education Review,* 8(1): 69–84.

Feinstein, L., Bynner, J., and Duckworth, K. (2005) *Leisure Contexts in Adolescence and Their Effects on Adult Outcomes.* London: Centre for Research on the Wider Benefits of Learning, Institute of Education.

Feinstein, L., Bynner, J., and Duckworth, K. (2007) 'Young people's leisure contexts and their relation to adult outcomes', *Journal of Youth Studies,* 9(3): 305–327.

Feinstein, L. Peck, S.C., Eccles, J.S., Zarrett, N., Brown, J., Sorhaindo, A., and Robson, K. (2008) 'Time use and mental health among young people in the UK, 1970–2006', *Wider Benefits of Leaning Newsletter. Winter 2008/09* (p. 4). London: Institute of Education. http://www.learningbenefits.net/News/Newsletters/WBL%20Newsletter%20Winter0809.pdf. Downloaded 3 February, 2009.

Fejgin, N. and Hanegby, R. (2001) 'Gender and cultural bias in perceptions of sexual harassment in sport', *International Review for the Sociology of Sport,* 36(4): 459–478.

Field, J. (2003) *Social Capital.* London, Routledge.

Findley, L.C., Garner, R.E., and Kohen, D.E. (2009) 'Children's organized physical activity patterns from childhood into adolescence', *Journal of Physical Activity & Health,* 6(6): 708–715.

Fisher, K. (2002) *Chewing the Fat: The Story Time Diaries Tell About Physical Activity in the United Kingdom. Working Papers of the Institute for Social and Economic Research, Paper 2002–13.* Colchester: University of Essex.

Fisher, R. (2003) 'Physical education in Europe: Policy into practice', in K. Hardman (ed) *Physical Education: Deconstruction and Reconstruction – Issues and Directions* (pp. 137–152). Schorndorf: Verlag Karl Hofmann.

Fitzgerald, H. (2006) 'Disability and physical education', in D. Kirk, D. Macdonald, and M. O'Sullivan (eds) *The Handbook of Physical Education* (pp. 752–766). London: Sage.

Fitzgerald, H. and Jobling, A. (2004) 'Student centred research: working with disabled students' in J. Wright, D. Macdonald, and L. Burrows (eds) *Critical Inquiry and Problem Solving in Physical Education: Working With Students in Schools* (pp. 74–92). London: Routledge.

Fleming, S., Hardman, A., Jones, C., and Sheridan, H. (2005) ' "Role models" among elite young male rugby league players in Britain', *European Physical Education Review,* 11(1): 51–70.

Flintoff, A. and Scraton, S. (2001) 'Stepping into active leisure? Young women's perceptions of active lifestyles and their experiences of school physical education', *Sport, Education and Society*, 6(1): 5–21.

Flintoff, A. and Scraton, S. (2006) 'Girls and physical education', in D. Kirk, D. Macdonald, and M. O'Sullivan (eds) *The Handbook of Physical Education* (pp. 767–783). London: Sage.

Fowler, J.H. and Christakis, N.A. (2008) 'Dynamic spread of happiness in a large social network: Longitudinal analysis over 20 years in the Framingham heart study', *British Medical Journal*, 337: 1–9. a2338.

Fraser, J. and Ziff, A. (2009) *Children and Young People's Participation in Organised Sport. Omnibus Survey*. Research Report DCSF-RR135. London: IPSOS Mori.

Fredricks, J.A. and Eccles, J.S. (2005a) 'Developmental benefits of extracurricular involvement: Do peer characteristics mediate the link between activities and youth outcomes?' *Journal of Youth and Adolescence*, 34(6): 507–520.

Fredricks, J.A. and Eccles, J.S. (2005b) 'Family socialization, gender, and sport motivation and involvement', *Journal of Sport and Exercise Psychology*, 27(1): 3–31.

Frew, M. and McGillivray, D. (2005) 'Health clubs and body politics: Aesthetics and the quest for physical capital', *Leisure Studies*, 24(2): 161–175.

Fuller, E. (2008) *Smoking, Drinking and Drug Use Among Young People in 2008*. London: National Centre for Social Research/National Foundation for Educational Research.

Furlong, A. and Cartmel, F. (1997) *Young People and Social Change. Individualization and Risk in Later Life*. Buckingham: Open University Press.

Furlong, A. and Cartmel, F. (2007) *Young People and Social Change. New Perspectives*. Buckingham: Open University Press.

Gabe, J., Bury, M., and Elston, M.A. (2004) *Key Concepts in Medical Sociology*. London: Sage Publications.

Gard, M. (2010) *The End of the Obesity Epidemic,* London: Routledge.

Gard, M. and Wright, J. (2005) *The Obesity Epidemic: Science, Morality and Ideology*. London: Routledge.

Garry, J.P. and Morrissey, S.L. (2000) 'Team sports participation and risk-taking behaviors among a biracial middle school population', *Clinical Journal of Sport Medicine*, 10(3): 185–190.

Gershuny, J. (2003) *Time, Through the Lifecourse, in the Family*, ISER Working Papers number 2003–3. University of Essex: Colchester.

Gorard, S., Taylor, C., and Fitz, J. (2003) *Schools, Markets and Choice Policies*. London: RoutledgeFalmer.

Gorely, T., Holroyd, R., and Kirk, D. (2003) 'Muscularity, the habitus and social construction of gender: Towards a gender-relevant physical education', *British Journal of Sociology of Education,* 24(4): 429–448.

Gould, D., Lauer, L., Rolo, C., Jannes, C., and Pennisi, N. (2006) 'Understanding the role parents play in tennis success: a national survey of junior tennis coaches', *British Journal of Sports Medicine*, 40(7): 632–636.

Granberg, E.M., Simons, R.L., Gibbons, F.X., and Melby, J.N. (2008) 'The relationship between body size and depressed mood. Findings from a sample of African-American middle school girls', *Youth & Society*, 39(3): 294–315.

Granberg, E.M., Simons, L.G., and Simons, R.L. (2009), 'Body size and social self-image among Adolescent African American girls. The moderating influence of family racial socialization', *Youth & Society*, 41(2): 256–277.

203

Green, K. (2008) *Understanding Physical Education*. Lopndon: Sage.

Green, K., Smith, A., and Roberts, K. (2005) 'Social class, young people, sport and physical education', in K. Green and K. Hardman (eds) *Physical Education: Essential Issues* (pp. 180–196). London: Sage Publications.

Green, M. (2009) 'Podium or participation? 'Analysing policy priorities under changing modes of sport governance in the United Kingdom', *International Journal of Sport Policy*, 1(2): 121–144.

Greydanus, D.E. and Patel, D.R. (2002) 'Sports doping in the adolescent athlete. The hope, hype, and hyperbole', *The Pediatric Clinics of North America*, 49(4): 829–855.

Gunn, S. (2005) 'Translating Bourdieu: cultural capital and the English middle-class in historical perspective', *British Journal of Sociology*, 56(1): 49–64.

Ha, A., Abbott, R., Macdonald, D., and Pang, B. (2009) 'Comparison of perceived support for physical activity and physical activity related practices of children and young adolescents in Hong Kong and Australia', *European Physical Education Review*, 15(2): 155–173.

Hagger, M.S. and Chatzisarantis, N. (2008) 'Youth attitudes', in Alan L. Smith and Stuart J.H. Biddle (eds) *Youth Physical Activity and Sedentary Behavior* (pp. 167–192). Champaign, IL: Human Kinetics.

Hanson, S.L. (2005) 'Hidden dragons: Asian American women and sport', *Journal of Sport & Social Issues*, 29(3): 279–312.

Hardman, K. and Marshall, J.J. (2000) 'The state and status of physical education in schools in international context', *European Physical Education Review*, 6(3): 203–229.

Hardman, K. and Marshall, J. (2005) 'Physical education in schools in European context: charter principles, promises and implementation realities', in K. Green and K. Hardman (ed) *Physical Education: Essential Issues*. (pp. 39–64). London: Sage Publications.

Hargreaves, D.J. (1985) 'Socialization', in Adam and Jessica Kuiper (eds) *The Social Science Encyclopedia* (pp. 775–776). London: Routledge & Kegan Paul.

Hargreaves, J. (1994) *Sporting Females. Critical Issues in the History and Sociology of Women's Sports*. London: Routledge.

Hargreaves, J. and McDonald, I. (2004) 'Series editors' foreword', in Wheaton, B. (2004) *Understanding Lifestyle Sport: Consumption, Identity and Difference* (pp. x–xi). London: Routledge.

Harrington, M. (2006) 'Family leisure', in Chris Rojek, Susan M. Shaw, and A.J. Veal (eds) *A Handbook of Leisure Studies* (pp. 417–432). Baisngstoke: Palgrave Macmillan.

Harrington, M. (2009) 'Sport mad., good dads. Australian fathering through leisure and sport practices', in Tess Kay (ed) *Fathering Through Sport and Leisure* (pp. 51–72). London: Routledge.

Harris, D. (2006) 'Articulation', in Chris Rojek, Susan M. Shaw, and A.J. Veal (eds) *A Handbook of Leisure Studies* (pp. 504–517). Baisngstoke: Palgrave Macmillan.

Harris, J. (2005) 'Health-related exercise and physical education', in K. Green and K. Hardman (eds) *Physical Education: Essential Issues* (pp. 78–97). London: Sage Publications.

Harris, J. and Cale, L. (2006) 'A review of children's fitness testing', *European Physical Education Review*, 12(2): 201–225.

Harrison, L. and Belcher, D. (2006) 'Race and ethnicity in physical education', in D. Kirk, D. Macdonald, and M. O'Sullivan (eds) *The Handbook of Physical Education* (pp. 740–751). London: Sage.

Harthill, M. (2005) 'Sport and the sexually abused male child', *Sport, Education and Society*, 10(3): 287–304.

Heinemann, K. (2005) 'Sport and the welfare state in Europe', *European Journal of Sport Science*, 5(4): 181–188.

Henderson, K.A. and Hickerson, B. (2007) 'Women and leisure: Premises and performances uncovered in an integrative review', *Journal of Leisure Research*, 39(4): 591–610.

Hendry, L., Kloep, M., Espnes, G.A., Ingebrigsten, J.E., Glendenning, A., and Wood, S. (2002) Leisure transitions – a rural perspective, *Leisure Studies*, 21(1): 1–14.

Hendry, L.B., Shucksmith, J., Love, J.G., and Glendenning, A. (1993) *Young People's Leisure and Lifestyles*. London: Routledge.

Hibell, B., Guttormsson, U., Ahlström, S., Balakireva, O., Bjarnason, T., Kokkevi, A., and Kraus, L. (2009) *The 2007 ESPAD Report. Substance Use Among Students in 35 European Countries*. Stockholm: The Swedish Council for Information on Alcohol and Other Drugs.

Hills, L. (2007) 'Friendship, physicality, and physical education: An exploration of the social and embodied dynamics of girls' physical education experiences', *Sport, Education and Society*, 12: 335–354.

Holt, N.L., Black, D.E. Tamminen, K.A., Fox, K.R., and Mandigo, J.L. (2008) 'Levels of social complexity and dimensions of peer experiences in youth sport', *Journal of Sport & Exercise Psychology*, 2008, 30: 411–431.

Holt, N.L., Tamminen, K.A., Black, D.E., Mandigo, J.L., and Fox, K.R. (2009) 'Youth sport parenting styles and practices', *Journal of Sport and Exercise Psychology*, 2009, 31: 37–59.

Holt, R. (1990) *Sport and the British. A Modern History*. Oxford: Oxford University Press.

Houlihan, B. (2002) 'Political involvement in sport, physical education and recreation', in A. Laker (ed) *The Sociology of Sport and Physical Education. An Introductory Reader* (pp. 190–210). Abingdon: Routledge Falmer.

Houlihan, B., Bloyce, D., and Smith, A. (2009) 'Editorial: Developing the research agenda in sport policy', *International Journal of Sport Policy*, 1(1): 1–12.

Hunter, P. (1995) *Community Use of Sports Facilities*. London: Office of Population, Censuses and Surveys.

Iacovou, M. and Berthoud, R. (2001) *Young People's Lives: A Map of Europe*. University of Essex, Colchester: Institute for Social and Economic Research.

Institute of Youth Sport (2008a) *School Sport Partnerships. Annual Monitoring and Evaluation Report for 2007: School Sport Coordinator Survey*. Loughborough: Institute of Youth Sport/Loughborough University.

Institute of Youth Sport (2008b) *School Sport Partnerships. Annual Monitoring and Evaluation Report for 2007: Primary Link Teacher Survey*. Loughborough: Institute of Youth Sport/Loughborough University.

Iwasaki, Y. and Havitz, M.E. (2004) 'Examining relationships between leisure involvement, psychological commitment, and loyalty to a recreation agency', *Journal of Leisure Research*, 36(1): 45–72.

Jackson, S. and Scott, S. (2006) 'Childhood', in G. Payne (ed) *Social Divisions* (pp. 216–250). Palgrave Macmillan (first edition, 2000).

James, A. and James, A. (2009) *Key Concepts in Childhood Studies*. London: Sage Publications.

Järvinen, M. and Østergaard, J. (2009) 'Governing adolescent drinking', *Youth & Society*, 40(3): 377–402.

Johnston, G. and Percy-Smith, J. (2003) 'In search of social capital', *Policy & Politics*, 31(3): 321–334.

Jones, G. (2009) *Youth*. Cambridge: Polity Press.

Jones, R. and Cheetham, R. (2001) 'Physical education in the National Curriculum: Its purpose and meaning for final year secondary school students', *European Journal of Physical Education*, 6(2): 81–100.

Kay, T. (2005) 'The voice of the family: Influences on Muslim girls' responses to sport', in A. Flintoff, J. Long, and K. Hylton (eds) *Youth, Sport and Active Leisure: Theory, Policy and Participation*. Eastbourne: Leisure Studies Association Publication No. 87: 91–114.

Kay, T. (2006) 'Editorial: Fathering through leisure', *Leisure Studies*, 25(2): 125–131.

Kay, T. (2009a) 'Introduction. Fathering through sport and leisure', in Tess Kay (ed) *Fathering Through Sport and Leisure* (pp. 1–6). London: Routledge.

Kay, T. (2009b) 'The landscape of fathering', in Tess Kay (ed) *Fathering Through Sport and Leisure* (pp. 7–22). London: Routledge.

Kehily, M.J. (2007a) 'A cultural perspective' in Mary Jane Kehily (ed) *Understanding Youth: Perspectives, Identities and Practices* (pp. 11–43). London: Sage Publication/ The Open University.

Kew, F. (1997) *Sport. Social Problems and Issues*. Oxford: Butterworth-Heinemann.

Khunti, K., Stone, M.A., Bankart, J., Sinfield, P.K., Talbot, D., Farooqi, A., and Davies, M.J. (2007), 'Physical activity and sedentary behaviours of South Asian and white European children in inner city secondary schools in the UK', *Family Practice*, 24: 237–244.

Kilminster, R. (1998) *The Sociological Revolution. From the Enlightenment to the Global Age*. London: Routledge.

Kirk, D. (2004) 'Towards a critical history of the body, identity and health. Corporeal power and school practice', in J. Evans, B. Davies, and J. Wright (eds) *Body Knowledge and Control. Studies in the Sociology of Physical Education and Health* (pp. 52–67). London: Routledge.

Kjønniksen, L., Wold, B., and Fjørtoft, I. (2009) 'Attitudes to physical education and participation in organized youth sports during adolescence related to physical activity in young adulthood: a 10-year longitudinal study', *European Physical Education Review*, 15(2): 139–154.

Klomsten, A.T., Marsh, H.W., and Skaalvik, E.M. (2005) 'Adolescents' perceptions of masculine and feminine values in sport and phsyical education: A study of gender differences', *Sex Roles*, 52(9–10): 625–636.

Kokko, S. (2005) 'Sports clubs as a setting for youth health promotion', in Tommi Hoikkala, Pekka Hakkareinen, and Sofia Laine (eds) *Beyond Health Literacy. Youth Cultures, Prevention and Policy* (pp. 338–854). Helsinki: Finnish Youth Research Society.

Koska, P. (2005) 'Sport: The road to health?' in Tommi Hoikkala, Pekka Hakkareinen, and Sofia Laine (eds) *Beyond Health Literacy. Youth Cultures, Prevention and Policy* (pp. 295–337). Helsinki: Finnish Youth Research Society.

Kovač, M., Sloan, S., and Starc, G. (2008) 'Competencies in physical education teaching: Slovenian teachers' views and future perspectives', *European Physical Education Review*, 14(3): 301–326.

Kristen, L., Patriksson, G., and Fridlund, B. (2003) 'Parents' conceptions of the influences of participation in a sports programme on their children and adolescents with physical disabilities', *European Physical Education Review*, 9(1): 23–41.

Laakso, L., Nupponen, H., Rimpela, A., Pere, L., and Telama, R. (2008) 'Trends in leisure time physical activity among young people in Finland 1997–2007', *European Physical Education Review*, 14(2): 139–155.

Lahelma, E. and Gordon, T. (2008) 'Resources and (in(ter))dependence', *Young*, 16(2): 209–226.

Laws, C. and Fisher, D. (1999) 'Pupils' interpretations of physical education', in C.A. Hardy and M. Mawer (eds) *Learning and Teaching in Physical Education* (pp. 23–37). London: The Falmer Press.

Lawson, T. and Garrod, J. (2003) *Complete A–Z Sociology Handbook*. London: Hoidder and Stoughton (first edition, 1996).

Layte, R. and Whelan, C.T. (2009) 'Explaining social class inequalities in smoking: The role of education, self-efficacy, and deprivation', *European Sociological Review*, 25(4): 399–410.

Lee, M.J., Whitehead, J., Ntoumanis, N., and Hatzigeorgiadis, A. (2008) 'Relationships among values, achievement orientations, and attitudes in youth sport', *Journal of Sport and Exercise Psychology*, 2008, 30: 588–610.

Lenskyj, H. and van Daalen, C. (2006) 'Look at that cow over there: Sexual harassment and shaming of adolescent girls in high school physical education', in E. Singleton and A. Varpalotai (eds) *Stones in the Sneaker: Active Theory for Secondary School Physical and Health Educators* (pp. 139–154). London, ON: Althouse.

Light, R. and Kirk, D. (2000) 'High school rugby, the body and the reproduction of hegemonic masculinity', *Sport, Education and Society*, 5(2): 163–176.

Lightfoot, L. (2008) 'School sport fails young hopefuls chasing glory at London Olympics', *The Observer*, 24th August, 2008, p. 25.

Lindström, M., Hanson, B.S., and Östergren, P.-O. (2001) 'Socioeconomic differences in leisure-time physical activity: the role of social participation and social capital in shaping health related behaviour', *Social Science and Medicine*, 52(3): 441–451.

Littlefield, R., Green, B., Forsyth, S., and Sharp, B. (2003) 'Physical education in Scottish schools – a national case study', *European Journal of Physical Education*, 8(2): 211–227.

Lorentzen, C. (2007) *Psychosocial Mediators of Stages of Change in Physical Activity*. Unpublished PhD thesis. Oslo: Norwegian School of Sport Sciences.

Lowrey, J. and Kay, T. (2005) 'Doing sport, doing inclusion: An analysis of provider and participant perceptions of targeted sport provision for young Muslims', in A. Flintoff, J. Long, and K. Hylton (eds) *Youth, Sport and Active Leisure: Theory, Policy and Participation* (pp. 73–90). Eastbourne: Leisure Studies Association Publication.

Lyng, S. (1990) 'Edgework: A social psychological analysis of voluntary risk taking', *American Journal of Sociology*, 95(4): 851–886.

MacDonald, D., Rodger, S., Ziviani, J., Jenkins, D., Batch, J., and Jones, J. (2004) 'Physical activity as a dimension of family life for lower primary school children', *Sport, Education and Society*, 9(3): 307–325.

MacDonald, R. and Marsh, J. (2002) 'Crossing the Rubicon: youth transitions, poverty, drugs and social exclusion', *International Journal of Drug Policy*, 13: 27–38.

MacDonald, R. and Shildrick, T. (2007) 'Street corner society: Leisure careers, youth (sub) culture and social exclusion', *Leisure Studies*, 26(3): 339–355.

McDermott, L. (2007) 'A governmental analysis of children "at risk" in a world of physical inactivity and obesity epidemics', *Sociology of Sport Journal*, 24(3): 302–324.

McElroy, M. (2008) 'A sociohistorical analysis of U.S. youth physical activity behavior', in Alan L. Smith and Stuart J.H. Biddle (eds) *Youth Physical Activity and Sedentary Behavior* (pp. 59–78). Champaign, IL: Human Kinetics.

McPhail, A., Collier, C., and O'Sullivan, M. (2009) 'Lifestyles and gendered patterns of leisure and sporting interests among Irish adolescents', *Sport, Education and Society*, 14(3): 281–299.

Malcolm, D. (2008) *The Sage Dictionary of Sports Studies*. London: Sage Publications.

Mallam, K.M., Metcalf, B.S., Kirkby, J., Voss, L.D., and Wilkin, T.J. (2003) 'Contribution of timetabled physical; education to total physical activity in primary school children: cross sectional study', *British Medical Journal*, 327: 592–593.

Marshall, S.J., Biddle, S.J.H., Sallis, J.F., McKenzie, T.L., and Conway, T. (2002) 'Clustering of sedentary behaviours and physical activity among youth: A cross-national study', *Pediatric Exercise Science*, 14: 401–417.

Marshall, S.J. and Welk, G.J. (2008) 'Definitions and measurement' in Alan L. Smith and Stuart J.H. Biddle (eds) *Youth Physical Activity and Sedentary Behavior* (pp. 3–29). Champaign, IL: Human Kinetics.

Martinez, S.M., Arredondo, E.M., Ayala, G.X., and Elder, J.P. (2008) 'Culturally appropriate research and interventions', in Alan L. Smith and Stuart J.H. Biddle (eds) *Youth Physical Activity and Sedentary Behavior* (pp. 453–477). Champaign, IL: Human Kinetics.

Martino, W. and Pallotta-Chiarolli, M. (2003) *So What's a Boy?* Maidenhead: Open University Press.

Mason, V. (1995) *Young People and Sport – A National Survey 1994*. London: Office of Population, Censuses and Surveys.

Maynard, M. (1989) *Sociological Theory*. London: Longman.

Meegan, S. and MacPhail, A. (2006) 'Irish physical educators' attitude toward teaching students with special educational needs', *European Physical Education Review*, 12(1): 75–97.

Mennell, S. (1998) *Norbert Elias: An Introduction*. Dublin: University College Dublin Press.

Metzl, J.D., Small, E., Levine, S.R., and Gershel, J.C. (2001) 'Creatine use among young athletes', *Pediatrics*, 108(2): 421–425.

Miles, S. (2000) *Youth Lifestyles in a Changing World*. Buckingham: Open University Press.

Miles, S. (2003) 'Researching young people as consumers: can they say why?' In S. Miles, A. Bennett, and C. Cieslik (eds) *Researching Youth: Issues, Themes, Controversies* (pp. 170–185). London: Palgrave MacMillan.

Miller, K.E. (2009) ' "They light the Christmas tree in our town" ', *International Review for the Sociology of Sport*, 44(4): 363–380.

Minnebo, J. and Eggermont, S. (2007) 'Watching the young use illicit drugs: Direct experience, exposure to television and the stereotyping of adolescents' substance use', *Young*, 15(2): 129–144.

Moran, A.P. (2004) *Sport and Exercise Psychology: A Critical Introduction*. London: Routledge.

Muggleton, D. (2005) 'From classlessness to clubculture: A genealogy of post-war British youth cultural analysis', *Young*, 13(2): 205–219.

Murphy, P. (1998) 'Reflections on the policy process', *M.Sc. in the Sociology of Sport and Sports Management*, Module 4, Unit 7, Part 15 (pp. 85–104). Leicester: Centre for Research into Sport and Society.

Naughton, J. (2006) 'Young people don't like us. Who can blame them?', *The Observer (Business and Media)*, Sunday, 12th November, 2006. p. 11.

National Institute for Health and Clinical Excellence (NIHCE) (2009) *NIHCE Public Health Guidance 17. Promoting Physical Activity, Active Play and Sport for Pre-School and School-Age Children and Young People in Family, Pre-School, School and Community Settings*. London: NIHCE. January 2009.

Nelson, T.F. and Wechsler, H. (2001) 'Alcohol and college athletes', *Medicine and Science in Sports and Exercise*, 33(1): 43–47.

Nicholson, M., Hoye, R., and Houlihan, B. (eds) (2009) *Participation in Sport: International Policy Perspectives*. Oxford: Routledge.

Nixon, K.L. (2007) 'Constructing diverse sports opportunities for people with disabilities', *Sport & Social Issues*, 31(4): 417–433.

O'Donnell, T. (2008) 'The body', in D. Kirk, C. Cooke, A. Flintoff, and J. McKenna (eds) *Key Concepts in Sport and Exercise Sciences* (pp. 137–139). London: Sage Publications.

O'Donovan, T. (2002) *Working with Young People in Physical Education: Methodological Consideration*, Paper presented at the British Educational Research Association, 11 September 2002, Exeter.

O'Donovan, T. (2003) 'Negotiating popularity: an ethnographic exploration of social motivation in physical education'. Paper presented at the British Educational Research Association, University of Edinburgh, 12th September.

O'Donovan, T. and Kay, T. (2005) Focus on 'Girls in Sport', *British Journal of Teaching Physical Education*, 36 (1): 29–31.

Office for National Statistics [ONS] (1999) *Living in Britain. Results from the 1998 General Household Survey*. London: The Stationary Office.

Office for National Statistics [ONS] (2005) *Social Trends*. London: ONS.

OFSTED (2008) *TellUs3 National Report*.http://www.ofsted.gov.uk/Ofsted-home/Publications-and-research/Documents-by-type/Statistics/TellUs3-National-Report Downloaded 28 October, 2008.

Oliver, M. (1996) *Understanding Disability: From Theory to Practice*. Basingstoke: Macmillan.

O'Sullivan, S. (2002) 'The physical activity of children: A study of 1,602 Irish school-children aged 11–12 years', *Irish Medical Journal*, 95(3): 78–81.

Pampel, F.C. and Aguilar, J. (2008) 'Changes in Youth Smoking, 1976–2002. A Time-Series Analysis', *Youth & Society*, 39(4): 453–479.

Parker, H. and Egginton, R. (2002) 'Adolescent recreational alcohol and drugs careers gone wrong: developing a strategy for reducing risks and harms', *International Journal of Drug Policy*, 13: 419–432.

Parker, H., Aldridge, J., and Measham, F. (1998) *Illegal Leisure: The Normalization of Adolescent Recreational Drug Use*. London: Routledge.

Parker, H., Williams, L., and Aldridge, J. (2002) 'The normalization of "sensible" recreational drug use: Further evidence from the north-west longitudinal study', *Sociology*, 36: 941–964.

Parry, J. (1988) 'Physical education, justification and the National Curriculum', *Physical Education Review*, 11(2): 106–118.

Parsai, M., Voisine, S., Marsiglia, F.F., Kulis, S., and Nieri, T. (2009) 'The protective and risk effects of parents and peers on substance use, attitudes, and behaviors of Mexican and Mexican–American female and male adolescents', *Youth & Society*, 40(3): 353–376.

Pate, R.R., Davis, M.G., Robinson, T.N., Stone, E.J., McKenzie, T.L., and Young, J.C. (2006) 'Promoting physical activity in children and youth. A leadership role for schools: A scientific statement from the American Heart Association Council on Nutrition, Physical Activity, and Metabolism (Physical Activity Committee) in collaboration with the Councils on Cardiovascular Disease in the Young and Cardiovascular Nursing', *American Heart Association Scientific Statement*. http://circ.ahajournals.org/cgi/content/full/114/11/1214. Downloaded 7 January, 2007.

Pate, R.R., Trost, S.G., Levin, S., and Dowda, M. (2000) 'Sports participation and health-related behaviors among US youth', *Archives of Pediatrics & Adolescent Medicine*, 154: 904–911.

Pate, R.R., Wang, C.-Y., Dowda, M., Farrell, S.W., and O'Neill, J.R. (2006) 'Cardiorespiratory fitness levels among US youth 12 to 19 years of age. Findings from the 1999–2002 National Health and Nutrition Examination Survey', *Archives of Pediatric Adolescent Medicine*, 160(10): 1005–1012.

Pattie, C., Seyd, P., and Whiteley, P. (2004) *Citizenship in Britain – Values, Participation and Democracy*. Cambridge: Cambridge University Press.

Payne, G. (2006) 'An introduction to "social divisions"', in G. Payne (ed) *Social Divisions* (pp. 3–22). Basingstoke: Palgrave MacMillan (first edition, 2000).

Peiro-Velert, C., Devis-Devis, J., Beltran-Carillo, V.J., and Fox, K.R. (2008) 'Variability of Spanish adolescents' physical activity patterns by seasonality, day of the week and demographic factors', *European Journal of Sports Science*, 8(3): 163–171.

Penney, D. and Evans, J. (1998) 'Dictating the play: Government direction in physical education and sport policy development in England and Wales', in K. Green and K. Hardman (eds) *Physical Education: A Reader* (pp. 84–101). Aachen: Meyer and Meyer Verlag.

Penney, D. and Evans, J. (2005) 'Policy, power and politics in physical education', in K. Green and K. Hardman (eds) *Physical Education: Essential Issues* (pp. 21–38). London: Sage Publications.

Penney, D. and Harris, J. (1997) 'Extra-curricular physical education: More of the same for the more able', *Sport, Education and Society*, 2(1): 41–54.

Peretti-Watel, P., Guagliardo, V., Verger, P., Pruvost, J., Mignon, P., and Obadia, Y. (2004) 'Risky behaviours among young elite-student-athletes. Results from a pilot survey in south-eastern France', *International Review for the Sociology of Sport*, 39(2): 233–244.

Philo, D., Mablethorpe, N., Conolly, A., and Toomse, M. (2009) *Families with Children in Britain: Findings from the 2007 Families and Children Study* (FACS). Department for Work and Pensions Research Report No.578. London: Department for Work and Pensions.

Pichler, F. and Wallace, C. (2007) 'Patterns of formal and informal social capital in Europe', European Sociological Review, 23(4): 423–435.

Pietiläinen, K.H., Kaprio, J., Borg, P., Plasqui, G., Yki-Järvinen, H., Kujala, U.M., Rose, R.J., Westerterp, K.R., and Rissanen, A. (2008) 'Physical inactivity and obesity: a vicious circle', *Obesity*, 16(2): 409–414.

Puig, N. (1996) 'Spain', in P. De Knop, L.-M. Engstrom, B. Skirstad, and M.R. Weiss (eds) *Worldwide Trends in Youth Sport* (pp. 245–259). Champaign, IL: Human Kinetics.

Putnam, R.D. (2000) *Bowling Alone. The Collapse and Revival of American Community*. New York: Simon & Schuster/Touchstone.

Qualifications and Curriculum Authority (QCA) (2001) *Physical Education And School Sport Project*, http://www.qca.org.uk/ca/subjects/pe/pess.asp. Downloaded 3 April, 2001.

Quick, S. (2007) *2006/07 School Sport Survey*. London: TNS.

Quick, S., Dalziel, D., Thornton, A., and Simon, A. (2009) *PE and School Sport Survey 2008/09*. London: TNS-BMRB.

Ratna, A. (2007) ' "Taking the power back!" The politics of British Asian female football players', *Leisure Studies Association Newsletter* No. 78 November, 19–23.

Redhead, S. (1997) *Subcultures to Clubcultures*. Oxford: Blackwell.

Reilly, J., Jackson, D., Montgomery, C., Kelly, L., Slater, C., Grant, S., and Paton, J. (2004) 'Total energy expenditure and physical activity in young Scottish children: mixed longitudinal study', *The Lancet*, 363: 211–212.

Rich, E. (2008) 'Eating disorders', in D. Malcolm (ed) *The Sage Dictionary of Sports Studies* (pp. 77–78). London: Sage Publications.

Rich, E., Holroyd, R., and Evans, J. (2004) ' "Hungry to be noticed": Young women, anorexia and schooling', in J. Evans, B. Davies and J. Wright (eds) *Body Knowledge and Control. Studies in the Sociology of Physical Education and Health* (pp. 173–190). London: Routledge.

Rich, E., Evans, J., and Allwood, R. (2005) *Problematising Perfection and Performance in Education: Learning from Young Women with Eating Disorders*, British Educational Research Association Annual Conference, University of Glamorgan, Treforest, Pontypridd, 14–17th September 2005.

Robb, M. (2007a) 'Relating', in Mary Jane Kehily (ed) *Understanding Youth: Perspectives, Identities and Practices* (pp. 313–344). London: Sage Publication/The Open University.

Robb, M. (2007b) 'Wellbeing', in Mary Jane Kehily (ed) *Understanding Youth: Perspectives, Identities and Practices* (pp. 181–213). London: Sage Publication/The Open University.

Robb, M. (2007c) 'Introduction', in Martin Robb (ed) *Youth in Context: Frameworks, Settings and Encounters* (pp. 5–11). London: Sage Publication/The Open University.

Roberts, K. (1996a) 'Young people, schools, sport and government policy', *Sport, Education and Society*, 1(1): 47–57.

Roberts, K. (1996b) 'Youth cultures and sport: The success of school and community sport provisions in Britain', *European Physical Education Review*, 1(2): 105–115.

Roberts, K. (1997) 'Same activities, different meanings: British youth cultures in the 1990s', *Leisure Studies*, 16(1): 1–15.

Roberts, K. (1999) *Leisure in Contemporary Society*. Wallingford: CABI Publishing.

Roberts, K. (2001) *Class in Modern Britain*. Basingstoke: Palgrave.

Roberts, K. (2003) 'Problems and priorities for the sociology of youth', in A. Bennett, M. Cieslik, and S. Miles (eds) *Researching Youth* (pp. 13–28). Basingstoke: Palgrave Macmillan.

Roberts, K. (2004) *The Leisure Industries*. Basingstoke: Palgrave.

Roberts, K. (2005) The Athenian dream in leisure studies, *Leisure Issues*, 7(1): 2–13.

Roberts, K. (2006a) *Leisure in Contemporary Society*. Wallingford: CABI Publishing.

Roberts, K. (2006b) 'Global youth: Is the future American?' Paper presented at the *XVI World Congress of Sociology*, Durban, South Africa, 23–29 July, 2006.

Roberts, K. (2007a) 'Leisure and ethnicity', *Leisure Studies Association Newsletter,* No. 78 November: 13–14.

Roberts, K. (2008) *Key Concepts in Sociology*. Basingstoke: Palgrave MacMillan.

Roberts, K. (2009) *Youth in Transition: Eastern Europe and the West*. Palgrave Macmillan: Basingstoke.

Roberts, K. (2010) 'Trends in leisure; trends in the study of leisure'. Invited lecture. University of Chester, 19th February, 2010.

Roberts, K. and Brodie, D. (1992) *Inner-City Sport: Who Plays and What Are the Benefits?* Giordano Bruno: Culemborg.

Roberts, K., Fagan, C., Boutenko, I., and Razlogov, K. (2001) 'Economic polarization, leisure practices and policies, and the quality of life: a study in post-communist Moscow', *Leisure Studies*, 20(3): 161–172.

Roberts, K., Pollock, G., Tholen, J., and Tarkhnishvili, L. (2009a) 'Young leisure careers during post-communist transition in the South Caucasus', *Leisure Studies*, 28(3): 261–277.

Roberts, K., Kamruzzaman, P., and Tholen, J. (2009b) 'Young people's education to work transitions and inter-generational social mobility in post-Soviet central Asia', *Young*, 17(1): 59–80.

Roberts, K., Pollock, G., Rustamove, S., Mammadova, Z., and Tholen, J. (2009c) 'Young adults' family and housing transitions during post-communist transition in the South Caucasus', *Journal of Youth Studies*, 12(2): 151–166.

Rojek, C. (1985) *Capitalism and Leisure Theory*. London: Tavistock.

Rojek, C. (2006) 'Representation', in Chris Rojek, Susan M. Shaw, and A.J. Veal (eds) *A Handbook of Leisure Studies* (pp. 459–474). Basingstoke: Palgrave Macmillan.

Rowe, N. (2005) 'Foreword', in C. Foster, M. Hillsdon, N. Cavill, S. Allender, and G. Cowburn (2005) *Understanding Participation in Sport – A Systematic Review* (p. 2). London: Sport England.

Rowlands, A. (2009) 'Invalid measures of physical activity threaten progress in health research: Physical activity and how to measure it better', Invited Lecture, University of Chester, 15th January, 2009.

Royal College of Physicians, Royal College of Paediatrics & Child Health, Faculty of Public Health (2004) *Storing up Problems: The Medical Case for a Slimmer Nation. Report of a Working Party.* London: Royal College of Physicians.

Royal Society for the Encouragement of Arts, Manufactures and Commerce (RSA) (2007) *The Report of the RSA Commission on Illegal Drugs, Communities and Public Policy.* London: RSA.

Sabo, D. and Veliz, P. (2008) *Go Out and Play. Youth Sports in America.* New York: Women's Sports Foundation.

Samdal, O., Tynjälä, J., Roberts, C., Sallis, J.F., Villberg, J., and Wold, B. (2006) 'Trends in vigorous physical activity and TV watching of adolescents from 1986 to 2002 in seven European countries', *European Journal of Public Health*, 17(3): 242–248.

Saelens, B.E. and Kerr, J. (2008) 'The family', in Alan L. Smith and Stuart J.H. Biddle (eds) *Youth Physical Activity and Sedentary Behavior* (pp. 267–294). Champaign, IL: Human Kinetics.

Sallis, J.F., Prochaska, J.J., and Taylor, W.C. (2000) 'A review of correlates of physical activity of children and adolescents', *Medicine and Science in Sports and Exercise*, 32: 963–975.

Salvara, M.I., Jess, M., Abbott, A. and Bognár, J. (2006) 'Preliminary study to investigate the influence of different teaching styles on pupils' goal orientations in physical education', *European Physical Education Review*, 12(1): 51–74.

Scheerder, J., Taks, M., Vanreusel, B., and Renson, R. (2005b) 'Social changes in youth sports participation styles 1969–1999: The case of Flanders (Belgium)', *Sport, Education and Society*, 10(3): 321–341.

Scheerder, J., Thomis, M., Vanreusel, B., Lefevre, J., Renson, R., Vanden Eynde, B., and Beunen, G.P. (2006) 'Sports participation among females from adolescence to adulthood: A longitudinal study', *International Review for the Sociology of Sport*, 41(3–4): 413–430.

Scheerder, J., Vanreusel, B., Taks, M., and Renson, R. (2002) 'Social sports stratification in Flanders 1969–1999: Intergenerational reproduction of social inequalities?' *International Review for the Sociology of Sport*, 37(3): 217–246.

Scheerder, J., Vanreusel, B., and Taks, M. (2003) 'Stratification patterns of active sport involvement among adults. Social change and persistence', *International Review for the Sociology of Sport*, 40(2): 139–162.

Scheerder, J., Vanreusel, B., and Taks, M. (2005a) 'Stratification patterns of active sport involvement of adults', *International Review for the Sociology of Sport*, 40(2): 139–162.

Scheerder, J., Vanreusel, B., Taks, M., and Renson, R. (2005c) 'Social stratification patterns in adolescents' active sports participation behaviour: a time trend analysis 1969–1999', *European Physical Education Review*, 11(1): 5–27.

Schenker, S. (2005) 'Tackling the obesity epidemic', *PE & Sport Today*, 17: 100–111.

Schizzerotto, A. and Lucchini, M. (2002) *Transitions to adulthood during the Twentieth Century. A Comparison of Great Britain, Italy and Sweden, EPAG Working Paper 2002–36.* Colchester: University of Essex.

Schools Health Education Unit (SHEU) (2007) Twenty one years of young people's reports. Schools Health Education Unit. http://www.sheu.org.uk/publications/yp07.htm#section7. Downloaded 12 December, 2007.

Scraton, S. (1992) *Shaping Up to Womanhood. Gender and Girls' Physical Education.* Buckingham: Open University Press.

Scraton, S. (1993) 'Equality, coeducation and physical education in secondary schooling', in J. Evans (ed) *Equality, Education and Physical Education* (pp. 139–153). Lewes: Falmer Press.

Seabra, A.F., Mendonca, D.M., Thomis, M.A., Malina, R.A., and Maia, J. (2007) 'Sports participation among Portuguese youth 10–18 years', *Journal of Physical Activity and Health*, 4(4): 370–380.

Seabrook, T. and Green, E. (2004) 'Streetwise or safe? Girls negotiating time and space', in W. Mitchell, R. Bunton, and E. Green (eds) *Young People, Risk and Leisure: Constructing Identities in Everyday Life.* London: Palgrave MacMillan.

Shanahan, M.J. (2000) 'Pathways to adulthood in changing societies: variability and mechanisms in life course perspective', *Annual Review of Sociology*, 26: 667–692.

Shildrick, T. (2002) 'Young people, illicit drug use, and the question of normalization', *Journal of Youth Studies,* 5: 35–48.

Shildrick, T. (2006) 'Youth culture, subculture and the importance of neighbourhood', *Young: Nordic Journal of Youth Research*, 14(1): 61–74.

Shilling, C. (1998) 'The body, schooling and social inequalities: physical capital and the politics of physical education', in K. Green and K. Hardman (eds) *Physical Education: A Reader* (pp. 243–271). Aachen: Meyer and Meyer Verlag.

Shilling, C. (2005) *The Body in Culture, Technology and Society.* London: Sage.

Sigman, A. (2007) 'Visual voodoo: The biological impact of watching TV', *Biologist*, 54(1): 12–17.

Sivan, A. (2006) 'Leisure and education', in Chris Rojek, Susan M. Shaw, and A.J. Veal (eds) *A Handbook of Leisure Studies* (pp. 433–447). Basingstoke: Palgrave Macmillan.

213

Skirstad, B. (2009) 'Ideological fights in School Sport'. Paper presented at the 1st World-wide Conference in School Sport. Catalonia, Spain November, 2009.

Sleap, M., Elliott, B., Paisi, M., and Reed, H. (2007) 'The lifestyles of affluent young people ages 9 to 15 years: A case study', *Journal of Physical Acvtivity and Health*, 4(4): 459–468.

Smith, A. (2006) *Young People, Sport and Leisure. A Sociological Study of Contemporary Youth.* Unpublished PhD thesis. Chester: University of Chester.

Smith, A. and Parr, M. (2007) 'Young people's views on the nature and purposes of physical education: A sociological analysis', *Sport, Education and Society*, 12(1): 37–58.

Smith, A., Green, K., and Thurston, M. (2009) '"Activity Choice" and Physical Education in England and Wales', *Sport, Education and Society*, 14(2): 203–222.

Smith, A., Thurston, M., Green, K., and Lamb, K. (2007a) 'Young people's participation in National Curriculum Physical Education: A study of 15–16 year olds in north-west England and north-east Wales', *European Physical Education Review*, 13(2): 165–194.

Smith, A., Thurston, M., Green, K., and Lamb, K. (2007b) 'Young people's participation in extracurricular physical education: A study of 15–16 year olds in the north-west of England and the north-east of Wales', *European Physical Education Review*, 13(3): 339–68.

Smith, A.L. and McDonough, M.H. (2008) 'Peers', in Alan L. Smith and Stuart J.H. Biddle (eds) *Youth Physical Activity and Sedentary Behavior* (pp. 295–320). Champaign, IL: Human Kinetics.

Smith, C., Stainton-Rogers, W., and Tucker, S. (2007) 'Risk' in M. Robb (ed) *Youth in Context: Frameworks, Settings and Encounters* (pp. 219–250). London: Sage.

Soule, B. (2008) '"Sports a risque" et "sports extremes": de quoi parle-t-on?', *Loisir & Societe*, 29(2): 321–345.

Sports Council for Wales (SCW) (2000) *A Strategy for Welsh Sport: Young People First.* Cardiff: SCW.

Sports Council for Wales (SCW) (2001) *Widening the Net? Young People's Participation in Sport 1999/2000.* Cardiff: SCW.

Sports Council for Wales (SCW) (2002) *Swimming Against the Tide? Physical Education and Sports Provision in Secondary Schools in Wales.* Cardiff: SCW.

Sports Council for Wales (SCW) (2003) *Secondary School Aged Children's Participation in Sport 2001.* Cardiff: SCW.

Sports Council for Wales (SCW) (2006) *Active Young People. Sports Update No. 58.* Cardiff: SCW.

Sport England (2000) *Sports Participation and Ethnicity in England. National Survey 1999/2000. Headline Findings.* London: Sport England.

Sport England (2001a) *Young People with a Disability and Sport. Headline Findings.* London: Sport England.

Sport England (2001b) *Young People and Sport in England 1999. A Survey of Young People and PE Teachers.* London: Sport England.

Sport England (2003a) *Young People and Sport in England. Trends in Participation 1994–2002.* London: Sport England.

Sport England (2003b) *Young People and Sport in England, 2002. A Survey of Young People and PE Teachers.* London: Sport England.

Sport England (2005) *Participation in Sport in Great Britain: Trends 1987 to 2002.* London: Sport England.

Sport England (2007) *Taking Part Survey*. London: Sport England.

Sport England (2008) *Active People Survey 2*. London: Sport England.

Sport England/UK Sport (2001) *General Household Survey: Participation in Sport – Past Trends and Future Prospects*. London: Sport England/ UK Sport.

SportScotland (2001) *Sports Participation in Scotland 2000*. Edinburgh: SportScotland.

SportScotland (2002) *Sports Participation in Scotland 2001*. Edinburgh: SportScotland.

SportScotland (2008) *Child protection legislation and volunteering in Scottish sport. LSA Newsletter No. 81*, November 2008: 28–30.

Staempfli, M. (2005) 'Book review: Suman,Verma and Larson, Reed (2003). Examining Adolescent Leisure Time Across Cultures: Developmental Opportunities and Risks', *Loisir & Societe*, 28(2): 679–681.

Stamatakis, E. and Chaudhury, M. (2008) 'Temporal trends in adults' sports participation patterns in England between 1997 and 2006: the Health Survey for England', *British Journal of Sports Medicine*, 42(11): 901–908.

Stensel, D.J., Gorely, T., and Biddle, S.J.H. (2008) 'Youth health outcomes', in Alan L. Smith and Stuart J.H. Biddle (eds) *Youth Physical Activity and Sedentary Behavior* (pp. 31–57). Champaign, IL: Human Kinetics.

Stroot, S.A. (2002) 'Socialization and participation in sport', in A. Laker (ed) *The Sociology of Sport and Physical Education. An Introductory Reader* (pp. 129–147). Abingdon: RoutledgeFalmer.

Such, L. (2009) 'Fatherhood, the morality of personal time and leisure-based parenting', in Tess Kay (ed) *Fathering Through Sport and Leisure* (pp. 73–87). London: Routledge.

Sunday Times Business Times [South Africa] (2006) 'The things youth yearn for most', *Sunday Times Business Times*, p. 1.

Svensson, R. (2003) 'Gender differences in adolescent drug use: The impact of parental monitoring and peer deviance', *Youth & Society*, 34(3): 300–329.

Sykes, F. (2008) 'Award-winner Paul puts success down to love of sport', *Future Fitness*, May 2008, p. 6.

Telama, R. and Yang, X. (2000) 'Decline of physical activity from youth to young adult-hood in Finland', *Medicine and Science in Sports and Exercise*, 32: 1617–1622.

Telama, R., Laakso, L., and Yang, X. (1994) 'Physical activity and participation in sports of young people in Finland', *Scandinavian Journal of Medicine and Science in Sports*, 4: 65–74.

Telama, R., Naul, R., Nupponen, H., Rychtecky, A., and Vuolle, P. (2002) *Physical Fitness, Sporting Lifestyles and Olympic ideals: Cross-Cultural Studies on Youth Sport in Europe*. Germany: Verlag Karl Hofmann Schorndorf.

Telama, R., Nupponen, H., and Pieron, M. (2005) 'Physical activity among young people in the context of lifestyle', *European Physical Education Review*, 11(2): 115–137.

Thomas, N. (2008) 'Disability' in D. Malcolm (ed) *The Sage Dictionary of Sports Studies* (pp. 67–69). London: Sage Publications.

Thomas, N. and Smith, A. (2008) *Disability, Sport and Society: An Introduction*. London: Routledge.

Tinning, R. (1991) 'Problem-setting and ideology in health-based physical education: an Australian perspective', *Physical Education Review*, 14(1): 40–49.

Tolonen, T. (2005) 'Locality and gendered capital of working-class youth', *Young*, 13(4): 343–361.

Tomkinson, G.R. and Olds,T.S. (2007) 'Secular changes in aerobic fitness test performance of Australasian children and adolescents', in J. Borms, M. Hebbelinck and A.P. Hink (eds) Pediatric Fitness. Secular trends and Geographic Variability', *Medicine and Sports Science*, Vol. 50. (pp. 168–182). Basel: Karger.

Tomlinson, A., Ravenscroft, N., Wheaton, B., and Gilchrist, P. (2005) *Lifestyle Sports and National Sports Policy: An Agenda for Research*. London: Sport England.

Tremblay D. and Thoemmes J. (2006) 'Temps sociaux et temporalités sociales', *Loisir et Société*, 29(1): 117-154.

Trost, S.G. (2006) 'Public health and physical education', in D. Kirk, D. Macdonald, and M. O'Sullivan (eds) *The Handbook of Physical Education* (pp. 163–187). London: Sage.

Twist, C. (2010) *Personal Communication*. 8th January, 2010.

UK Sport/Sport England (2001) *Participation in Sport, Past Trends and Future Prospects*. London: Sport England.

Vaage, O.F. (2009) *Mosjon, Friluftsliv og Kulturaktiviteter. Resultater fra Levekarsundersøkelsene fra 1997–2007. Rapport 2009/15*. Oslo-Kongsvinger: Statistisk Sentralbyra.

Van Bottenburg, M., Rijnen, B., and Sterkenburg, J. (2005) *Sport Participation in the European Union: Trends and Differences*. Mulier Institute.

Van Krieken, R. (1998) *Norbert Elias*. London: Routledge.

Van Putten, A.E., Dykstra, P.A. and Schippers, J.J. (2008) 'Just like mom? The intergenerational reproduction of women's paid work', *European Sociological Review*, 24(4): 435–449.

Van Wel, F., Maarsingh, W., Ter Bogt, T., and Raaijmakers, Q. (2008) 'Youth cultures: From snob to pop?' *Young*, 16(3): 325–340.

Vanreusel, B., Renson, R., Beunen, G., Albrecht, L., Lefevre, J., Lysens, R., and Vanden Eynde, B. (1997) 'A longitudinal study of youth sports participation and adherence to sport in adulthood', *International Review for the Sociology of Sport*, 32(4): 373–387.

Verma, G.K. and Darby, D.S. (1994) *Winners and Losers: Ethnic Minorities in Sport and Recreation*. London: The Falmer Press.

Vescio, J., Wilde, K., and Crosswhite, J. (2005) 'Profiling sport role models to enhance initiatives for adolescent girls in physical education and sport', *European Physical Education Review*, 11(2): 153–170.

Vincent, J.A. (2006) 'Age and old age', in G. Payne (ed) *Social Divisions* (pp. 194–215). PalgraveMacmillan (first edition, 2000).

Voss, L.D., Hosking, J., Metcalf, B.S., Jeffery, A.N., and Wilkin, T.J. (2007) 'Children from low-income families have less access to sports facilities, but are no less physically-active: cross sectional study (EarlyBird 35)', *Child: Care, Health and Development*, 34(4): 470–474.

Wacquant, L. (1995) 'Pugs at work: Bodily capital and bodily labour among professional boxers', *Body and Society*, 1(1): 65–93.

Waddington, I. (2000) *Sport, Health and Drugs. A Critical Sociological Perspective*. London: E. & F.N. Spon.

Waddington, I., Malcolm, D., and Green, K. (1997) 'Sport, Health and Physical Education: A Reconsideration', *European Physical Education Review*, 3(2): 165–182.

Waine, C. (2007) 'Chair's report', *Obesity News Review*, 16 (June 2007): 1.

Wallace, C., and Kovatcheva, S. (1998) *Youth in Society*. London: Macmillan.

Wallhead, T.L., and Buckworth, J. (2004) 'The role of physical education in the promotion of youth physical activity', *QUEST*, 56: 285–301.

Walseth, K. (2006a) 'Sport and belonging', *International Review for the Sociology of Sport*, 41(3–4): 447–464.

Walseth, K. (2006b) 'Young Muslim women and sport: the impact of identity work', *Leisure Studies*, 25(1): 75–94.

Wang, C.K.J. and Liu, W.C. (2007) 'Promoting enjoyment in girls' physical education: The impact of goals, beliefs, and self-determination', *European Physical Education Review*, 13(2): 145–164.

Wanless, D. (2004) *Securing Good Health for the Whole Population. Final Report*. London: Department of Health.

Warikoo, N. (2005) 'Gender and ethnic identity among second-generation Indo-Caribbeans', *Ethnic and Racial Studies*, 28(5): 803–831.

Watt, T.T. and Rogers, J.M. (2007) 'Factors contributing to differences in substance use among back and white adolescents', *Youth & Society*, 39(1): 54–74.

Weber, M. (1949) *The Methodology of the Social Sciences*. New York: The Free Press.

Weber, R. (2009) 'Protection of children in competitive sport: Some critical questions for London 2012', *International Review for the Sociology of Sport*, 44(1): 55–69.

Welch, M., Price, E.A., and Yankey, N. (2002) 'Moral panic over youth violence wilding and the manufacture of menace in the media', *Youth & Society*, 34(1): 3–30.

Welk, G.J., Eisenmann, J.C., and Dollman, J. (2006) 'Health-related physical activity in children and adolescents: a bio-behavioral perspective', in D. Kirk, D. Macdonald, and M. O'Sullivan (eds) *The Handbook of Physical Education* (pp. 665–684). London: Sage.

Wheaton, B. (2004) 'Introduction. Mapping the lifestyle sport-scape', in Wheaton, B. (2004) *Understanding Lifestyle Sport: Consumption, Identity and Difference* (pp. 1–28). London: Routledge.

Wheaton, B. (2008) 'Lifestyle sports' in D. Malcolm (ed) *The Sage Dictionary of Sports Studies* (pp. 155–157). London: Sage Publications.

Wheeler, K. and Nauright, J. (2006) 'A global perspective on the environmental impact of golf', *Sport in Society*, 9(3): 427–443.

Whitson, D. (1990) 'Sport in the social construction of masculinity', in M.A. Messner and D.F. Sabo (eds) *Sport, Men and the Gender Order. Critical Feminist Perspectives* (pp. 19–29). Champaign, IL: Human Kinetics.

Whyte, G. (2006) 'Exercise is BAD for you …', *The Sport and Exercise Scientist*, 10 (December 2006): 14.

Wilkin, T. (2007) 'The Early Bird study – Peninsula Medical School, Plymouth Campus', *Obesity News Review*, 16 (June 2007): 3.

Williams, B., Davies, L., and Wright, V. (2010) *Children, Young People and Alcohol. Research Report DCSF-RR195*. London: DCSF.

Wilson, T.C. (2002) 'The paradox of social class and sports involvement', *International Review for the Sociology of Sport*, 37(1): 5–16.

Winsley, R. and Armstrong, N. (2005) 'Physical activity, physical fitness, health and young people', in K. Green and K. Hardman (eds) *Physical Education: Essential Issues* (pp. 65–77). London: Sage Publications.

Womack, S. (2008) 'Making a difference: internet security', *The Edge*, 27: 26–27.

World Heath Organization (WHO) Regional Office for Europe (2006) *Framework for Alcohol Policy in the WHO European Region*. Copenhagen: WHO.

Wouters, C. (2007) Informalization, *Manners and Emotions Since 1890*. London: Sage Publications.

Wray, R. (2006) 'Surfing booms as TV watching stalls', *The Guardian*, 29 November, 2006. p. 26.

Wright, J. (1999) 'Changing gendered practice in physical education: Working with teachers', *European Physical Education Review*, 5(3): 181–198.

Wu, Y. (2006) 'Editorial: overweight and obesity in China', *British Medical Journal*, 333: 362–363.

Wyn, J., Tyler, D., and Willis, E. (2002) *Researching the Post-1970 Generation: Reflections on the Life-Patterns Study of Australian Youth*. Paper presented at XV World Congress of the International Sociological Association, Brisbane, Australia, 7–13 July 2002.

Xiong, H. (2007) 'The evolution of urban society and socials changes in sports partici-pation at the grassroots in China', *International Review for the Sociology of Sport*, 42(4): 441–447.

Zeijl, E., du Bois Raymond, M., and de Poel, Y. (2001) 'Young adolescents' leisure patterns', *Loisir and Societe*, 24(2): 379–402.

Zick, C.D., Smith, K.R., Brown, B.B., Fan, J.X., and Kowaleski-Jones, L. (2007) 'Physical activity during the transition from adolescence to adulthood', *Journal of Physical Acvtivity and Health*, 4(2): 125–137.

Zuzanek, J. (2005) 'Adolescent time use and well-being from a comparative perspective', *Loisir & Societe*, 28(2): 379–423.

INDEX

Page number followed by 'n' denotes notes.